P9-CKT-420

second edition

Reading *with* Meaning

Teaching
Comprehension
in the
Primary Grades

Stenhouse Publishers
Portland, Maine

Debbie
Miller

Stenhouse Publishers
www.stenhouse.com

Credits
Pages 106 and 130: "Ducks on a Winter Night" and "Dressing Like a Snake" from *Creatures of Earth, Sea, and Sky* by Georgia Heard. Copyright © 1997 by Georgia Heard. Published by Wordsong, an imprint of Boyds Mills. Reprinted by permission.

Library of Congress Cataloging-in-Publication Data
Miller, Debbie, 1948–
    Reading with meaning : teaching comprehension in the primary grades / Debbie Miller. — 2nd ed.
      p. cm.
    Includes bibliographical references and index.
    ISBN 978-1-57110-955-2 (pbk. : alk. paper) — ISBN 978-1-57110-977-4 (ebook)
    1. Reading (Primary) 2. Reading comprehension. I. Title.
    LB1525.7.M55 2002
    372.4—dc23
                          2012029982

Back cover photograph by Jack Gloeckler
Cover design, interior design, and typesetting by Martha Drury
Manufactured in the United States of America

PRINTED ON 30% PCW
RECYCLED PAPER

19 18 17 16 15 14   9 8 7 6 5 4

To the Public Education and Business Coalition, an organization whose commitment to education inspires us to teach and learn with passion, rigor, and joy

Contents

In Appreciation

To all of you I thanked the first time, I thank you again. I will never, ever forget you.

And now, this time around . . .

To Philippa Stratton at Stenhouse—thank you (again!) for your continued encouragement and support of me, and teachers everywhere. Your work has meant so much to so many, and I'm honored to be your friend. And thank you for suggesting this second edition—I'm happy we did it!

To Samantha Bennett—thank you for your happy spirit, sage advice, and firm belief in the unlimited capacity of teachers and children. You inspire me whenever we're together, and give me the energy I need to keep writing. Thank you for helping me think through this edition of *Reading with Meaning* and making me smarter in the process. (P.S. I want to dress like you in my next life.)

To teachers and children in the classrooms where we've worked together—I always learn more from you than you do from me. You bring me joy and keep my faith in the future strong.

To my love, Don—thank you for everything! Can it really be forty years and counting? In *Teaching with Intention* I wrote, "Grab the snorkels, pack the shorts, and let's sail away for a year and a day . . ." (*Psst!* Are we ever going to do it?)

To Noah and Courtney, Chad and Rachel, and our three irresistible granddaughters, Eliot, Finley, and Francesca—thank you for filling us up with happiness and love, and reminding me of what's most important. (And if we really do sail away, all seven of you have to come with us . . .)

Prologue
It Doesn't Get Better Than This

New crayons in bright red baskets sit at the children's tables, flanking caddies filled with sharpened pencils, markers, scissors, and glue. The pencils stand tall, their erasers intact. All sixty-four crayons point in the same direction. Markers fresh from familiar yellow-and-green boxes have their lids capped tight. And the glue comes out of its dispenser with an easy twist of its orange cap and a gentle squeeze.

A basket of songbooks sits atop the small clusters of tables. Each holds one or two copies of *Five Little Ducks, Oh, A-Hunting We Will Go, Little Rabbit Foo Foo, Twenty-Four Robbers, Dr. Seuss's ABC, My First Real Mother Goose, Chicka Chicka Boom Boom, The Lady with the Alligator Purse,* and *Chicken Soup with Rice.* Assorted fairy tales, picture books, and nonfiction text round out the selection.

In the meeting area, an old floor lamp and several small table lamps glow softly, their shades decorated by children from years past. Plants that have survived the summer are back home on the window ledge; paper flowerpots stick to the windowpanes, waiting for children to paint their bouquets. Empty picture frames await the smiles of this year's girls and boys.

Low bookshelves filled with books sorted into labeled tubs define the meeting area; ABC books sit alongside Arnold Lobel and Henry and Mudge; space and underwater books nestle with the reptiles; and tubs labeled "Predictable Books," "Song Books," "Fairy Tales," and "Little Bear" join "Insects," "Poetry," and "Biographies." Picture books stand tall on shelves of their own.

The Kissing Hand by Audrey Penn, this year's choice for the first day of school read-aloud, stands ready at the chalk ledge. The rocker and the braided rug await us.

The writing table seems to say, "Get over here!" Paper of all sizes and colors, lined and unlined, duplicator and construction, lies straight in organizers that are just the right size. Six staplers and as many tape dispensers line the back of the table, with refills close by. Small containers hold paper clips, pushpins, sticky notes, hole punches, and staple removers. Children's dictionaries and thesauruses stand at the ready on the ledge behind.

Unifix cubes, pattern blocks, calculators, and Judy Clocks; microscopes, magnifying glasses, slides, maps, globes, and atlases fill the shelves in the math, science, and geography areas.

Wooden blocks and Legos left behind years ago by my own children occupy another shelf. Buckets of plastic dinosaurs, insects, reptiles, and other assorted animals are ready for play. Nearby, small tubs labeled "Pastels," "Beads," "Buttons," "Yarn," "Needles and Thread," "Fabric," "Stuffing," "Clay," and "Watercolors" are stocked and ready for work activity time.

Professional books stretch from one end of my desk to the other. Ellin Keene and Susan Zimmermann line up next to Lucy Calkins, Shelley Harwayne, Georgia Heard, and Richard Allington. Brenda Power, Ralph

Fletcher, Brian Cambourne, Joanne Hindley, Ralph Peterson, Stephanie Harvey, Anne Goudvis, Smokey Daniels, and others join them and are there when I need their counsel.

These authors have new colleagues now, including Peter Johnston, David Perkins, David Pearson, Samantha Bennett, Cris Tovani, Carol Dweck, Connie Moss and Susan Brookhart, Richard Stiggins, and Grant Wiggins and Jay McTighe. Their expertise and inspiration have enriched my practice and strengthened my beliefs about teaching and learning.

My plan book is open, all subjects and specials penciled in and accounted for. Paper for individual portraits, first-day interviews, and forms for the Reader Observation Survey and Developmental Reading Assessment are ready to go.

In these luscious days before school starts, I also think about the things I need to do to ensure that learning happens—sometimes we can focus so much of our time and attention on setting up our rooms and perfecting the space that we neglect to engage in the intellectual work it takes to plan the learning we want to happen in the first few weeks and throughout the year. I use this quiet time to think through the year in chunks of time—making sure to leave room within these chunks for lots of surprises as I come to know children over time. When we spend as much time and effort on planning as we do in setting up our rooms, we give ourselves the gifts of clarity and confidence as we embark on another year of learning and teaching.

And now—at last—the time has come. Yellow, orange, purple, and green magnetic letters march across the radiator, spelling "Welcome to First Grade"; the class list is posted in the hall under my nameplate. Sweetheart, Speedy, and Flopsy are fed, and their cages are pristine. As I take one last look before I leave for the day, I wonder, *Does it get any better than this?*

Twenty-four hours later I find myself under those same clusters of tables, picking up stray Unifix cubes, assorted crayons and marker lids, two butterfly barrettes, an animal cracker, and one small white sock with lace. On the tables, the crayons have abandoned the caddies; pencils are mysteriously dented and have mixed themselves in with the markers, and the glue looks as if it's had more than just a gentle squeeze.

My desk is piled high. Registration forms, emergency cards, testing dates, and memos from the office mingle with money and checks for the PTA, today's lunch, and school sweatshirts. Notes from parents request Girl Scout information, an overview of this year's curriculum, and the date and time of the Halloween parade. Two more parents have written to let me know their children are gifted.

I plop into my chair and take another look. This time I notice the tiny bouquet of dandelions in the red plastic glass, the happy purple, orange, yellow, and green chains that now hang from our doors, and the "I luv U Mlr" written on the dry erase board.

Magnetic letters that once marched across the radiator now dance, spelling *Mom, Dad, LOVE, Zac, cat,* and *IrNsTPq.*

Yesterday's empty flowerpots hold painted bouquets of what I think might be daisies, roses, geraniums, and tulips. Children's self-portraits, with their too-high-on-the-forehead eyes, crinkled paper hair, glued-on earrings, and bright red lips, smile back at me.

I read over their interviews. Hannah wants to learn to write her little letters; Cole wonders why the octopus squirts ink. If they could do anything in the world they wanted, Eric would be a fireman, Will would go to the moon, and Jake would live in the theater district in New York City. When I asked Grace, "What's one more thing I should know about you?" she answered, "You should know I believe in fairies." And Breck's answer? "I really want you to teach me." Now I know for sure. It really doesn't get better than this.

Introduction
to the Second Edition

When I was contemplating a second edition to *Reading with Meaning*, I made a pot of coffee, put a couple of raspberry fig bars on my favorite blue plate, and sat myself down to read it, cover to cover. *What will I think when I finish?* I wondered. *Will I wince at the words I wrote so long ago?*

A few hours later I was filled with relief, happiness, and pride. (And, um, more than "a couple" of raspberry fig bars.) In all the important ways, *Reading with Meaning* still rang true: much of what was relevant back then is just as—and maybe even more—relevant today. The emphasis on higher-level comprehension skills and strategies in the current standards makes me smile—it's about time making meaning is deemed "cutting edge" when it comes to teaching children (even our youngest) to read!

So What's New?

Thinking About Comprehension Strategies as the How Instead of the What

You'll notice that for the most part, comprehension strategies are no longer the organizing feature of the curriculum—now it's content and standards that lead me to the big ideas. Skills and strategies are the essential tools that children need to actively engage with content, construct meaning, and grow their understanding of big ideas in the world. Comprehension strategies are the how—the specific processes learners flexibly use—to get smarter about big, important topics that are relevant to them and help them become powerful and thoughtful human beings.

Planning Documents

Near the beginning of each chapter, you'll find a set of planning documents that offer possibilities for in-depth teaching and learning. These documents include plans for the following:

> *Big ideas*—What big ideas do I want students to walk away with at the end of this study and remember ten years from now?
> *Summative assessments*—What end-of-study assessments will students create that exist in the real world and have real purpose and audience?
> *Guiding questions*—What compelling questions will foster inquiry, understanding, and the transfer of learning?
> *Learning targets*—What are our long-term and short-term goals?
> *Matching formative assessments for learning*—What will students make, do, say, or write to demonstrate understanding?

Use these documents to get yourself and your colleagues thinking about your big ideas, guiding questions, and the rest—there's something empowering about being part of the figuring out!

New Titles

You'll find new book titles throughout. I've kept some old favorites— remember *Oliver Button Is a Sissy* and *Amazing Grace*?—but I'm always on the lookout, as I'm sure you are, for new books that will engage children and help me teach well. There's also an appendix that includes favorite picture books— fiction and nonfiction—as well as predictable books, wordless books, alphabet books, books in a series, and books of poetry and rhyme.

Frequently Asked Questions

These really are the questions I get asked most. They're at the end of the book, and I suspect that if we were to sit down and chat, these might be the kinds of things we'd talk about. (I'll bring raspberry fig bars if you bring the coffee . . .).

And a Little Note About the Common Core State Standards . . .

Remember No Child Left Behind, where comprehension was grouped with phonics, phonemic awareness, fluency, and vocabulary, with each receiving equal importance? The Common Core State Standards changes all that—now higher-level comprehension work is emphasized for all children, even our youngest readers. Reading, in the Common Core, is all about making meaning. (Do I hear applause out there?)

And this, too, is heartening: the Common Core focuses on results, rather than means, leaving room for teachers to determine how these goals should be reached and what additional topics might be addressed. Authors of the Common Core say, "The Standards do not mandate such things as a particular writing process or the full range of metacognitive strategies that students may need to monitor and direct their thinking and learning."

I take that to mean they're leaving that up to us. We do get to decide, based on what we know about comprehension instruction and the children sitting in front of us, how best to go about teaching children to comprehend at the high levels required. Common Core work needs to be placed in the context of real teaching and learning, and not treated as an isolated list of skills to teach.

Think about these big ideas first: How will I organize my curriculum? What structures and practices for teaching and learning will I put into place for this in-depth work? Does my classroom library need beefing up? Do I have a fifty-fifty balance between fiction and nonfiction? How will I provide for close, in-depth reading?

This is about complex work over time—rushing through won't get children where they need to be. So let's slow down and think about what's most important. Breathe. Remain calm. And teach and be our best selves. I hope this book will help with that.

Happy reading!

Debbie

1

Guiding Principles

Torin and Jack work together to sound out words.

Independence is the goal!

When I think about the principles that guide my teaching of reading comprehension, I realize that they are the same principles that guide my work throughout the day. Making certain that children and I are crystal clear about where we're going. Why it matters, and the hard work we need to do to get there. Keeping an eye on the amount of time children have to engage with and produce evidence of their learning, thinking, and growth, and trusting and supporting them as they assume responsibility for new learning and big ideas right from the start. All of these allow me to make thoughtful decisions based on the principles I believe in.

It was Brian Cambourne who encouraged me to make explicit my beliefs about teaching and learning. He supported me and my colleagues at Regis University as we explored the beliefs, theories, and practices of others, considered their implications for teaching in general, tried out new practices in our classrooms, and finally synthesized and made explicit our personal beliefs about teaching and learning.

When we know the theory behind our work, when our practices match our beliefs, and when we clearly articulate what we do and why we do it, people listen. At back-to-school night, when I get questions like "Do you do phonics or something else?" or "My child is reading at the sixth-grade level. How will you challenge him?" or "Do you believe in 'real spelling' or 'invented spelling'?" my stomach no longer churns. I know what to say. No longer are my answers vague, my demeanor tentative, my attitude defensive. No longer do I say things because it's what someone wants to hear. I'm clear. I'm confident. I'm calm. Parents appreciate and respect a teacher who "knows her stuff," even when it doesn't quite agree with theirs.

Or maybe the district is thinking of adopting a new spelling program. I can look at it and know fairly quickly if it's something I could work with. When an administrator asks us about leveling all the books in our school library or the new assistant principal asks us to dye our hair green if children read a certain number of books, I really don't have to ponder. I know just what to say.

What if you are mandated to do something that you know in your heart is not best for kids? Look at it carefully. Maybe there is a piece of it that will work. As for the rest? Chances are good that both your method and the new one have the same goals; maybe you just believe in going after it a little differently. Think about how you believe reading needs to be taught, and be ready to thoughtfully explain how and why. Then make an appointment with your principal and do it. Most administrators listen to and support teachers when we speak with conviction, know the research behind our beliefs, and present our point of view in respectful, rational ways.

This is even more important now. Envision yourself as a social activist, in your building and maybe even beyond. After all, we're the ones who spend our days with children, and we're the ones who see and feel the effect of ill-conceived policies and programs in the faces, hearts, and minds of the children we teach. I'm sometimes told by those in power, "What you say makes a lot of sense, but we've adopted a new program and have mandated teachers to teach it with 'fidelity' for at least the first three years."

I used to think, *What? You're asking teachers to pledge fidelity to a program over fidelity to children? For three YEARS?* Now I say it right out loud. Nicely.

But we can't say that if we can't show how what we're doing is working for student learning and getting them where they need to be. We have to ask the people making the mandates to articulate the purpose behind them, and work to find out if we are meeting children's needs in different ways. If we don't want people to tell us what to do and how to do it, we must be clear about what we are doing and why we're doing it, and back it up with strong evidence that shows all students are on their way to achieving at least one year of growth in their time with us.

There are many effective ways to teach children and live our lives. No one has a patent on the truth. Find yours. Read. Reflect. Think about what you already know about good teaching and how it fits with new learning. Read some more. Think about the implications for your classroom. Collaborate with colleagues. Try new things and spend time defining your beliefs and aligning your practices. Once you've found what's true for you, stand up for what you know is right. Live it every day, and be confident and clear about why you believe as you do. People will listen!

So now, when someone asks you those big important questions or makes requests of you that don't put children first, you'll think it *and* say it, right? (How does it feel to be an activist? ☺)

Establishing a Framework

Think about yourself as a reader. You probably choose what you want to read for a variety of purposes; have opportunities to read for long periods of time; respond mostly through reflection, conversation, and collaboration; and sometimes share your thinking and insights with others. In a reading workshop, children have daily opportunities to learn how to do the same.

Reading workshop is a simple framework for teaching and learning that beautifully accommodates my beliefs about how children learn. Based on the principles of time, choice, response, and community, a workshop format allows for in-depth teaching and learning, flexibility, differentiation, and ultimately, independence.

I used to structure workshops around a fifteen-minute (or sometimes longer) mini-lesson; a thirty- to forty-five-minute extended work time in which children had daily opportunities to read, write, talk, and apply what I was working to teach them; and ten to fifteen minutes for reflection and sharing. Nice and tidy, right?

Yes. But to what end? Is nice and tidy what we're all about? If so, it's tempting to want to tell/show children too much, keep them with us too long, in a good-faith effort to ensure their success. "They're with me," I used to say to myself again and again as the mini-lesson minutes ticked by, taking away precious minutes from student work time. But were they really with me? The truth is, some were and some weren't. And so the question becomes "Is this about getting those who are 'far, far, away' into the nice and tidy 'with me' column?"

No. Not when we believe in the power of student agency and independence. Not when we understand that over-scaffolding diminishes student energy, engagement, and motivation and increases student conformity and compliance. And not when it's clear that the one who is doing the reading, writing, and talking is also the one who is doing the thinking and the one who is getting smarter! When we know that learning is a consequence of thinking, just who should be doing it?

So now, instead of keeping the whole group together in way-too-long mini-lessons, I send children off—release them—much earlier, so that they get to be the ones doing the reading, writing, talking, and *learning*. It's messier—nurturing creativity and independence always is—but now the children are the ones digging in, figuring out, and working hard to read words and make sense of stories, content, and big ideas. And I get to be the one listening in, conferring with children, and supporting them as needed.

What if I notice that student stamina is fading? Or learn something from listening in that would be important for everyone to know? Instead of addressing these issues during the share, or in a lesson the next day, now I attend to them right then and there, when my actions and words can be most useful and powerful. Bringing children back together, briefly addressing what they need to do or think about to move forward, then sending them back to work, breathes energy, life, and a renewed sense of purpose into the workshop.

Samantha Bennett describes this process as the "catch-and-release" workshop model, and explains it this way in *That Workshop Book*:

> Picture the rhythm of the fly fisherman. During the mini-lesson, the teacher (or fisherman) has the students "out of the water." The trick is to throw the fish back into the river before they stop breathing and die. Clever, huh? That's why the word *mini* before *lesson* is important.
>
> During the work time, student stamina for work may wane, and it is time for another "catch" from the fisherman. So, we pull students out of the river of learning for another round of teacher talk—to show students how and remind them why the task we are asking them to do is important. But only for a few minutes! It's crucial to

throw them back in to reading, writing, talking, and learning before they stop breathing. Students need lots of time to swim in texts and talk in order to learn. If teachers are doing all of the talking, they are the ones swimming, and doing all the work. (2008, 10)

Samantha's circle diagram captures this catch-and-release process perfectly . . .

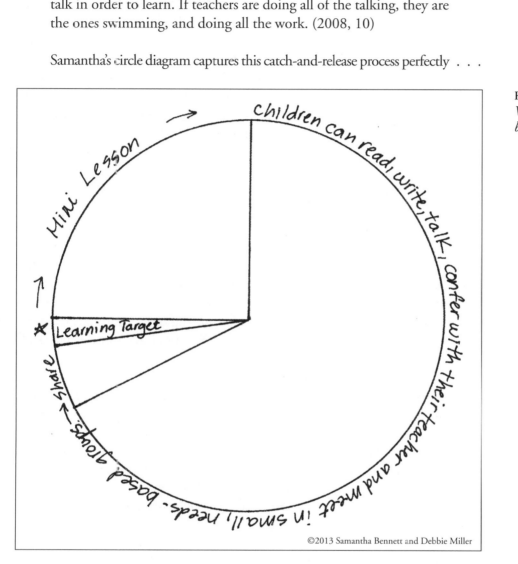

©2013 Samantha Bennett and Debbie Miller

FIGURE 1.1
Workshop as a time-based structure

Sometimes visitors ask me, "You mean you have a reading workshop every day? Don't the kids get bored? Don't you?" Yes, no, and no. The truth is, I can't imagine having a workshop only two or three days a week, or leaving out a component here and there, depending on my mood. Such questions always draw my eye (and subsequently the visitors') to the quote by Lucy Calkins that hangs above my desk:

It is significant to realize that the most creative environments in our society are not the ever-changing ones. The artist's studio, the researcher's laboratory, the scholar's library are each deliberately kept simple so as to support the complexities of the work-in-progress. They are deliberately kept predictable so the unpredictable can happen. (1983, 32)

To get started, find at least sixty to ninety uninterrupted minutes in your day and put your reading workshop there. No time like that in the morning? Look at your afternoon. I'd choose a big block of uninterrupted time in the afternoon over a chopped-up morning any day. The workshop won't run the full time until after the first four or five weeks, but teach well and you'll be amazed at how quickly your children get there!

Proficient Reader Research

When Ellin Keene, then director of programs at the Public Education and Business Coalition, handed me a copy of the proficient reader research synthesized by Pearson, Dole, Duffy, and Roehler (1992), my eyes glazed over. Who were these guys, anyway? And what did they know about teaching real kids in real classrooms? Yes, I knew something was missing in my reading workshop. I'd been saying I wanted rigor. And yes, I trusted Ellin. But come on! This stuff seemed way too ivory tower to me.

The chapter was published in the early 1990s; researchers had spent much of the previous ten years investigating what proficient readers do to comprehend text, what less successful readers fail to do, and how to best move novices toward expertise. From this work, Pearson et al. identified comprehension strategies that successful readers of all ages use routinely to construct meaning when they read and suggested that teachers need to teach these strategies explicitly, using well-written literature and nonfiction.

The research showed that active, thoughtful, proficient readers construct meaning by using the following strategies:

- Activating relevant, prior knowledge (schema) before, during, and after reading text (Anderson and Pearson 1984).
- Creating visual and other sensory images from text during and after reading (Pressley 1976).
- Drawing inferences from text to form conclusions, make critical judgments, and create unique interpretations (Hansen 1981).
- Asking questions of themselves, the authors, and the texts they read (Raphael 1984).
- Determining the most important ideas and themes in a text (Palincsar and Brown 1984).
- Synthesizing what they read (Brown, Day, and Jones 1983).

Sounds simple enough, right? But how exactly does one go about teaching a few strategies, in depth, and over time? Especially one who, after wading through the research, is seriously wondering if she is a proficient reader herself?

I was always a fast reader, and therefore, I figured, a good one. In school, I remember being among the bluebirds, flying high through story after story, zipping through the questions at the end, and turning in pages of neatly written seatwork with the pictures colored in just so.

But this stuff was different. What did they mean, think about your thinking? I'm reading too fast to think. Interact with the text? Forget it; I just want to find out what's going to happen next. Draw inferences? Determine importance? Synthesize? I'm not sure what those terms *mean*, and I sure don't know if I do them!

Still, I was intrigued. I wanted to learn more. And because of Ellin, who recognized that the research had merit long before many of the rest of us did, small groups of us began meeting once a week to try to make sense of it all. Ellin understood that first we needed to learn about ourselves as readers. She challenged us to be metacognitive—to think about our thinking as we read. We'd read books and short pieces, keep track of our thinking by jotting notes in the margins, and then talk about the pieces and what we were thinking as we read.

When we began to pay attention to what was going on inside our heads as we read, we were amazed at what we learned about ourselves as readers. We were making connections, asking questions, drawing inferences, and synthesizing information. We began to create working definitions for each of these strategies, realizing early on that the dictionary definition was not going to cut it. (We fancied ourselves way beyond Webster!) Although friends chided us to "get a life," we knew Ellin was right. Only when we took the time to really get to know ourselves as readers were we able to seriously consider the implications of the research for the children in our classrooms.

Were we proficient readers all along? I'm not sure. Did all this heightened awareness simply bring to the forefront what was already going on inside our heads when we read? Maybe. Regardless, I'm a different reader now. I've learned to slow down and enjoy the ride; getting there no longer consumes me. Twenty years later, I'm still paying attention!

I find myself asking questions, inferring, making connections, and smiling when I silently name what I'm doing. It's not a loud, in-your-face consciousness like it was in the beginning, but a soft, quiet, more natural one, holding conversations with myself when I read.

The proficient reader research kept me in teaching. Not only was it the "something missing" I'd been searching for, but it systematically raised my expectations for children as well as for learning and teaching. And the best part? Teaching isn't as predictable as it once was. Every day I know children are going to surprise me with their thinking, teach me to see and understand things in new ways, motivate me to think deeply about my teaching, and help me make thoughtful decisions about where to go next because of what they say and do.

It's been ten years now since I wrote these words, and they still ring true. My expectations for children, and my expectations for myself as a teacher and learner, are forever and significantly raised. But have I revised my thinking about other aspects of strategy instruction? Yes! I wouldn't be much of a teacher and learner if my answer were no, right?

I used to think of comprehension strategies as the organizing feature of my curriculum. Making connections, asking questions, determining importance, and so on were the big ideas of my curriculum, and everything else came underneath. When asked what we were working on in the classroom, I'd say, "Inferring" or "Synthesizing information" or "Asking questions." But now those answers seem vague.

I'm surprised no one asked, "So, what are you synthesizing information about?" Or, "Inferring and asking questions about what?" Or, "What content are you tackling right now?"

Now I think of the content and standards as the organizing features—they lead me to the big ideas of my curriculum. So now, when asked what we're working on in the classroom, I might say, "We're synthesizing our learning about life cycles," or, "We're building background knowledge about people in other parts of the world," or, "We're learning how readers ask and answer questions, determine importance, and synthesize information to help them access, remember, and understand nonfiction texts and materials."

Skills and strategies are the essential tools that children need to actively engage with content, construct meaning, and grow their understanding of big ideas in the world. Strategies are the how—the specific processes learners flexibly use—to get smarter about big, important topics that are relevant to them and help them become powerful and thoughtful human beings in school, their neighborhoods, and beyond.

Take a look at this from the Common Core State Standards document:

> Students habitually perform the critical reading necessary to pick carefully through the staggering amount of information available today in print and digitally. They actively seek the wide, deep, and thoughtful engagement with high-quality literary and informational texts that builds knowledge, enlarges experience, and broadens world views. They reflexively demonstrate the cogent reasoning and use of evidence that is essential to both private deliberation and responsible citizenship in a democratic republic. (2010, 3)

And yes, this starts in *kindergarten*! To learn how to read in these sophisticated ways, to seek the "wide, deep, and thoughtful engagement with high-quality literary and informational text," is there any doubt that giving children the tools they need to make meaning is more important than ever?

The Common Core standards focus on results rather than means—this leaves it up to us to decide how the goals should best be met. They say right up front that "the Standards do not mandate a particular writing process or the full range of metacognitive strategies that students may need to monitor and direct their thinking and learning" (Common Core State Standards 2010, 4).

How do you begin to plan for a four- to six-week study focused on content standards, and the skills and strategies needed to access them? First, think big picture. Ask yourself questions like these:

- What do I want children to understand and remember ten years from now?
- Why does this study matter?
- What essential questions will guide us—what are our beacons of hope and big understandings?
- What are our long-term targets/goals? Do I have a balance of knowledge, strategy, and demonstration-of-understanding goals for children?
- What skills and strategies will children need to actively engage with the content, construct meaning, and grow understanding?
- How will children demonstrate their understanding?
- How can I combine reading, writing, listening, and speaking standards into this content study?
- How much time do I have? Exactly how many days? (Put the end date on a calendar and plan backward.)

These questions may seem daunting at first, but stay with me! In the chapters that follow I'll show just how they help me plan for student learning.

Once you know what you want to teach, think about how you will teach it. What books, materials, websites, and other resources will you and your students need to teach and learn well? What kinds of formative assessments will you use so that you *and* your children know where they are and where they need to go?

I know it's difficult just to think about planning a four- to six-week course of study—in fact, I used to think it was counterproductive. After all, how could I possibly know where we'd be six weeks from now? But this isn't about the day-to-day planning—that still needs to be done. Rather, this "big picture" planning is about creating a well-thought-out, *overall* plan that guides my work and gives direction to our day-to-day learning goals, or targets. Once we know where we're going, we know what we need to do to get there!

There's nothing worse than walking into school each morning having to figure out what to teach, scramble for a book, come up with a plan. When we get caught in that trap, our teaching becomes disconnected and is just a series of lessons rather than a coherent plan for teaching and learning.

Do I ever deviate from the big picture? Absolutely. I never know when a child or a colleague will cause me to think about things in new ways, lead me in new directions, and refine my thinking. As David Pearson says, "Good planning, like good instruction, is as intentional as it is adaptable" (Pearson 1995, personal interview).

Gradual Release of Responsibility

Chances are good that if you think back to a time when you learned how to do something new, the gradual release of responsibility model (Pearson and Gallagher 1983) comes into play. Maybe you learned how to snowboard, canoe, play golf, or drive a car. If you watched somebody do it first, practiced under that person's watchful eye, listened to his or her feedback, and then one fine day went off and did it by yourself, adding your own special twist to it in the process, you know what this model is all about.

Pearson and Gallagher use a model of explicit reading instruction using these four stages that guide children toward independence:

1. Teacher modeling and demonstration
2. Guided practice, where teachers gradually give students more responsibility for task completion
3. Independent practice accompanied by descriptive feedback
4. Application of the strategy in real reading situations

Many have described this model in a variety of ways, but, essentially, gradually releasing responsibility is all about teachers reducing the amount of scaffolding across time, and lessons, as students gain independent control of applying what they've been taught.

But did you know that this model doesn't have to be linear? We don't always have to begin with modeling, then move to guided practice, independent practice, and finally application. We might even *begin* with guided practice! That way we'll learn quickly where children are, *then* model, so that our explicit teaching—modeling and demonstration—is based on actual student needs, not on assumptions about what we *think* they need.

In *Comprehension Going Forward*, David Pearson writes:

> There is no inherent virtue in explicit instruction and modeling. We offer it if and when students demonstrate less than completely independent control over an activity; and we provide just enough scaffolding so that students can perform the activity successfully. It is a "Goldilocks" phenomenon—not too much, not too little, but just the right amount. (Daniels 2011, 248)

Are you thinking, *Aha! I see the way a catch-and-release workshop model and the gradual release instructional model (maybe we should call it the not-so-gradual-release model!) work together?*

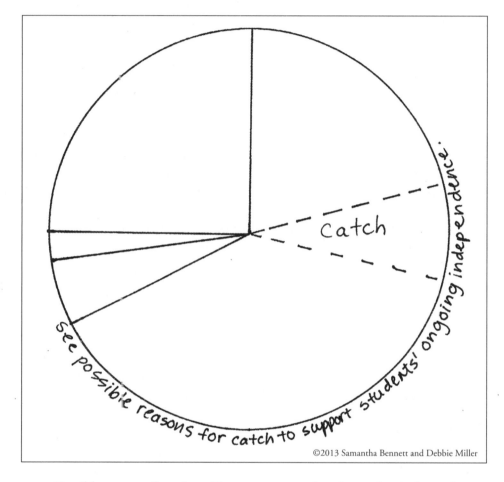

©2013 Samantha Bennett and Debbie Miller

FIGURE 1.2
Workshop with (not-so) gradual release as "catch and release" to support independence

Possible reasons for a "catch" to support students' ongoing independence:

- To notice patterns of confusion (multiple learners) as children are working
- A shift in task; for example, "Now that you've talked about what you already know about butterflies, we're going to read what the experts say."
- To publicly affirm a child's thinking or work
- To notice patterns of understanding to share with everyone so they continue to repeat it
- To scaffold different genres or lengths of text within one lesson

So what does all this mean for kids? How can we help them find their own soft and quiet voices? From my reading of the research, late-night and after-school conversations with colleagues, and years of personal experience as a reader and a teacher, here are my daily ten principles and practices that guide me in my work with children:

Because I believe that learning is a consequence of thinking . . . every day in my classroom you'll see children reading, writing, and talking more than you'll see me reading, writing, and talking!

Because I believe children need time to practice what I'm working so hard to teach them . . . every day you'll see them engaged in workshops with a one-third/two-thirds balance of time: one-third of the time for me to teach and two-thirds of the time for them to work.

Because I believe in the gradual release of responsibility instructional model and its goals for student independence . . . every day you'll see me modeling *just enough* to show children how and why, sending them off to have a go, and catching them back if and when they need it.

Because I believe in instilling the spark of agency within children . . . every day you'll see children working hard, and me asking questions like "How did you figure that out?" and "What did you learn about yourself as a reader today that you will use in the days and weeks to come?"

Because I believe every learner needs descriptive feedback to grow and get smarter . . . every day you'll see me conferring with children individually, looking at the work they create, and often writing notes to give children concrete feedback.

Because I believe in assessment for learning . . . every day you'll hear children and me reflecting and thinking aloud about where we're going, where we are now, and what we will do today to move forward.

Because I believe that surface structures and deep structures are best taught side by side . . . every day you'll see lessons that focus on word work *and* lessons that focus on comprehension, and lots of time for children to practice consolidating them in real books.

Because I believe in the connections between student ownership and engagement . . . every day you'll see children making thoughtful choices about what to read, where to read, and with whom.

Because I believe that every child deserves a year of growth . . . every day you'll see all children developing a clear understanding of their goals and working hard to meet them.

Because I believe in the power of classroom communities and the emotional engagement they offer . . . every day you'll see children interacting with each other in collaborative, thoughtful, and respectful ways.

Community: Creating a Culture and Climate for Thinking

If you had asked me about the importance of creating a sense of community in my classroom ten years ago, I'd have said it was everything. I'd have talked about the interviews and surveys we do at the beginning of the year, the self-portraits taped above the chalkboard, the photographs everywhere of children playing and working together. I'd have told you about Talent Show Tuesdays, about writing and signing "Our Promise to Each Other," and about the children's work that hangs not only on the boards and doors but also from the wires that crisscross our room. I'd have told you about the cozy spaces where children work in small groups, pairs, and independently, and about rituals for birthdays, losing a tooth, and saying good-bye. And finally, I'd have mentioned that each day begins with our singing "Oh, What a Beautiful Morning" with Joanie Bartels, and ends with an a cappella version of "Happy Trails to You" written by cowgirl Dale Evans.

And if you asked me about the importance of creating community today? I'd still say it's everything. But now I know that once the promises are written and signed, the room is beautifully and thoughtfully arranged, and the photographs are taken, developed, and sitting prettily in a frame, our work has just begun. Real classroom communities are more than just a look. Real communities flourish when we bring together the voices, hearts, and souls of the people who inhabit them.

When our vision of community expands to create a culture and climate for thinking (Perkins 1993)—when rigor, inquiry, and intimacy become key components of our definition—it's essential that we work first to build genuine relationships, establish mutual trust, and create working literate environments. If we look to the months ahead and envision children constructing meaning by spontaneously engaging in thoughtful conversation about books and ideas, asking questions that matter to them and exploring their solutions, and responding independently to a variety of text in meaningful ways, we must be deliberate in those first days and weeks of school.

Building Relationships

I begin by paying attention to the little things. It's noticing Paige's cool new haircut, Grant's oversized Avalanche jersey, Kendal's sparkly blue nail polish, and Cody's washable tattoos. It's asking about Palmer's soccer game, Jane's dance recital, Elizabeth's visiting grandpa, and Hannah's brand-new baby brother.

It's giving Ailey a heart rock to add to her collection, copying a poem about cats and giving it to Gina because I know she loves them, and even putting a Band-Aid on Grace's tiny paper cut. Showing children we care about them and love being their teacher is an important first message. And at the same time, I'm modeling for children how to show someone you care about them; I'm modeling how you go about creating lasting friendships.

Teaching children how to listen and respond to each other in respectful, thoughtful ways also helps foster new relationships and caring communities. I used to have long conversations with children about this, telling them how important it was to listen carefully to each other and to really think about what their classmates have to say. I'd talk about responding respectfully, looking at the person you're speaking to, calling them by name, and on and on. But the very next day a child might groan at a song another had chosen, wildly wave a hand when someone else was talking, or flip through the pages of a book while another child was sharing. And I'd go into the whole respect routine again. During these conversations, the children were just as eloquent. They *sounded* just like me! But their behavior didn't change. And I'd wonder, *What's going on here? Why don't they get it?* And even sometimes, *What's wrong with these kids, anyway?*

Eventually I realized, of course, that nothing was wrong with "these kids." They didn't get it because I hadn't *shown them how*. I'd *told* them to be respectful, thoughtful, and kind, but I hadn't shown them what that looks and sounds like.

The best opportunities to show kids how to behave occur in the moment. When Frankie says to Colleen, "Colleen, could you please speak up? I can't hear what you have to say," I can't let that pass without making sure everyone heard. I can't let that pass without pointing out how smart it is to want to hear what someone has to say. I say, "You guys, did you just hear Frankie? Frankie, could you say that again?" She does, and I ask, "So boys and girls, why was that such a smart thing for Frankie to do?" They respond, and then I use their words and mine to bring our thoughts together.

And when Max tells Jack that his idea is "a little bit dumb," I can't let that pass either. I say, "Max, I'm sure you didn't mean to be rude to Jack, but when you said his idea was a 'little bit dumb,' that's just what it was. It's okay to disagree with someone, but there are nicer, more polite ways to do it. You might say something like, 'Jack, I don't understand what you mean' or 'Jack, why do you think that?' Try it again, Max." He does, beautifully this time, and I don't miss the opportunity to let everyone know how much we've learned from Max today.

Or when Sean is trying to find a place in the circle and he starts nudging himself into a spot four inches wide, I say, "Sean, could you think of a better way to get yourself into the circle?" Sean's stumped. "Well, how about this? The next time you need to be in the circle and there isn't room, how about asking someone to scoot back so you can fit in? Let's try it right now. Just say, 'Sunny, could you please scoot back so I can fit into the circle?'" He does. Next, I turn my attention to Sunny. "Okay, Sunny, Sean has asked you nicely to scoot back. What could you say back to him?" She says, "Sure, Sean, I'll scoot back for you." With smiles all around, she does.

Is the first time the charm? No. And probably not the third time either. But remain diligent. Remain calm. Don't give up the good fight! Once the flagrant violations are in check, watch closely for the rolling of eyes, the private conversations, the exasperated sighs. Don't let those go by either.

You can use these first lessons—we can call them "anchor lessons"—to refer to. For example, when Sarah snaps at Troy, I say, "Oops, Sarah, what's another way you could tell Troy what you're thinking? Think back to how Max handled something like this." We'll assist her if she needs it, but a gentle reminder is usually enough.

Here are a few more teachable moments.

To the children with the wildly waving hand when someone is talking: "You know what? I know you're not meaning to be rude, but when your hand is up and someone else is talking, I'm thinking you're probably focusing on what you're going to say rather than listening to the person who is speaking. What do you think? Since we can learn so much from each other, remember to keep your hands down and really listen and think about what your friends are saying. When they're finished, you can share what you're thinking."

To the children who abruptly get up in the middle of a story or discussion: "Oh my goodness, you're going to leave us now? Think of the learning you'll miss! Can you wait until the story [or discussion] is over? Thanks."

To the children who always have something to say, no matter the topic or the day, and the ones who hardly have anything to say, ever: "Today I want you to think about yourselves as listeners and speakers. If you're someone who's great at talking a lot, I want you to be a listener today. See what you can learn. If you're someone who is a great listener, I want you to do some talking today. We want to know what you are thinking, too. Raise your hand if you think you do a lot of listening. Raise your hand if you think you do a lot of talking. Wow! You really know yourselves. That's so smart. Let's try it."

To those who have already heard every book in your library and can't wait to let you know the minute you hold one up: "That's so great you've heard this book before. And you know what? Since we know how much more we can learn and understand when we reread, I want you to pay special attention when you hear the story today. Think about what you notice this time that you didn't notice before. Think about what puzzled you the first time, and what you think about that this time. Will you let us know?"

Doesn't all this take a lot of time? You bet. But it sets the tone for learning and thoughtful conversation; it paves the way for the work that lies ahead. Once children realize you're not going to relent, once they realize that this is not just a "sometime thing," and once they understand what you want them to do and why it's important, it becomes habit. It becomes part of the language of the classroom.

Establishing Mutual Trust

Like building relationships, establishing trust takes time. And it must begin with me, the teacher. Every time I value a child's idea by acting on it, think out loud to make sense of a question or response because I really want to understand, or ask children what they think and then listen carefully, I let them know I respect their thinking and trust that they have something smart to say.

I don't mean in a superficial "they're only seven" kind of way; I mean trusting children enough to give them the time and the tools to think for themselves, to pose and solve problems, and to make informed decisions about their learning. Respecting their ideas, opinions, and decisions doesn't mean carte blanche acceptance, but it does mean giving their voices sincere consideration. Trust needs to be mutual. If we're asking children to thoughtfully consider the thinking of others, we must expect no less from ourselves.

It was Lauren who made me a believer. It was early in her first-grade year, and she'd been happily reading books like *Whose Mouse Are You?* by Robert Kraus and *Cookie's Week* by Cindy Ward. But the day I read aloud Mary Hoffman's *Amazing Grace*, things changed. She had to have that book. I gave her my usual line: "You know, Lauren, I'm thinking this book is too challenging for you right now. How about waiting a while, then giving it a try? You can keep it safe in your cubby until then. Let's find *Where Are You Going, Little Mouse?* I think that would be perfect for you." But she'd have none of the mouse. It was *Amazing Grace* she wanted.

In the end, she won me over. But once I'd said yes, I couldn't just give her the book and say, "You go, girl." Once I'd relented, I needed to do everything I could to help make her decision—now ours—a good one. I had to figure out how best to support her and maximize her chances for success. This wasn't about power or proving a point; this was about helping a little girl learn to trust herself and make good decisions about her learning.

We made a plan together: I'd help her learn a page a day at school, she'd reread what she'd learned already, and she'd take the book home every night to practice. Five weeks later, the kids and I were calling her Amazing Lauren! And she was amazing. Not only was she able to read *Amazing Grace*, but she was off and running, reading books like *Oliver Button Is a Sissy* by Tomie dePaola, *Wild Wild Wolves* by Joyce Milton, *The Paper Bag Princess* by Robert Munsch, and *Honey, I Love* by Eloise Greenfield.

What if I'd said no? Would she have learned to read *Oliver Button Is a Sissy*; *Honey, I Love*; and the others? Probably. But I want to do more than teach kids how to read. I want to teach them how to go after something if they really want it, I want to teach them the rewards of hard work and determination, and I want to teach them that if they're sincere, I'll do everything I can to support them.

I've taken the time to figure out my guiding principles and work hard to ensure that everything I do with children aligns with what I believe. When you need the courage or energy to do the same, reread this passage from earlier in this chapter:

There are many effective ways to teach children and live our lives. No one has a patent on the truth. Find yours. Read. Reflect. Think about what you already know about good teaching and how it fits with new learning. Read some more. Think about the implications for your classroom. Collaborate with colleagues. Try new things and spend time defining your beliefs and aligning your practices. Once you've found what's true for you, stand up for what you know is right. Live it every day and be confident and clear about why you believe as you do. People will listen!

Books † LYLE

"Books are lovely " by Frankie

Frankie's response to the question "What do we know about books?"

In September, Part One

Setting Students Up for Success—The Structures and Routines of Workshop

Sharing a snack is the perfect time for practicing good manners and the civility of conversation.

■ ■ ■ ■

It's late afternoon. The children have gone for the day, and save for a lone cricket chirping from its bug box in a faraway corner, the room is quiet. It's the second week of school, and despite vows that this year it's going to be different, that this year there really will be balance in my life, I'm already feeling overwhelmed and out of sync. And instead of being smart and heading out for the gym, or even staying to get ready for Wednesday's back-to-school night, score the district's newest assessment, or check my voice mail for the messages I know await me, I find myself watching the sunlight as it streams in through the windows.

My eye catches a stack of letters peeking out from under a pile of books. Realizing they're the ones I'd asked parents to write, and mortified I'd forgotten them in the rush of the first week, I sink (or is it slink?) into the once-white overstuffed chair in the corner and begin to read.

I'd invited parents to take a few moments to write to me about their children, asking them to think about things that might be important for me to know as well as their hopes and expectations for the coming year. As I read, I learn that this year's children are animal lovers, Irish step dancers, Kenny Loggins enthusiasts, pianists, creative artists, Lego-maniacs, gymnasts, soccer players, geniuses, and budding geniuses. They are dubbed silly, smart, sweet, caring, serious, mature, young, sensitive, gregarious, shy, confident, playful, and imaginative.

Matthew's parents write that from the day he was born, he had a sparkle in his eye, and now they do, too. They say that "more than anything, Matt would love to read." Caitlin's family tells me they waited ten years for her and that she is "the light of our lives." And Danny's parents write, "We moved into the neighborhood because our dearest wish was for you to be his first-grade teacher." (Yikes!)

As I read the letters from the parents, I'm struck by the love between the lines, the hopes and dreams that live in their words, and the faith and trust they have in me. No one wrote that they wanted their child to score high on the Iowa Test of Basic Skills, or attain Level 20 by the end of first grade, or even meet the highly publicized state standards. It's not that they don't want those things for their children, but the things they chose to write to me about—the things they considered most important for me to know—were not about test scores, reading levels, or state standards.

I remind myself that in the incessant push for higher test scores, and in the face of endless editorials about the demise of public schools and misguided politicians and their plans for reform, I must not let myself—or my budding geniuses—get caught up in some kind of frenzied, frantic pace that knows no end. I remind myself to not let go of what I know is best for kids. For me, September is all about building relationships, establishing trust, creating working literate environments, and getting to know children as readers, writers, thinkers, and learners—and remembering that our classrooms still need to be joyful places where we take the time to appreciate Matthew's sparkling eye, Isabella's shy poetic spirit, and Kendal's boundless energy.

How do I plan for this important, beginning-of-the-year work? I begin with the big picture—I think about what I want students to walk away with at the end of this year, and what I want them to remember ten years from now and forever. These big ideas reflect who I am and what I believe, and guide me and my work with children throughout the months, weeks, and days of the school year. You'll see their influence in what students make and do to demonstrate key understandings, and how they're rooted in my guiding questions, long- and short-term learning targets, or goals, and day-to-day planning. In the pages that follow, you'll see evidence of how children and I move from seemingly abstract big ideas to tangible, day-to-day lessons and demonstrations of understanding and independence.

Some of these goals, or learning targets—and their matching assessments—won't be just right for your children. The important thing is to be mindful of what your students need to know, what they need to be able to do, and what they need to make or do to demonstrate understanding. When crafting learning targets, we need to make sure to share them with all students and show them how they can achieve them—that way they'll understand just what is being asked of them. Other targets will come to you (of course!) as you observe your learners and notice how they respond to different lessons—you're the one who knows your students best.

So . . . how about you? What do you want your students to walk away with this year and remember ten years from now and beyond? Why does reading matter? (I'll share my list if you share yours!)

Big Ideas: Why Do Reading and Learning Matter?
- I want children to understand that readers read to get smarter, and to learn about themselves, other people, and the world—that reading is something they can do independently that empowers them to control their lives and make the world a better place.
- I want children to know that smart is something you get, and that through hard work, effort, and determination, they can accomplish their goals.
- I want children to know that readers read, write, think, and learn with purpose and enthusiasm, and see themselves as problem-posing, problem-solving citizens of the world who have what it takes to figure things out.
- I want children to engage in conversations and discussions about big ideas with open hearts and minds, to be willing to share their own thinking, and to appreciate, learn from, and respect the ideas and opinions of others.
- I want children to understand that learning is for always—it's ongoing, lifelong, and vital.

These big ideas come from my background knowledge, including years and years of classroom experience, ongoing discussions with great teachers and thinkers, and reading a great many professional texts. Current reads include *Understanding by Design, That Workshop Book, Seven Strategies of Assessment for Learning, Talk About Understanding, Making Learning Whole, Opening Minds, Mindset, What Research Has to Say About Reading Instruction* (fourth edition), *Pathways to the Common Core*, and the Common Core State Standards "key design considerations" and vision for students.

Routines of Reading Workshop

Flash forward to the last week of September. The voice of Joanie Bartels singing "Oh, What a Beautiful Morning" is the signal for children to finish selecting their books and gather in the meeting area. By the last "I've got a beautiful feeling, everything's going my way," everyone's singing along with Joanie. Reading workshop in first grade is in full swing. We've been at it for almost three weeks now, and children have learned how to select their books for the day, how to gather for a story and mini-lesson, how to practice reading behaviors in authentic situations using real books, how to use workshop procedures, and how to share with their classmates what they've learned about themselves as readers.

Hold the phone, you might be thinking. *How could they learn all that in just three weeks?* or *How can you have a reading workshop when they can't even read?* Hang on. The fact is, many children haven't learned to decode or comprehend. Not yet. And still, they see themselves and their classmates as readers. They clearly look the part, and right now, that's precisely the point.

Reading workshop in September is less about teaching children how to read and more about modeling and teaching children what good readers do, setting the tone for the workshop and establishing its expectations and procedures, and engaging and motivating children to want to learn to read. Once these are in place, we can move forward quickly without the distraction of management, procedural, and behavioral issues.

Learning to read should be a joyful experience. Give children the luxury of listening to well-written stories with interesting plots, singing songs and playing with their words, and exploring a wide variety of fiction, nonfiction, poetry, and rhymes. Let them know when they say or do something smart; give them credit and ask them to share. Help children access what they already know and figure out how to help them make connections to something new. Be genuine. Laugh. Love. Be patient. You're creating a community of readers and thinkers; you're building relationships and establishing trust. Come October, you'll be glad you did.

▣ SEPTEMBER PLAN ▣
Setting Students Up for Success—The Structures and Routines of Workshop

Big Ideas for the Year: Why Do Reading and Learning Matter?	Demonstration of Understanding
What do I want students to walk away with at the end of this year and remember ten years from now and beyond?	*What kind of summative, end-of-study assessment can we create that exists in the world and has a real purpose and audience?*
I want students to understand the following:	"Celebration of Readers" night focusing on what readers do and the surface structure systems—letters, sounds, and words in context
Readers read to get smarter and learn about themselves, other people, and the world. Reading is something they can do independently that empowers them to control their own lives and make the world a better place.	Children will do the following:
	Host and lead a reading workshop, explaining the structures, rituals, and routines they live and practice every day.
Smart is something you *get*, and through hard work, effort, and determination students have the power to make themselves smarter.	Read aloud a songbook, a predictable book, or a nonfiction book and explain how they've grown as readers since the first day of school.
Readers read, write, think, and learn with purpose and enthusiasm, and see themselves as problem-solving citizens who have what it takes to figure things out.	Big questions for children to think about:
	What can I do as a reader now that I couldn't do when school started?
Readers, writers, and learners engage in conversations and discussions with open hearts and minds; are willing to share their thinking; and appreciate, learn from, and respect the ideas and opinions of others.	What did I do to get smarter?
	What might be next for me?
Learning is for always—it's ongoing, lifelong, and vital.	

(continued)

■ **SEPTEMBER PLAN** ■ *(continued)*

Possible Guiding Questions

What compelling questions will foster inquiry, understanding, and transfer of learning?
- What do readers do?
- Why does reading matter?
- How will reading make me bigger and stronger?
- How do readers grow?
- How do readers interact with other readers?

Possible Supporting Targets	Possible Assessments for Learning
Long-term targets are in bold, and daily targets are listed below them.	*These formative assessments match the daily targets and let kids and me know where we are and where we need to go.*
I can describe *what* readers do. • I can read a variety of books. • I can read and think out loud about my book. • I can recommend books to my classmates.	• Children record titles in reading journal over time • Conferring and listening in to partner work, and turn and talk sessions • "Love a book? Recommend it to a buddy!" chart (page 167)
I can describe *how* readers read and get better over time. • I can read for a longer time today than I did yesterday. • I can reread my books. • I can teach someone how to read a book that I know how to read.	• Place sticky note on class number line—move forward as minutes increase • Children tally rereadings on sticky note, place on front cover of book • "Want to learn to read a book?" chart: three columns include child's name, book he or she can read, and name of child who wants to learn how
I can explain "Why read?" and describe how reading makes me stronger and more powerful in the world. • I can pay attention to my thinking when I read. • I can talk with a friend about my book. • I can retell stories using key details.	• Conferring and sharing with a partner • Listening in, conferring, and reflection and share time • Partner work during read-aloud
I can plan and facilitate a reading workshop to help learners get smarter about reading. • I can explain expectations for reading workshop. • I can name the elements of a reading workshop that help me grow as a reader. • I can read/sing aloud three books!	• Anchor chart: "What is reading workshop and how does it help me grow?" • Partner work, whole-group reflection, and share sessions • Conferring and the "Celebration of Readers" night

■ SEPTEMBER CALENDAR ■

SUNDAYMONDAYTUESDAYWEDNESDAYTHURSDAYFRIDAYSATURDAY

By the end of September, I want my first graders to be able to host a reading workshop for their families at back-to-school night. With that goal in mind, here are some ideas for how I would structure the weeks leading up to that event.

■ Weeks 1 and 2
Guiding questions: What do readers do? Why does reading matter?
- Learning focus on the systems, structures, rituals, and routines of reading workshop that help us answer the guiding question
- Read aloud: songbooks, predictable books, alphabet books, stories, nonfiction
- Possible first week mini-lessons:
  - What readers do and why they do them:
    + How readers get started in a book
    + How readers choose a book
    + What readers do when they finish a book
    + How to get ready to talk with someone else about a book
  - Procedural mini-lessons based on things that come up and interfere with learning:
    + How, when, and where to sharpen pencils, replace sticky notes, and so on
    + How to get questions answered
    + What to do when we're "finished"
  - Procedural mini-lessons that help students track thinking and learning, such as marking places where they learned something about themselves as readers
- Key instructional language from the beginning: "What's working well for you? What's not working so well? How do you know? What makes you think that? Tell me more about your thinking."

■ Week 3
- Guiding questions: How do readers get better over time? How do readers grow?
- Focus on the how of reading (This continues throughout the year in different iterations and contexts.)
- Possible mini-lessons:
  - What does it mean to read "independently"?
  - How do I know a book is just right for me?
  - How do we choose books thoughtfully so we can grow? (vocabulary load, sentence length, amount of print on a page, predictability, purpose)
  - How do we attend to the things that will help us most? (content, schema, motivation, variety)
  - How do we track the books we read? Why does it matter?

■ Week 4: Putting it all together
Explicit instruction, practice, and reflection on the elements of reading workshop we've been using for the past three weeks, and what we want to share with the grown-ups who will visit our classroom on Friday afternoon
- Possible mini-lessons:
  - How to share thinking and show evidence on how I've grown as a reader so far and how I want to grow throughout the year, how we work together as a class, and so on
  - Figuring out roles on back-to-school night, how each reader will have time to share with their grown-up, and how they will lead groups of grown-ups through a workshop

End of Week 4: Student-hosted and student-led back-to-school night/afternoon

Texts That Engage and Delight Young Readers

See the appendix, "A Collection of Books to Start the Year and Use All Year Long," for a list of texts young readers will enjoy. These titles aren't a must-have list—they signify the spirit of the types of text that are perfect for reading aloud and putting in the hands (and hearts!) of children in September and all year long. These books are in addition to early readers and/or leveled texts.

Book Selection: In the Beginning

Remember the red baskets of books sitting atop children's tables I mentioned earlier? For the first two or three weeks of school, children select their books each day from these. I include a variety of books in the baskets—mostly the songbooks we've been learning, but also familiar fairy tales, ABC books, picture books, wordless books, books of rhymes and poetry, predictable books, and well-illustrated nonfiction. I add new books to the baskets as we read them, as well as enlarged, photocopied, and laminated copies of poems, songs, snippets of text, and rhymes children especially love. Each basket (ours are the 12-by-18-inch plastic ones) holds around twenty-five books and serves four to six children.

In September, the books and materials I've chosen are most likely not at the children's instructional level; whether a child can or cannot read them doesn't matter right now. I've chosen them because the familiar songs and story lines, the short text, and the lively illustrations are perfect for children to work with books, learn how active readers read (see Figure 2.1), practice reading behaviors, become engaged and motivated to want to learn to read, and build community.

When children arrive each morning, they select four or five books from the basket at their table, place them at their seats, chat a bit with their friends, and begin reading.

In addition, the New Standards Committee's *Reading and Writing Grade by Grade* (Resnick and Hampton 2008) says that first graders should do the following:

- Read four or more books every day, independently or with assistance
- Discuss at least one of them with another student or in a group
- Read some favorite books many times, gaining deeper comprehension
- Read their own writing and sometimes the writing of their classmates
- Read functional messages they encounter in the classroom (for example, labels, signs, instructions). (80)

FIGURE 2.1

How Do Active Readers Read a Book?

Before reading, active readers:
- Read (or find out) the title and the author, and look at and think about what they notice on the cover and the back of the book
- Ask: What do I know about this type of text? This story? This topic? This author?
- Take a thoughtful peek inside and predict what the story might be about, or what they might learn

During reading, active readers:
- Read the pictures
- Read the words they know
- Use their own words to read a book they've heard before

After reading, active readers:
- Ask: What was this book about?
- Ask: What did I learn?
- Ask: What do I understand now that I didn't understand before?
- Ask: What did I learn about myself as a reader?

And to think that we can put children in these kinds of learning situations in the first days and weeks of school!

In a couple of weeks, children may choose to sit almost anywhere in the room, but in the beginning, when we're establishing procedures, reading behaviors, and the tone of the workshop, they sit at the tables. I use this time to say hello, have brief conversations with the children about what's going on in their lives, and offer reassuring words to the few parents who still have a hard time saying good-bye. I also do some noticing ("love those bright red sneakers!") and check to see if anyone needs help with book selection. After most of the children have arrived, I put on the music and children gather in the meeting area for shared reading and the day's read-aloud and mini-lesson.

The tone for the beginning of the school day has a relaxed, social, "I'm glad you're here" sort of feel. It's very similar to the way I begin my own day; I can't imagine walking into the building, striding down the long hall to my room, unlocking my door, and immediately creating a chart or reviewing the day's lessons. First I need to feel connected in some way to the people I work with, whether it's asking Sue about her new baby girl, talking with Barb about the class we teach together, or stopping in to check out Michelle's tadpoles and chat about why hers are again twice the size of mine. I need to take the time to light a candle, put on a little Eric Clapton or Keb Mo, and ease myself into the day.

Reading Aloud

My first read-aloud is almost always a songbook, poem, or rhyme. I introduce a new selection each day, have two or three favorites ready to go, and then ask for requests. Most days we end up reading or singing six or seven—children love the predictable text, rhythm, and rhyme. This continues well into October, and although we might "graduate" from *Five Little Ducks* by Raffi and *Oh, A-Hunting We Will Go* by John Langstaff, we begin the day with music all year long. Often I'll type up the words to favorite songs from CDs, tapes, books, and my Girl Scout days. The children follow along, and once they know the words, laminated copies go into the baskets and plain copies are sent home.

In addition to their repetition, rhythm, and rhyme, my reasons for choosing songbooks, poems, and rhymes are many:

- They're fun!
- Children are instantly engaged and motivated to learn to read the words. I have multiple copies, and children can't wait to get their hands on them.
- Repeated readings increase phonemic awareness, build sight-word vocabularies, and help students with fluency.
- The words and tunes are easy to learn; children read along right away and feel part of the "reading club" almost immediately.
- They build community. Where else would "Little Rabbit Foo Foo" be declared "our song"?
- Children love to take these books, poems, and songs home to share with parents, brothers, and sisters. I send a note with the copies, telling parents the purpose of the songbooks, ways to support their early reader, and reassurances that yes, right now, pointing to words and memorizing are good things. Parents appreciate being connected to the classroom so early in the year and sometimes respond by sending in words to songs they learned as kids.

Once we've warmed up with songbooks, I read aloud one or two other types of books, depending on their length and the children's disposition. Sometimes I'll read one of the books out of the baskets at the children's tables; I try to vary genre, author, format, and style and think about books this particular group of kids can easily connect with or that might pique their interest.

September fictional read-alouds often focus on relationships, school, and learning. Favorites include *The Falling Raindrop, Odd Velvet, Oliver Button Is a Sissy, Amber on the Mountain,* and *The Little Yellow Leaf.* Nonfiction read-alouds focus on topics I know will engage and interest children; these favorites include *Actual Size, Bugs Up Close,* and *Life-Size Aquarium.*

This month during read-alouds, I emphasize *all* the thinking strategies. I make my thinking visible when I have a question, make a connection, or create an image in a natural, informal way. I'm simply doing—demonstrating—what active readers do.

We'll focus on specific strategies in the months ahead, but in September, I'm all about the big picture.

Reading aloud also comes into play throughout the day. After lunch and/or at the end of the day, I often read aloud from a chapter book. Perennial favorites include *The Trumpet of the Swan* by E. B. White, *Mr. Popper's Penguins* by Richard and Florence Atwater, *Pippi Longstocking* by Astrid Lindgren, *Poppy* and *Poppy and Rye* by Avi, and the My Father's Dragon series by Ruth Stiles Gannet.

Reading aloud is one of the most important things I do. Reading aloud motivates kids to want to learn to read, extends their oral language, and gives them opportunities to connect new information to what they already know. Reading aloud offers teachers opportunities to

- model thinking strategies, fluent reading, and reading behaviors;
- build background knowledge for different types of text;
- build community;
- enhance vocabulary; and
- share with kids our love of reading and learning.

Mini-Lessons

At the beginning of the school year mini-lessons focus primarily on modeling and identifying reading behaviors, and teaching and learning the expectations and procedures of the workshop. Reading behaviors are the observable things that readers do—the deliberate actions we take that connect us to our lives as readers. Think of them as the habits we keep, like keeping a running list of books we want to read, recommending books to friends, participating in book groups, or even marking our places with a paper clip, bookmark, or sticky note. When we want children to develop habits that readers keep, we must heighten their awareness by explicitly modeling and pointing out what it is that readers do and giving them time to practice these behaviors in authentic situations using real books. Focusing first on what readers do prepares children for learning *how* they do it.

A first lesson on reading behaviors could begin this way: "Boys and girls, from talking with you and reading letters from your parents, I've learned that this is a class that wants to learn all about reading. Is that true? It is? Well, guess what—I love to teach kids all about reading, so this is going to be perfect! I'm thinking that you guys are like a lot of other kids I know: I'm thinking that you know a lot of things about reading already. Let me show you what I mean. Think about somebody you know who loves to read. Can you get a picture of that person in your head? Good. Now, this person you know who loves to read, what do you see him or her doing? What do you know about this person as a reader?"

Children respond:

"They have book clubs; my mom's in one!"

"They go to the library all the time and check out a ton of books."

"They read lots of different stuff, like my dad. He reads newspapers and books and magazines and papers from his work."

"They read a lot."

"Listen to you!" I tell them. "You *do* know a lot about what readers do! I'll record your words on sentence strips like this one, and then I'll tape them on the door there. That way we won't forget. Over the next couple of days, let's do some investigating—let's watch carefully for people who are readers and notice what else they do. Let's see how many more things we can add to our list."

At the end of the week, the door is covered. Children and I observed readers

"talking about books and ideas."

"recommending books to each other."

"asking questions about the stories."

"reading with friends."

"trading books with each other."

"pointing to the words as they read."

"rereading books."

"buying books."

"sounding out words."

"laughing, crying, smiling, frowning."

"reading out loud."

"using a bookmark."

"finishing one book and starting another one."

"writing on sticky notes and sticking them in the book."

"looking at the pictures and reading the little words under them."

"reading really fast."

"reading slowly."

"looking up a word in the dictionary."

Children also started paying attention to where readers read, and they insisted on recording this information, too (on another door). So, where do readers read?

In bed
Under a tree
On the porch
Up in a tree house
Under the covers
In school
At a soccer game
In a bubble bath
On an airplane
In the bookstore
At the checkout stand
In the car
Waiting in line
On the couch, and
In a big red chair (I think we have the makings of a poem here!)

From the first lesson on, I model and children begin practicing the things that readers do, and we talk about the reasons why. For example, one day we might begin a series of lessons on what readers do when they finish reading a book. From discussion and our class-generated list, we learn that they might stop and think about the big ideas, reread the book, choose another one, talk about their book with a friend, or read it with a buddy. We also speculate (and soon find out firsthand) why we might do each of these things. For example, we might choose to reread to better understand the story, get better at reading the words, get ready for a book group, or maybe just because we love the book.

Because the list of reading behaviors is long, I choose the most important behaviors—that is, the ones I think are most important for beginning readers to practice early on. I put my energy, and theirs, into those.

What's my purpose here? Why spend time modeling and practicing reading behaviors? I've learned that doing these things

- sets the tone for creating a working literate environment.
- lets children know that they share in the responsibility for their learning.
- builds community—together we investigate, learn, and practice what it is that readers do.
- offers kids opportunities to make informed choices about their learning.
- fosters independence.
- actively engages readers early on and builds confidence.
- sends the message, "You are smart, I know you can do this, I'll show you how."

Mini-lessons this early in the year also establish workshop (and classroom) procedures. I begin by asking myself just two questions: What are the things that consistently interfere with teaching and learning? What procedures can be put in place to eliminate or lessen their effect?

What drives me crazy? It's the grinding of the pencil sharpener when children are working, the plaintive voices asking to get a drink or go to the bathroom, children lining up or calling out to ask how to read or spell a word. It's being interrupted during a conference with a child or a conversation with an adult, transition times that take too long, children telling me, "I'm done," or asking, "What do I do now?" It's kids' abandoning books without making the effort to have a go, my asking for their attention over and over, and announcements over the intercom about candy sales, Brownie meetings, and the band.

What keeps me sane? If the problem can be solved in the classroom, I quickly initiate conversations and/or mini-lessons about what it is that's interfering with teaching and learning, why it's a problem, and how we might solve it.

A procedural mini-lesson might begin this way: "You know, yesterday I was conferring with Cody, and all of a sudden we heard the loud, grinding sound of the pencil sharpener. Do you know the sound I mean?" Their nods and big eyes tell me they do. "It seemed to go on forever, and Cody and I couldn't focus on our work. We couldn't even remember what we were talking and thinking about. Right, Cody? And I'm wondering, did the pencil sharpener interfere with anyone else's learning?" Tales of woe follow.

"I have an idea that might help us—let me know what you think about this. See these two cans? One is labeled 'I'm sharp!'; the other is labeled 'Please sharpen me.' If your pencil lead breaks or it gets dull from so much writing, put it in this can labeled 'Please sharpen me.' Then, just take a sharpened pencil from this one, the 'I'm sharp!' can, and keep working. What do you think?" Everyone thinks it's a very smart idea.

Another day during reading, two children behind me keep repeating my name, another is softly tapping my shoulder, and one more is doing something with my hair. I turn and face them. "Hey, you guys, I'd love to talk with you, but I'm in the middle of a conference. Please find a place to read quietly, and right before we share we'll talk about other ways for you to let me know you need me when I'm working with someone else. Be thinking about what might work." Then, during the "How's it going?" part of the share, I say, "Girls and boys, before we begin sharing, there's something we need to talk and think about. I know there are times during reading when you really need to talk to me and I'm busy conferring with someone else. I do want to help you, but I can't just stop in the middle of a conference. What do you think we could do to make this better? Take a couple of minutes to talk with those next to you and see what you can come up with."

Jake and Olivia propose that "if there's something that only Mrs. Miller can help you with, you could write her a little note and stick it on the dry erase board. Then keep on reading until she comes to you; don't just, well, you know, sit there." Olivia reminds everyone to "sign your name." After the initial flurry of messages, we agree: it's a hit.

Why not just post a list of rules on the first day of school and be done? I remember those days, but that was when the room was mine, not ours; that was when I was the only teacher, and they were the only learners; and that was when I asked all the questions, and had all the answers, too. Before sending children off to read, I'm explicit about what I want them to do, how they can go about doing it, and why it's important. I want them to begin this part of the workshop with a clear sense of purpose; I want them to be thinking, "I get it. Now let me have at it!" So how do kids "have at it" when most are not yet reading? Reading books and working with books are two different things. Although learning to read and comprehend books is our goal, working with books helps get us there and introduces children to the real world of reading.

Let's say the mini-lesson had been on using sticky notes to mark the places in your book where you learned something about yourself as a reader. Before sending the children off, I'd say, "In your reading today, if you find yourself thinking, *Hmm. I just learned something about myself as a reader today—I figured out the words* space *and* suit *by looking at the picture*, remember to mark that page with a sticky note, just the way I showed you. That way, you can keep track of your learning and thinking, *and* if you share, you'll know the exact page to open your book to. Got it? Good. Think, too, about *why* marking your learning and thinking is an important thing for readers to do. Let's talk later about what you discovered during the share. Happy reading!"

I know that not all children will keep track of their learning and thinking by marking the text with sticky notes today, but some will. The enthusiasm and excitement generated by even one or two children as they model and share how it helped them as readers and learners are contagious.

Okay. Let's say you agree with the importance of reading aloud, and you're comfortable with mini-lessons. But sending kids off to read and work with books so early in the year? What would that look like with twenty-seven first graders? Well . . . It's Jamie and Grace singing "Five Little Ducks" over in a corner while Jane's carefully pointing to the words I've copied onto chart paper, and Torin and Palmer looking at a book about snakes, gleefully poring over the bulge that has got to be a mouse. It's Brodie and Frankie, each signing out a copy of *The Lady with the Alligator Purse* by Nadine Bernard Westcott and *Chicken Soup with Rice* by Maurice Sendak—they have a playdate after school, and already they're making plans to make Rice Krispies Treats and read in Brodie's tree house. It's Sheldon, Cain, and Conner wandering a bit—how many drinks have they had? Cole's in a corner following the tiny black-and-white drawings in *Hand Rhymes* by Marc Tolon Brown, trying to manipulate his fingers and read "Two Little Monkeys" at the same time; Grant's working at my desk with *Touch the Poem* by Arnold Adoff, making a list of every word he knows—already he's up to seven! Nickie's just read *It Looked Like Spilt Milk* by

Charles Green Shaw three times and *Twenty-Four Robbers* by Audrey Wood twice, and now she's searching the basket for a copy of *Little Rabbit Foo Foo* by Michael Rosen. It's Julianna and Jake, giggling and marking their pages with sticky notes every time they figure out a new word, their books overflowing with the bright yellow flags of their learning. Troy's snuggling in that once-white chair leafing through *Dr. Seuss's ABC*, singing the alphabet song to no one in particular. And at one table, Jamie's reading all about Henry and his big dog, Mudge; it looks like Colin is coloring circles on sticky notes and putting them in his book, *Gemstones* by Ann Squire; and Colleen has spread out three different versions of *The Three Little Pigs*, comparing illustrations and story lines.

What am I doing in the midst of all this? I'm conferring with children, taking notes, and learning as much as I can about them as readers. I'm intrigued by Colin: what's with all the colored circles on his sticky notes, and what has this very social little boy so engaged?

"Hey," I say, sliding a chair up next to him. "Colin, it looks like you're really into that book. Can you talk with me about it?"

"Well, I think it's a really good learning book for me."

"What do you mean, a really good learning book?"

"Well, I always like to learn new stuff, and I like rocks and this book gets me to know more stuff about 'em."

"Like . . ."

"Well, you see here on this page"—he finds the slip on which he's drawn a red circle—"see, on this page, it's all about rubies. Red, red rubies."

"That's so smart. How did you know this page was all about rubies?"

"See?" He points to each letter. "R-U-B-Y, that says *ruby*. And here's a picture of a ruby. It's red. And here it says *red*—see, R-E-D."

"Ruby. That's kind of a tricky word. How did you figure it out?"

"It's not tricky! It's my grandma's name!"

"That's funny! Do you see any other words on this page that you know?"

Colin squints. "Let's see. Um, there's *the*, and *see*, and oh! There's *ruby* again!" More squinting. "That's all for today."

"Good reading, Colin. Thank you. You know what else? I'm so interested in all your sticky notes with the colored circles. How does that work?"

Deep breath. "Okay. So say I want to learn about rubies, I just put my finger right in front of the sticky note and open it up. See? And here's where the blue rocks are, and the purple ones, and the green ones. Get it?"

"I do get it! That's so smart to mark your place that way. I'm thinking that would be a smart thing to share with everyone. Would you do that? Share with them what you shared with me?"

"Sure!"

"Thank you for talking with me, Colin. I learned a lot from you today! See? I wrote it all down here. Look at all you know!"

"What's it say?"

"It says that you like nonfiction books—they're the kind that give you information, like *Gemstones*. And that you're confident—that means you believe in yourself and try new things. Here it says you can work with other kids, like you did yesterday, and by yourself, too, like today. And here? See these words? These are the words you read to me. Want to read them again? . . . Good job! And these words next to the star? I wrote a note to myself to try to find some other books about precious stones or colored rocks for you—some that have fewer words on a page. All these things show me how smart you are, and help me know how I can teach you best. Did I get everything?"

"Did you write that my grandma's name is Ruby?"

"Oops! I forgot that. I'll put that right here, next to the words you know. Before I go, do you need my help with anything?"

"I want to know the names of all the rocks, like the purple ones, the green ones, all the different colors. Will you teach 'em to me?"

"I'd love to teach them to you! Why don't you pick two or three right now? We could make a book that has all the names of the gems you know during work activity time if you'd like. We could keep adding to it every time you learn a new one. What do you think?"

Huge grin. "I want to know this purple one."

"That's an amethyst." I write the word under the purple circle on his sticky note.

"And this green one."

"That's an emerald." I write *emerald*.

"Do we really get to make a book during work activity?"

"We do."

"Will you write it down in your notebook? With a star?"

"You bet."

"This is the best day of my life! Hey, Colleen, I get to make a book all about colored rocks in work activity!" Colleen raises an eye.

"Well, I'll still be studying *The Three Little Pigs*."

"So, Colin," I say, "what will you do next?"

"I'm just gonna stick with this book, and next I want to read *Way Down South*, this one right here."

"Good plan. Thanks, Colin. Bye."

"Adios." I slide my chair over to Colleen. "Hi, Colleen, what's going on over here? . . ."

Reflection and Sharing

I signal that share time is about to begin by singing, "Everybody listen!" Children sing back, "Right now!" I ask them to think about what they've learned about themselves as readers today and to think a minute about how they might best share that with the group. I slip a CD into the player, and before the final chorus of Keb Mo's song "I'm Amazing," children have arranged themselves in a large circle and are singing along. Some have books in front of them, indicating they'd like to share.

This part of the workshop has evolved over the years into more than a time for children to share their learning. It's that, for sure, but some days it's also a forum for exchanging ideas and discussing issues, making connections from our reading lives to the world, and constructing meaning for ourselves and each other, one idea at a time. This part of the workshop, just like the mini-lesson and conferring, gives me daily opportunities to explicitly address our learning goals. I can teach in the mini-lesson, in conferences, and the share. You'll see examples of how this can sound during the share in just a bit with my exchanges with Colin, Jamie, Grant, and Olivia.

In September, much of our time is spent setting the tone and establishing procedures. Although I'm interested in what children have to say about what they've learned about themselves as readers, I'm not focusing so much on the content of what they have to say right now. I'm not worried when their thinking seems muddled or off the mark—we're learning! Right now I want them to practice oral language and the civility of conversation, I want them to know how it feels to think about their thinking, and I want them to become familiar with the routines and procedures of reflection and share time.

Because I know that some of the most significant learning will come from this part of the workshop, it's important that I make clear what the sharing will look and sound like, and why. Once again, I think about what I want for kids in March, April, and May, and set about getting them there.

I know I want children to be reflective and thoughtful not only about books and ideas, but also about how they view the world and their place in it. That's why we spend the first few minutes of the share reflecting on the day so far. I ask them to think about questions like "How did reading go for you today? What's working well for you?" and "What's not working so well?" When a chorus of children answers the first question with "Good!" (they always do), I know I've got work to do. I'll say, "Think back. What was good? What about today was good for you? Can you think out loud about that?" Then I give them time to formulate their answers. Or maybe I've asked, "Is there anything that didn't go well today?" and a child answers, "It was too noisy for me." In that case, I respond with, "What was too noisy? How did it get in the way of your learning? Think back and think out loud about what we could do to make it better tomorrow."

Children don't always know that they know something. My modeling, guiding, and nudging them to think back, think out loud, and take a reflective, thoughtful stance often shows them that they do. Later in the year, when I ask them, "So how do you know?" or "What makes you think that?" or "Tell me more about your thinking," they've had practice being reflective and thoughtful. The time we spend thinking out loud about the day sets the tone for the rest of the share. Children come to understand that I expect a respectful, thoughtful, time-to-listen-and-learn-from-each-other frame of mind.

I model and talk with children about their responsibilities for sharing, listening, and learning. Every day I remind them, "If you'd like to share, remember you need to be prepared: bring your book, think about how you can best share your learning, and speak loudly enough so that everyone can hear." I tell the rest of the children, "If you're the ones who are learning, you'll need to be looking at the person speaking, listening carefully, and thinking about what he or she has to say. Is everybody ready?"

I take a look around the circle and notice those who want to share. I usually begin with children I've conferred with that day, particularly those who I know have something pertinent to share (most likely this means something connected to the mini-lesson). I invite children by saying something like, "Colin, would you like to share?"

Colin answers, "Yes, thank you. The title of my book is *Gemstones*, and when I was reading today, I did this really cool thing. See all these sticky notes? If I want to study about rubies, I find the red circle—that's the color rubies are—and I just open it up to this page. If I want to study the purple rock, it's called a—um, what is it, Mrs. Miller?"

"It's called an amethyst."

"Yeah, *amethyst*. If I want to study about them, I go to the purple circle and open up to this page. See? And we're going to make a book at work activity, and I'm going to learn to read all the names of every one in the book."

"Colin," I ask, "can you talk a little about how you're using the sticky notes to help you as a reader?"

"Um . . . they help me find my place so I don't have to take forever trying to find stuff?"

"You've got it—that's just what thoughtful readers do. Thank you, Colin. Boys and girls, what did we learn from Colin today?" Hands fly. Jamie, Grace, and Jane each have a copy of *Five Little Ducks* in front of them. I invite them to share, and they begin singing. "Oops!" I say. "What do you need to say back? Let's start again. Jamie, Grace, and Jane, would you like to share?"

"Yes, thank you," they answer together.

"Perfect. Now, tell us about what you're going to do, and what you learned about yourselves as readers."

Grace begins. "Well, we learned all of the words in *Five Little Ducks*, and we want to sing for everyone. You can clap, but only at the end." They sing, and we clap at the end.

After a brief lesson on clapping (how long is too long?) I ask them, "So, how did you get so good at reading the words? What did you learn about yourselves as readers?"

Jamie nails it. "We kept practicing and practicing. And we learned that sometimes it's fun to learn a book together."

Grant shares the ten words he already knows from his book today. He thinks writing them down on sticky notes is a good idea, but he's not sure how it will help him as a reader. I'm not sure, either, but Olivia knows. "Now he's learning to write the words he can read."

"So what do you think, Grant? What do you think about what Olivia said?" Grant smiles and gives a little shrug.

People who visit often say to me, "That's so cute how they say, 'Yes, thank you.' How did you get them to do that?" Maybe it is cute, but that's not why I ask the children to respond that way. It's about tone, it's about respect, and it's part of the language we use as we live and learn together for six and a half hours every day. Later in the year, visitors ask, "How do you get your kids to talk and share their thinking like that? My kids could never do that." How did I get them to do that? It's really pretty simple. I taught them.

What About Phonics and Word Work?

My focus in this book is on helping children develop strategies for constructing meaning and learning content. But you might be wondering how children learn about letters, sounds, and words. I believe the surface structure systems—those skills and strategies that help readers identify words and read fluently, and the deeper structure systems—those skills and strategies that help readers comprehend—are best taught side by side.

In *Comprehension Instruction: Research-Based Best Practices* (Block and Pressley 2002), Pearson and Duke write that "'comprehension instruction' and 'primary grades' should appear together often . . . comprehension instruction in the primary grades is not only possible but wise and beneficial rather than detrimental to overall reading development" (247).

But that's a tall order! How do we go about teaching children in the primary grades both the surface structure systems and the deep structure systems? And what can we do to ensure that no one falls through the cracks? Take a look at our daily schedule—reading, writing, talking, and learning take place all day long!

It's essential that children have significant time every day to practice applying what they're learning in context, with real books. Explicit instruction and practice time in reading and writing workshop, the reading children do in science and social studies investigations, and all the reading options in work activity time give children an amazing number of minutes to read, practice, and consolidate the surface and deep structure systems. Count the number of minutes throughout the day that your children have to read. What do you notice? What are you thinking?

To emphasize my belief in the side-by-side teaching of decoding and comprehension, we have a chart in the classroom titled "We are learning strategies that readers use to construct meaning and decode words" (see Figure 2.2). The chart is divided into two columns: "What do readers do to help themselves understand and enjoy their reading?" and "What do readers do when they come to a word they don't know?" We add new learning and information to the chart throughout the year.

Children love to learn about words and are fascinated by their growing ability to use them in new ways. To capitalize on this enthusiasm, I use the same strategies for teaching words as I use for teaching comprehension. Explicit instruction, modeling, reading high-quality literature and children's writing, and giving children time to practice real reading and writing are the cornerstones of my teaching. I find that much of the work we do is integrated into our whole-group discussions, small-group meetings, and independent practice sessions every day.

I use the morning message as an opportunity to teach and reinforce earlier lessons on sentence structure, vocabulary, sound-symbol relationships, and strategies for decoding. I record a couple of simple sentences on the whiteboard, and we investigate these words and sentences in a variety of ways. We might focus on identifying sight words, recognizing spelling patterns, finding little words in big words, chunking sounds together, or learning word meanings—all using the morning message.

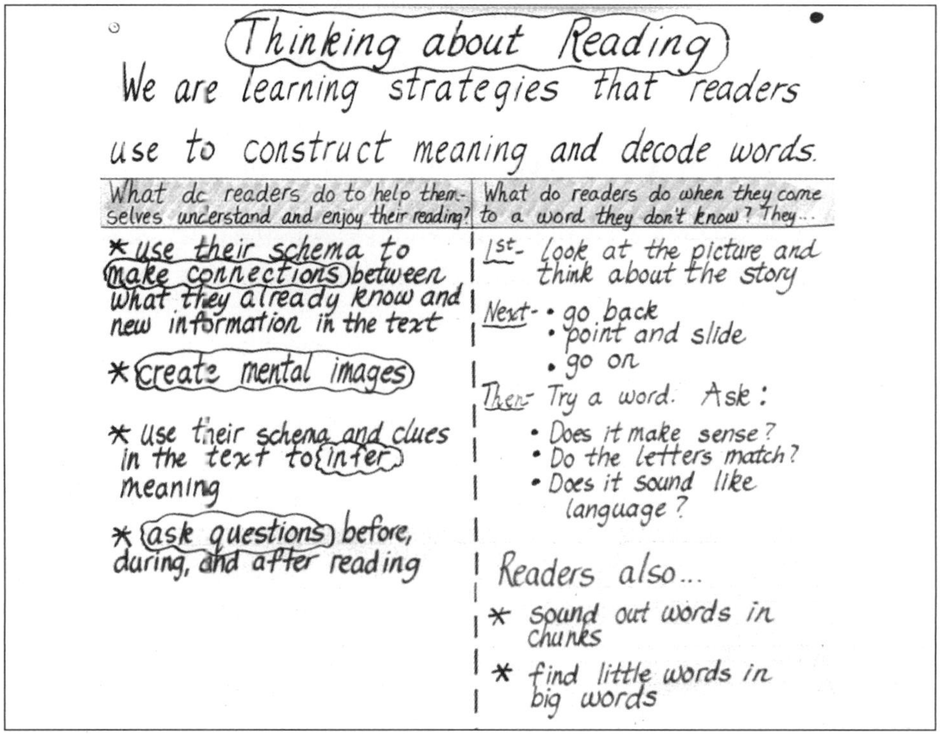

FIGURE 2.2
An in-progress classroom chart shows the side-by-side teaching of decoding and comprehension.

Singing breathes life into the classroom and provides opportunities to investigate words, letters, and sounds. When the whole class is gathered on the rug and we sing "Dr. Seuss's ABC's," the children learn the names of the letters and the sounds associated with them. When children listen to stories, I explain what they can observe about concepts of print and language, how stories are structured, and how to figure out the meanings of words. Or I give children copies of songs we've learned and ask them to point to the words as we sing, matching voice and print, associating letters and sounds, and building sight-word vocabularies.

In small- or whole-group meetings (within the workshop and also in a specific word work block of time—see daily schedule) we often work with spelling patterns or word families. We begin by talking about a particular spelling pattern—I find several examples in a couple of books and, after discussing the words, send the children off to collect their own words with the same pattern. We chart and share what we've noticed and learned. When children recite and read nursery rhymes, play with tongue twisters, and read snippets of text I've retyped from favorite read-alouds, they develop a sense of the predictability of language, the repetitive nature of words, and the relationships between letters and sounds.

Children have daily opportunities to learn about words and sentences during independent reading and writing. They learn about sound-symbol relationships and features of words when I ask them to write down all the sounds they hear in writing workshop. Every moment children spend reading and writing is a chance to apply what they know about words in a real, relevant context. I often transform the snippets of text I've retyped from favorite books and songs into cloze activities. By eliminating several nouns, for example, or even omitting every sixth or seventh word from the text, I encourage children to use their developing knowledge of syntax to fill in the blanks that make sense and sound like language.

I make a point to stop with the class on the way to the lunchroom to read a few words or sentences from a third grader's pond project or point out the words they already know around the lunchroom. When we're on our way to a field trip, the children revel in reading the words they know from every billboard and fast-food restaurant we pass. I know that they are acquiring a sight-word vocabulary they will build on for a lifetime.

While introducing children to the fascinating quirks and essentials in the world of words, I try to remember that a real context in reading and writing is just as important when I am teaching comprehension. The most effective ways to teach comprehension are also the most effective ways to teach children about letters, sounds, and words. I model, think aloud about how I use particular strategies to figure out unknown words, and list our learning on chart paper. I use a variety of literature as well as the children's writing, and I encourage the children to think aloud during share time about their success in pronouncing words they never thought they could.

A balance of word-work lessons occurs in reading and writing workshop, during the morning message, during shared reading of poems, songs, or rhymes, and in specific word-work blocks of time (see the schedule in Chapter 4, Figure 4.1). Again, having a clear understanding of what kids need to know and do (see the foundational skills section of the Common Core State Standards) will guide you and help ensure that no child falls through the cracks.

Now What?

We've spent lots of time on the structures and routines of workshop. Now, to make sure that students can and will read for two-thirds of the workshop time, we need to pay careful attention to helping them choose books that they are interested in *and* that will move them forward as readers. We also need to figure out our structures for assessment—how we know where they are as readers and what they need to grow.

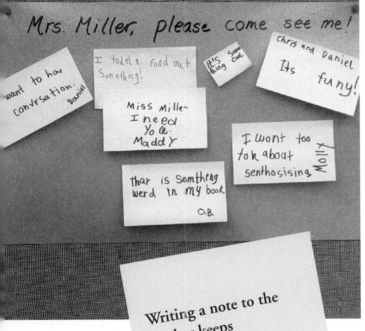

Writing a note to the teacher keeps interruptions to a minimum during conferences.

In September, Part Two

How Do I Know They Are Growing? How Do They Know?

Camille chooses to read (and fingerplay) Marc Tolon Brown's *Hand Rhymes* during reading workshop.

Book Selection: Showing Students How

John Guthrie and Nicole Humenick (2004) found that ensuring that students had access to an array of interesting texts produced reading achievement gains roughly four times as large as the small effect of producing systematic phonics instruction as reported by the National Reading Panel (2000). In addition, they found that providing students with choices about what to read, where, and with whom produced an effect on reading achievement more than three times as large as that reported for systematic phonics instruction. This doesn't mean that systematic phonics instruction is not supported, just that there are other aspects of research-based reading instruction that are at least as important as phonics lessons. (For examples of an array of interesting texts, see the appendix.)

So now the jury is in. Not only is choice about student ownership—important in and of itself—but it produces significant gains in achievement. In light of this research, are there any valid reasons why we shouldn't give children access to interesting texts and provide them with at least some choices about what to read, where, and with whom?

Early mini-lessons on book selection (children choose books once a week, usually on Friday afternoons) focus on the ways readers make good choices. Much of the word on the street has to do with matching kids with books based on such features of text as vocabulary load, sentence length, amount of print on a page, and predictability. I also teach children to consider

- the size of the print: Is it too little? Too big? Just right?
- the words and lines on a page: Are there too many? Too few? Just the right amount?
- the pictures: Do they seem like they will help me read the words?
- repetition: Is a predictable text what I need?
- the words: Can I read all of them? Most of them? None of them at all?

In my years of teaching children how to make thoughtful and appropriate choices, however, I've learned that there's more to book selection than being able to read the words. If we mean it when we say we want children to become lifelong readers, if we mean it when we say we want children to actively engage in text for a variety of purposes and for increasingly long periods of time, we can't teach them to make book selections based on words alone. If we really mean it, we also need to teach children to pay attention to

Content Schema: What's my schema for this? What do I know about this topic, author, or type of text?

Myself as a Reader Schema: What do I know about myself as a reader and the books in the classroom to help me make a good choice?

Motivation: How hard am I willing to work to learn to read this book? (Remember Lauren, the mouse, and *Amazing Grace*?)

Variety and Purpose: Have I selected more than one type of text and level of difficulty? Do I have books that are good for practicing what I'm learning or we're learning how to do?

Content

We all know kids who have extensive knowledge about a specific topic. Adam is this year's dinosaur expert—he's been passionate about them since he was three. Now he's six, and he's found his way over to the dinosaur tub. I don't know the level of the book he's chosen, but it's clear it's way too difficult for him according to traditional leveling guidelines. As I confer with him, I learn not only that Adam can read the word *dinosaur*, but that when I teach him how to activate and apply what he already knows about dinosaurs, he can also read words and phrases like *triceratops, stegosaurus, plant eater, asteroid,* and *millions of years ago* Because he knows so much about the topic and his motivation is high, he's able to read a book of greater difficulty than a traditional assessment might indicate.

Think, too, about children who know about certain types of stories. Caroline, Devon, and Nicole, like Adam and his dinosaurs, know fairy tales. Because these stories have a language all their own, it's no surprise that with only a little nudging, they can read words and phrases like *Once upon a time, "Who's that sleeping in my bed?" "Not I," said the pig, Trip, trap, trip, trap,* and *"I'll huff and I'll puff, and I'll blow your house down!"* The story lines are so well known to them that they can navigate text that, based on readability alone, would appear too challenging.

Schema for Themselves as Readers and the Books Available to Them

When we begin to talk about using schema, or prior knowledge, to comprehend text, it makes sense to talk with kids about combining what they know about themselves as readers and what they know about the books available to them in the classroom to help them make thoughtful choices. One day I might read four or five books from the tub labeled "Learn to Read." I'll point out things I notice as I read, and after reading several volumes in this series, children begin to join in with things they notice, too.

When I've finished reading, I'll ask, "So, what do we know about these kinds of books? Let's make a list of what we know to help us remember." I write "Learn to Read" at the top of the sheet, record the class's thinking, and tape the sheet on the wall above the tub. In the days to come we do this for six or seven tubs of books. Throughout the year, children assume responsibility for researching other tubs of books as they build schema for new series, authors, or types of text.

I also ask, "What kind of a reader would this type of book be best for? Do you think these books would be smart choices for kids just learning to read, those who have had a little more practice reading, or someone who has been practicing a long time? Why?" We decide that because the print is large, the songs, rhymes, and stories are familiar, the text is predictable, and the pictures match the words, the "Learn to Read" books would be good for kids just learning to read or for someone wanting to read something that's short and fun.

Connecting what children know about the books in the classroom to what they know about themselves as readers helps narrow their selections. When a child knows that he is just starting to read, and that the "Ready Set Read" books usually contain familiar fairy tales, with only a few sentences on a page, attractive pictures, and big print, he knows right where to go. Or if a child is a more fluent reader, and she knows that the Frog and Toad books are about two friends and their adventures, and that the books have quite a few words on a page and a few pictures, she knows she might be interested.

Motivation

What was it about the story *Amazing Grace* that so motivated Lauren to want to read it? Her story is not as unique as it once was. Now I know more about the power of the read-aloud and the discussions that ensue, the value of student choice, the importance of creating literate environments that are purposeful, accessible, and organized, and the significance of teacher attitudes and expectations.

When I read aloud a favorite book to children, I'm doing more than reading a good story. I'm showing my love and enthusiasm for reading and learning, I'm sharing my thinking and inviting children to join me, and I'm encouraging and expecting students to do the same in their reading. My message is clear: I love reading. I know you will, too. Let me show you how.

Children know I'm not going to ask them to do something beyond their capabilities. I want them to succeed, and I offer recommendations that are just within their reach. And because they trust me to know them well, they respond in ways that sometimes surprise both of us. Success begets motivation.

Visitors to our classroom sometimes wonder how children as young as six, seven, and eight can sustain reading for forty-five or fifty minutes a day. When children understand that they share in the responsibility for their learning, when they have a say in the books they read, and when what they are asked to do has meaning, they are able to read for long stretches at a time.

When children recommend books to each other, share their thinking and learning at the end of a workshop, or sign up as an expert on the "Want to learn to read a new book?" chart, they motivate each other. When several children decide to tackle a challenging text together, stay in the meeting area after a read-aloud to reread parts of a text, and take the day's conversation deeper, they set the standard for thinking and learning in the classroom.

Variety and Purpose

Can you imagine reading only professional books, only poetry, or only the books on the *Oprah* table? I can't either. But what about limiting kids to only one level and/or type of text day after day? That's hard to imagine, too. I worry when we methodically move children through book after book, level after level, all to achieve some target number that labels them—and us—proficient.

I worry about their engagement and enthusiasm for reading and learning, I worry about their concluding that reading fast is reading well, and I worry about losing the Adams, the Carolines, the Devons, and the Nicoles along the way. Readers of all ages need a variety of text type and level of difficulty.

How do I teach children how to thoughtfully select a variety of text that meets their needs as readers? I begin by bringing in the odd assortment of reading that's stacked beside my bed. I show them the Pottery Barn catalog and the dog-eared page that shows the quilt I'm thinking of ordering for my son Noah. I hold up my book group book, *Flags of Our Fathers*, and share some of what I've written on the sticky notes jutting out everywhere. They see my *Language Arts* magazine, and the article where I've highlighted parts I want to remember. I show them *I Read It, but I Don't Get It* by Cris Tovani; *This Same Sky, A Collection of Poems from Around the World* selected by Naomi Shihab Nye; and Michael Cunningham's book *The Hours*, recommended to me by my friend Chryse Hutchins.

I talk about how some of my reading is easy for me, like the catalog; *just right*, like *Language Arts, Flags of Our Fathers,* and *I Read It, but I Don't Get It*; and challenging, like *The Hours* and many of the poems in the poetry book. I point out the variety of texts I'm reading—a magazine, a catalog, a nonfiction text, poetry, and fiction—and my reasons for choosing them.

Then I say, "Let's take about fifteen minutes right now to make new book selections. Think about choosing a variety of books, both in the type of text you are choosing and the level of difficulty. Think about whether they are easy for you, just right, or challenging. Remember, readers mostly read books that are just right, but you could decide on an easy one or a challenging one, too. Think about what you know about yourself as a reader *and* the books in the classroom to help you make good choices. Last of all, make sure you are able to talk about *why* you've made the choices you've made. Let me know if I can help."

Twenty minutes later, the children are seated in a circle, their stacks of books in front of them. They're eager to share their selections. Everyone is browsing through the various choices; many are sharing their books with each other. This is exactly what I'd hoped for. I love it when I have a stack of new books to read, and I want the children to feel the same way.

To help everyone focus, I ask a question: "Griffy, would you like to share your books and tell us why you chose them?"

"Yes, thank you." Griffy holds up *Little Bear's Friend* by Else Holmelund Minarik. "Well, you see, I got this one because I've read all the other Little Bears, and this is my last one. Little Bear books are just perfect for me. And then this one, *Mouse Soup*, Mrs. Miller gave it to me because she thinks it's just right for me, too, and it's funny and she knows I like funny ones. I got this one, *Tough Boris*, because I have lots of schema for pirates. It's cinchy for me, but I still like to read it. Let me show you my favorite page! I got *Mouse Tales* because it looks sort of like *Mouse Soup*, and it was in the same tub so it's the same author—there's lots more in there if you want one, too. And then I found this huge book about space. See?" He struggles to lift the heavy text. "I know a lot about space. This book looks like fiction, but it's really nonfiction, and it's about the planets and all that stuff we're learning about. Remember about Venus, and how it's the hottest planet? It shows how the gases are all trapped up, see, right here? The words are very tiny and hard for me, but it's still good for me."

"Wow, Griffy," I say, "you made some very thoughtful choices! What do the rest of you notice about Griffy's book selection?"

I believe children need to spend their time reading text that is "just right"—and I believe we need to broaden our definition of what "just right" means. Singing and pointing to the words of "Long Tall Texan" with a friend, looking at a shark book and learning from its pictures and captions, and reading *Hush Little Baby* by Sylvia Long because you've been working hard and need a break were all just-right choices for Griffy.

So what do you think? Can the term *just right* be fluid? Could the term *just right* depend on the reader's purpose, interest, motivation, background knowledge, and level? Consider these questions:

- Could a book that's easy to read be just right for a child working on fluency?
- Could a book above a child's level be just right if he or she has extensive background knowledge about its content?
- Could a book be just right for a child working on comprehension if the words are easy to read, but the content is challenging?
- Could a book be just right for a child working on decoding if he or she knows most of the words, but not all of them, and the content is easy?
- Could a challenging book be just right for the child who is highly motivated to read it?
- Could a book that's easy to read be just right for the child who needs to build background knowledge on a specific topic?

■ Could a book that's easy to read and easy to understand ever be just right? When?

Now that I've modeled and the children have practiced many of the ways readers make good choices, how else might I support children as they choose? How else might I ensure that most of their chosen books are at their instructional level? I take an active role. What's most effective?

Book talks. About once a week, all year long, right before the mini-lesson, I showcase three or four books that I know will be just the right match for specific children. I read the title and the first three or four pages, and I browse out loud through the book. Then I say, "You know, Matt, I'm thinking this book might be perfect for you. Would you like to give it a try?"

Sticky notes. If I know a child might not like a public recommendation, or if I find a book before or after school that I think would be a good choice for a child, I often write a personal message on a sticky note, place it on the cover, and put it in the child's cubby. I might write, "Hi, Nicole! I saw this book and thought of you. It's another version of *The Three Billy Goats Gruff.* Let me know what you think of it. Love, Mrs. Miller. P.S. Who's that tripping over my bridge?"

Read-aloud. Remember to read aloud some of the titles children are reading, too. Not only does it elevate the status of the book *and* the status of the child you recommend it to, but it also gives children a preview of the text. Once I've finished, I'll say to a child I know would benefit from reading the book, "Grant, would you like to try this one?"

Recommending charts. Though I certainly do my share, I'm not the only one doing the recommending! Children love recommending books to each other. To facilitate this process, I divide a large piece of chart paper into three columns headed "To and From," "I Recommend," and "Why?"

Go looking together. Sometimes a child just needs you to take him by the hand to several tubs that you know would offer good choices. Browse through the books with him, thinking out loud about the kinds of things you want him to be thinking about when he begins to choose independently.

Pick one. Offer three choices, all of which you know are just right. Ask the child to pick one.

Conferring. Conferences are the best time to talk with children individually about books and book selection. If a child is making consistently poor choices, you can talk about why these choices are not going to help her become a better reader, and recommend some that would. When you make recommendations, think out loud about why you think these books would be just right.

For example, to Sean, who is comfortable reading *The Lady with the Alligator Purse* by Nadine Bernard Westcott, *Little Green Frog* by Beth Coombe Harris, and *The Bear Went Over the Mountain* by Robert Bingham Downs day after day, I say during a conference, "Wow, Sean, you really know these books. How did you learn to read them so well?"

He says, "I just kept practicing."

I say, "That's so smart. And you know what? I think you're ready for something a little more challenging. You know how you can read all the words and you understand everything that is going on? That tells me you're ready for some books that will help you become an even better reader. Are you up for a challenge?" The slight nod gives me the go-ahead. "Let's go look at the tub of 'Start-Off Stories'—do you remember where they are?"

Sure enough, he leads me to the "Start-Off Stories" and we have a seat on the floor. "Remember these books?" I say, pointing to the tub and the "What do we know about 'Start-Off Stories'?" sheet taped above it. "They have a few more words on the page than your other books, but you have schema for lots of them already. The pictures match the words, and the text is predictable. And you're not going to believe this, but some of them are fairy tales, and I know you like those. See? Here's *The Little Yellow Duck*—it's kind of like *The Ugly Duckling*. And here's *The Ant and the Dove*—it's a good story, too. You want to try *The Little Yellow Duck*? Wow, I love it when kids are up for a challenge! That's smart thinking." At this point I'm thinking, *Come on, Sean, I'm the one doing all the work here! Are you listening?* But I say, "Let's read a little of it together. . . ."

I check in on Sean now and then to see how he's doing, and I ask him if he'd like to share what he learned about himself as a reader today. He declines. Unwilling to let the opportunity pass—both for him and for other kids who could learn from him—I say, "You did such a smart thing today, Sean. Would you mind if I shared how you tried something new?"

He relents, and in the end decides to do it himself. At share time, Sean tells the class, "Today I got a new book, and here it is. I didn't think I could read it, but Mrs. Miller thought I could, and I can. I'm going to practice it some more." (Hey, maybe he *was* listening!)

Once we decide that it's important for children to have a say in the books they read, we must not only teach them how to make wise choices, but also make available high-quality selections that offer a wide variety of levels, topics, and types of text. This probably sounds as though I have a huge collection of books in the classroom. I do. But it hasn't always been that way.

Check out your school and local libraries. They almost always have great children's collections, both for reading and thinking aloud and for independent reading. Get to know librarians—they can be wonderful resources, and they'll often let you check out large numbers of books for long periods of time if they know your purpose. Borrowing books from libraries also lets you try them out first and decide which ones you might want to own or order.

Be choosy. Build your collection slowly. For thinking aloud, look for high-quality literature that is likely to prompt thinking and discussion, has believable, compelling characters, and deals with real childhood issues, especially complex ones. When we believe it's important for children to construct meaning by interacting with the text and developing personal perspectives, we must select books that give them the opportunity to do so. Childhood is not all happy, not all sad, not all good, and not all bad. Don't be afraid to let kids know you know this.

Many first graders would give their eyeteeth (if they had them) to read chapter books. I do have a few in the room, but even if the children can read them, I don't encourage them to do so—picture books are often better written and more thought-provoking for young readers. And besides, what's the rush? Children have years and years of chapter books ahead of them.

Beware, too, of the giant boxes of books dropped off in the lounge from the Kiwanis Club's annual book drive. I know they mean well, but do we really want our children learning to read with someone else's old basal readers, Walt Disney's cartoon versions of the classics, pop-up books that no longer pop, or picture books scribbled on by a three-year-old long since grown? Yes, there will be treasures. Just don't get into thinking that all books are equal. Just like the outcast computers that come our way, quality really is better than quantity!

Assessment: OURS (Kids' *and* Mine)

I used to think that formative assessments were for me—I'd ask children to do something to demonstrate evidence of their understanding, take a close look at the body of work as a whole, and then use the information to consider the implications for individual students, partnerships, invitational groups, or whole-class instruction.

But I was missing an important partner in all this assessing: the child. And although I'd always said, "My children share in the responsibility for their learning," when it came to assessment, it was pretty much all about me.

When teachers and children truly share in the responsibility for their learning, it's about shared ownership of growth over time. We want children to be aware of what they can do today that they couldn't do yesterday, and to be aware of the processes they used—exactly what they did—to get there. I want them to have evidence that all their effort and hard work has paid off—that there is purpose in what I've asked them to do. We help them understand their growth as readers over time by asking children to reflect and respond in their notebooks all year long to questions like these:

How long could I read on my own at the beginning of the year, and how long can I read now? What helps me build stamina? What are my stamina goals?

How many sight words did I know at the beginning of the year, and how many do I know now? What helps me learn and remember new words? What words am I working on now?

What kind of thinking did I used to do when I read, and what kind of thinking do I do now? What helps me be an active reader? What thinking strategies am I working on now?

What did I used to know about a particular topic, (content/big ideas) and what do I know now? What strategies do I use to remember and understand new learning? What big ideas am I learning about now?

How many books have I read so far this year? What kinds of books do I like? What kinds of books do I want to explore? What will I read next?

What am I learning about myself as a reader? What did I learn today that I will do again tomorrow, and in the days, weeks, and months to come? What skills and strategies am I working on now?

In order to respond in thoughtful ways to big questions like these, *children* need to know and understand the following:

Where am I going?
Where am I now?
How can I close the gap (Chappuis 2009)

Here's the shift—I always knew the answers to the three questions above. But my kids weren't as clear. When children have a clear vision about where they and we are going, when we offer them regular, descriptive feedback, and when we teach them to self-reflect and to keep track of and share their learning, we motivate them and help them understand that they have control over their learning (Stiggins et al. 2004, 12–13). In time, they learn that smart is something that you get—that through hard work and effort, they have the power to *make themselves smarter and achieve their goals*. How cool is that?

Making Thinking Visible

Once I gave up the basal reader, it took a while to figure out what kids should be doing instead of those neatly stapled stacks of worksheets. I thought that surely they needed to do *something* when they finished reading a book. But what? Design book jackets? Draw a picture of their favorite part? Make puppets of the book's characters? Rewrite endings? My kids did all these things—and loved every minute.

But my colleagues and I began to notice that whereas it took children ten minutes to read a book, it could take them thirty minutes to design a book jacket. And for what? Most likely it would wind up on a bulletin board underneath a snappy heading. It dawned on me that these activities were keeping children from doing what we know helps them learn to read best: *reading.*

If reading workshop is all about real reading, it must be about responding in real ways, too. Nowadays when children in my class respond to their reading, the focus is on what they're thinking and learning. Nowadays the purpose of their response is to enhance and demonstrate understanding. And those time-consuming projects? They've gone the way of the worksheet.

Teaching children how to use a variety of open-ended responses helps them remember their thinking as they read, heightens their awareness of their learning goals, or targets, and lets us (and them!) know just where they are now.

What are the kinds of responses that focus and engage young readers, helping them hold on to their thinking and enhance understanding? Which ones show the children and me how they're gaining knowledge and applying strategy skills and thinking strategies? And which ones are the most universal, the kind we might use throughout the day? Options for response are many, but the following are those I use and teach most consistently:

Sticky notes. This is probably the most authentic, and what kids use most. Keeping track of thinking on sticky notes is a lot like writing in the margins or highlighting text in your own book. The uses of sticky notes are almost limitless—children use them to record strategy use, draw images, make and confirm predictions, form opinions, think their way through a text, write exit tickets, and so on.

Notebook entries. I teach children to use their notebooks because of their accessibility and versatility, both at school and at home. Notebooks are great for both written and artistic responses, as well as a place for children to reflect on themselves as readers. I sometimes ask children to bring their notebooks to a read-aloud to help them keep track of their thinking, record their questions, reflect on themselves as learners, synthesize information, and so on.

Step into the story. During a read-aloud, I often ask children to step into the story and think aloud about what a particular character is thinking or feeling. For example, in a study about the civil rights movement, I read aloud *The Story of Ruby Bridges* by Robert Coles. When we come to the picture of Ruby entering her new school, and the angry mob surrounding her, I ask, "Think about what you know about the civil rights movement in our country, and think about what you know about Ruby Bridges so far in this story. Who wants to step into the story and think aloud for Ruby? What must she be thinking right now?"

This is a great in-the-moment assessment: How are children connecting what they know to their new learning? Are they understanding what's happening in the story? Do they have misconceptions?

Exit tickets. Quick and easy, exit tickets give us an immediate assessment about children's understanding of the day's learning goal.

Two-column notes. Almost as versatile as sticky notes and notebooks, a two-column setup for notes is also open-ended and can be used in a variety of ways. For example, one column might be headed "Quote from text" and the other "My thinking"; "I learned"/"I wonder"; "Quote from text"/"My image"; and the like.

Venn diagrams. These are useful when comparing relationships between characters, authors, types of text, skills, strategies, and even such specific things as meteors, comets, and asteroids.

Webs. These are useful in "putting it all out on the table" in the process of answering questions, determining important ideas, drawing inferences, and forming conclusions.

Story maps. These are useful in helping children understand how story elements work together to create meaning.

I teach children how and when to use each response one at a time. I take my time introducing each one, waiting for just the moment a particular approach will be the most helpful and make the most sense, when the experience might be anchored in the child's mind. That way, when kids encounter similar problems in their own reading, they will connect their current situation to the earlier experience.

Teaching children a new way to respond is not unlike teaching a new strategy. Once I've modeled the response, I need to provide opportunities for children to gradually assume responsibility for its use. In addition to asking them to work through a new response option in small groups and pairs, I sometimes ask them to bring clipboards and pencils to the meeting area, where they'll practice using the response in the course of a read-aloud. This way, their focus can be on listening to the story and using the response rather than having to be responsible for reading the text, too. When children experience and understand the purpose of each response, it becomes easier for them to apply it in their own reading in purposeful ways.

When teaching children how to respond in a new way, I want them to understand that this is now another option, or tool, they can use to help themselves make sense of their reading and demonstrate understanding; it's another technique they can add to those they already know. I want the children to understand how to use each type of response flexibly, to adapt the responses in

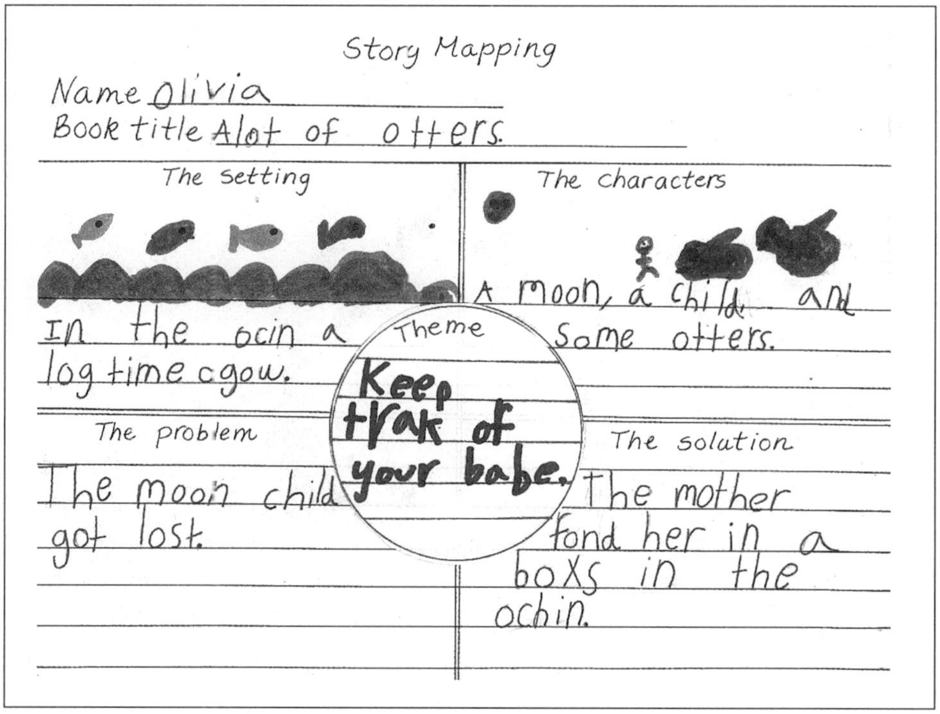

FIGURE 3.1
*Olivia suggested how
to add "Theme" to
this story map form.*

ways that are most useful, and, most important, to create their own ways of building understanding.

For example, after teaching children how to use story maps to identify important information in fiction, I moved into showing them how to identify the key ideas, or themes, in stories. Olivia was puzzled. She brought me the story map form (Figure 3.1) and said, "Where's the place for the theme? I think it should be on here somewhere." When I asked her where, she didn't hesitate. I incorporated her suggestion on the form that night.

Looking closely at children's responses, conferring, listening carefully, and taking notes about what children have to say throughout the day give me a clear indication of where they are as learners, both independently and as a group. I learn which children need more individual or small-group support, and which ones are ready to move forward into more challenging or different types of text.

Record-Keeping

Most schools require some sort of baseline assessment of children's reading skills at the beginning of the year, and my school is no exception. In first grade we use the Reader Observation Survey developed by Marie Clay and the

Developmental Reading Assessment 2 (DRA2) to evaluate early literacy achievement. The survey assesses letter identification, concepts of print, sight words, writing vocabulary, and dictation. The DRA2 measures a child's reading level through running records and retellings.

We administer the Reader Observation Survey as needed and the DRA2 at the end of the year as well as at the beginning to give teachers, children, and parents a clear indication of how children have grown as readers in the areas mentioned above. But how do we measure a child's developing expertise in other areas of reading comprehension? It's very different from evaluating a child's skills in decoding. I can't give comparative levels or numbers to parents and say they represent how their child has grown in his or her ability to comprehend.

I can share what I've learned from children during conferences, observations I've written in my notebook detailing what I've seen and heard the children say, and artifacts that demonstrate evidence of understanding and show how children acquire new knowledge and construct meaning.

You'll find examples of these kinds of responses in the monthly plans included in Chapters 2 and 4–8. A wide range of artifacts is included—children's work, their comments and strategy definitions, exit tickets, and classroom charts we've constructed together. You'll notice that examples of comprehension ability or development aren't only about a child's ability to decode. Children with few decoding skills can make an amazingly complex inference while reading a beginning picture book. Likewise, children who are accomplished decoders may struggle to make even the simplest connections between their reading and their life experience. You'll notice from the syntax and spelling in the classroom artifacts that the children are clearly beginning readers, yet they are able to use their developing comprehension skills in sophisticated ways.

I've experimented with many different ways of record-keeping, and have finally settled on small 4-by-6-inch notebooks that I keep in a basket near my desk. There is a notebook for each child, and every day before our literacy workshops I scoop up four or five from the front of the basket. Throughout the work sessions, I confer individually with these four or five children and make notes about what I've learned about them as readers, writers, and learners.

Entries might include words the child wrote on a sticky note, oral responses, a quick running record, and/or strategies the child uses for decoding and comprehension. I also make note of a child's specific strengths and areas where he or she needs more support. Listing specific examples from conferences and observations keeps my comments real and in context, and puts me back in the scene when I need to refresh my memory.

At the end of each week or so, I look at these notebooks, along with entries from my own notebook and children's response sheets, and determine if there are children with similar needs who would benefit from small-group work. I meet with these small, needs-based groups for ten to fifteen minutes during the independent-practice part of the workshop. Small groups may need additional instruction, modeling, and practice making relevant connections, sounding out words, or working with vocabulary development. Or a small group may need to challenge themselves by choosing more sophisticated texts, applying a strategy in a new genre, or sharing their thinking and learning with others.

And remember our earlier conversation about catch-and-release in the workshop? I can also bring small groups of children together (in addition to the whole group) and meet their needs right on the spot. Sometimes needs arise that we haven't planned for, and this allows for teaching and learning flexibility.

In these small-group lessons, children often use the same text, but I also ask them to bring a book they are reading independently. We use the same text so we have the same point of reference; they bring the books they are reading independently so we can make a plan for independent practice. In the lesson, I model what I want them to practice, and we discuss why it's important.

Small groups like these give children opportunities to teach and learn from each other as they work together to apply and practice strategies for comprehension, decoding, and the meaning of words. We chart our learning, and children share their new insights during share time. Groups stay together for one, two, or three work sessions over a one- or two-week period. I meet with just one small group a day as needed, ensuring time to confer with individual children, too.

Taking the Learning Deeper: Work Activity Time

It's the last forty minutes of the day—work activity time in Room 104. As I take a minute to stand back and reflect, I'm struck by the realization that at this very moment, not one child is calling my name, tugging at my sleeve, or tapping my shoulder. I take the opportunity to pick up my notebook, find a corner, and take a closer look.

I love what I see. Perched on my grandmother's small spindle rocker, Olivia is reading aloud from *Oliver Button Is a Sissy* by Tomie dePaola. Whitney, Jaron, Daniel, and Tate sit cross-legged in a semicircle below her, their fingers following along in copies of the book as she reads. Shoulders straight and legs crossed, Olivia stops reading and puts the book in her lap.

"Here's what I'm wondering right now," she says in a voice vaguely familiar. "On this page, where the boys took Oliver Button's shoes and wouldn't give them back, I just keep wondering, why would they do that? Why do you think they would do that?"

She's drawn a questioning web on the dry erase board and written, "Why would they do that?" in the circle at the center.

"Maybe they're just jealous of him," Whitney volunteers.

"Well, that *could* be it," Olivia responds as she writes Whitney's response on the web. "What do the rest of you think about that?"

I'd love to know what the rest of them think about that, but Chris catches my eye across the room. Surrounded by a stack of volcano books, he's glued about a mile of red yarn on top of a volcano he's made from brown construction paper, and now he's taping six long pages of writing, end to end, to the volcano's base. Titled "Pompeii Buried Alive!" his piece begins, "A large cloud appeared over the volcano. WOW! I can see the ashes falling on the people and the houses in my head. That had to hurt. . . ."

In another part of the room, Sunny, Paige, Grace, Brodie, Frankie, and Torin are preparing for their play, which was inspired by the book *Heckedy Peg* by Audrey Wood. Copies of the text, along with fabric, thread, needles, paper, staplers, scissors, markers, and glue cover the tabletop as they work to create costumes, props, tickets, scripts, a program, and signs.

The Lego kids are busy, too. Mitchell's building a deinonychus for his dinosaur research ("How can deinonychus run so fast?") and Thad's creating a model of the Texas School Book Depository Building. He's fascinated with JFK and is preparing for a class he'll be teaching this time tomorrow. Five kids and I have signed up already, and he's asked us in writing to bring notebooks, pencils, and "all your questions."

Maggie, Bret, Nina, and Madi are trying to figure out how they can adapt their Irish step-dancing moves to the tune "Rockin' Robin," and right behind them Meghan, Nicole, and Caroline are working on their dog research. They've stuffed their notebooks full of dog poems, pictures, notes, and observations, real examples of dog biscuits and treats, and photographs of dogs they know. Today, according to plan, they've brought in samples of fur from all those dogs they know and are sorting them into plastic bags, labeling each bag with a permanent marker.

Whit and Frank are building "Little Bear World" out of wooden blocks, and just outside the room a small chorus of girls and boys are singing their way through their three-ring binders. The binders are filled with copies of the songs we've learned so far, and the children are on the fourth, with about twenty more to go. Cory, Madison, and Kenta gingerly sidestep them on their way out to the playground for gravel and sand. We read *Where Are You Going, Manyoni?* by Catherine Stock earlier, and they're intent on creating Tobwani Dam in an old aquarium.

I smile as I watch them, remembering the raised eyebrows of those who earlier in the year wondered how in the world I could find the time to let children "just play"—and every day, too, for goodness' sake.

Work Activity Time: In the Beginning

In the beginning of the year, children use work activity time to investigate and explore the materials in the classroom. I explain the options they will have during this part of the day and trust them to make good choices. Together, we work to create the expectations and procedures we will follow. It's a time for building relationships and establishing community, playing together and making new friends, practicing being thoughtful and respectful to each other, and learning the art of sharing a room and everything in it with twenty-six other people.

And it's the perfect time for children to transfer and generalize new knowledge, either independently or with their peers; it's the time when children can put into practice what they've learned during other parts of the day. But before we can expect the Tobwani Dams, Little Bear Worlds, and classes on JFK, children need time to explore, investigate, and, yes, play.

They need time to build with blocks, draw, paint, cut and paste, play with clay, make beaded necklaces, finger-knit friendship bracelets, sew, take care of the animals, and listen to stories. They need time to read and write, listen to music, sing and dance, play school, do experiments, work with magnetic letters, and play board games like Sorry, checkers, and chess.

I don't worry about who goes where or for how long, or how many are already there. There are no sign-ups, rotations, or elaborate plans for children to fill out. I simply ask them where they'd like to go and what they'd like to do, and remind them of what we've learned about being respectful and thoughtful to each other and the materials in the classroom.

The principles that guide my work throughout the rest of the day guide my work here, too. Just as in reading and writing workshop, providing time, choice, a variety of materials for a wide range of responses, and a predictable structure children can count on allows the unpredictable to happen. If I want to challenge children's imagination, promote their love of learning and inquiry, and encourage them to become independent learners and thinkers, they need to be the ones deciding where they'll go and what they'll do.

And if I'm patient, one fine day someone will think to paint an image from a poem he or she has written or read, or start a dinosaur book club, or create a cutaway of Earth out of clay. One fine day someone will ask a question about the whereabouts of our missing frog and write a note to everyone to help him or her infer where it might have gone. And one fine day someone may choose to make a chart that synthesizes his or her learning about Planet X.

When that day comes, I shout it from the rooftops. I ask the child to share his work, and when he's finished, I say, "How did you come up with such a good idea?" I let everyone know how making connections from what they already know to another situation or time of day is a brilliant thing to do. And because it happens every year, I know that the share circle will soon be filled with other kids who have plenty of brilliant ideas of their own.

Children's talk changes from "I want to make pizzas out of clay" to "I want to make the planets out of clay and put them in order from the sun. And then I want to share it with the kindergartners." Once children begin to integrate their learning into their play, the materials are no longer ends unto themselves; they've become another means for creating understanding and constructing meaning. They've become a means for living the learning.

Late September

The zucchini is piling up in the teachers' lounge. Halloween costumes and giant bags of bite-sized candy bars have replaced wading pools and charcoal briquettes at the local Kmart. And I'm just about ready to admit that yes, this year's group has potential! Reading workshop has taken on a new look, too. By late September, children understand its procedures and expectations. They know all about *what* readers do; now they're ready to learn *how*.

In October

Digging into the Thinking Strategies; Focus on Schema

A reminder to help children make thoughtful and appropriate book selections is always a good idea.

Children combine what they know about decoding and comprehension as they read and think about text.

I t is early October, and I'm getting anxious. *Are they ready?* I wonder. Twenty-seven first graders sit together on the carpet in our small meeting area. The lamps are lit, the Pumpkin Spice candle is burning, and my lesson is ready to go. I scan the crowd. Kenta has his hands inside his bright orange Broncos shirt. Bret is braiding Maggie's hair. And Whit is rolling his socks down, up, then down again.

My mind flashes back to last year's class. *Were they ever like this? Will this group learn to read as well, and think as deeply?* I remember what my husband said when I ran this by him last night. "You say the same thing every year," he told me, "and then in November, you can't believe how smart they are." With his words in my head, I begin.

Thinking Aloud: Showing Kids How

I thought that once I became aware of the thought processes going on inside my head as I read, modeling this activity—thinking out loud while reading a picture book to first graders—would be a piece of cake. Not exactly . . .

I cringe when I think of one particularly awkward attempt, using Eve Bunting's book *The Wall.* Colleagues had told me what a fabulous book it was, and I lost no time grabbing it off the shelf of my local library. I flipped through its pages that night at home, unsure of what I'd say as I read, but oddly confident that something would come to me.

Nothing did. The next morning in class I heard myself rambling on, unsure of what to say and making things up as I went. Flustered and embarrassed, I realized from this experience that I could no longer continue to blithely read away, making a comment about beautiful language, throwing out a question or two, sharing a random connection. No longer could I grab just any book off the shelf merely because it had been recommended to me, or because it had been written by an author I knew and loved. The bar had been raised. Now when I model the thought processes proficient readers use to make meaning, I'm deliberate. I make sure my think-alouds are genuine, my language is precise, and my focus is clear. Here's how to make that happen.

Proper Planning Prevents Poor Performance!

Do you know the book *Understanding by Design* by Grant Wiggins and Jay McTighe (2005)? When I read it, I found myself writing in the margins, nodding again and again, and thinking, *Yes! This makes sense.* This book is all about backward planning, or planning with the end in mind.

When we plan with the end in mind, we set our goals for children first. We ask ourselves, "What do I want children to know, understand, and be able to do at the end of a study and remember ten years from now? What guiding questions will foster inquiry, understanding, and transfer of learning? What books and resources are rich in content, provoke discussion, offer a variety of perspectives, and focus on big ideas?" I use the Common Core State Standards, along with district and school expectations and my goals for children, to help me determine what content and which strategies are most worthy of our time, hard work, and effort each year.

Thinking about assessment up front—before designing specific lessons and activities—gets us away from "covering the curriculum" with a bunch of set lessons and activities, and moves us toward more thoughtful, intentional teaching and moves children toward more thoughtful, focused learning. Once we know where we're going and what we're going for, there's purpose, motivation, and ownership in our daily work with children. Likewise, when children know where they're going and what they're going for, there's purpose, motivation, and ownership in their work, too. And a whole lot of positive energy all around!

Once the steps above are in place—once I know just where I am going and we are going—I can think through how we're going to get there. Now it's time to ask, "What knowledge, skills, and strategies will children need to accomplish these goals? What are our long-term learning targets? What will some of our short-term, daily targets be, and what matching assessments will let students and me in on where they are now and where they need to go next?"

I know I can't plan all the short-term targets ahead of time—we'll need to live the plan to do that—but I do know that if I plan my work and work my plan, every child, every day, will be closer to achieving their long-term goals than they were the day before. Every child deserves a year's growth, and taking these actions helps ensure that they will get one. As in the sections on September in Chapters 2 and 3, you'll find examples of backward planning in the planning documents that accompany each chapter.

Why does this work, year after year after year? I believe it's because of the number of minutes—across days, weeks, and months—that children spend reading, writing, and talking. Take a look at Figure 4.1—a duplicate of my schedule.

If you add up the number of minutes in each chunk of time that I ask students to read and write, it can be as much as 120 minutes a day and more than a whopping 600 minutes a week. Who is doing most of the reading, writing, and talking? Who is getting smarter? When we're charged with accelerating readers' ability to comprehend increasingly complex texts, the "engine that motors readers' development is the time spent in engaged reading and in talking and writing about that reading. It will be important, therefore, to organize the school day so that students have long blocks of time for reading" (Calkins, Ehrenworth, and Lehman 2011, 50).

Knowing students deeply through conferring and running records, listening in, small-group work, observation, and their demonstrations of

	Monday	**Tuesday**	**Wednesday**	**Thursday**	**Friday**	**Minutes of reading per week**
8:45–9	Books out! Reading and talking about books	Books out! Reading and talking about books	Books out! Reading and talking about books	Books out! Reading and talking about books	Books out! Reading and talking about books	25–50
9–9:10	Morning Message	Morning Message	Morning Message	Morning Message	Morning Message	25
9:10–10:30	Reading Workshop	Reading Workshop	Reading Workshop	Reading Workshop	Reading Workshop	225
10:30–11:20	Writing Workshop	Writing Workshop	Writing Workshop	Writing Workshop	Writing Workshop	0–50
11:25–11:50	Phys Ed	Phys Ed	Phys Ed	Phys Ed	Phys Ed	0
11:50–12:30	Lunch	Lunch	Lunch	Lunch	Lunch	0
12:30–12:45	Read Aloud	Read Aloud	Read Aloud	Read Aloud	Read Aloud	75
12:45–1:45	Math	Math	Math	Math	Math	50
1:45–2:10	Music	Word Work	Art	Word Work	Drama	30
2:10–2:50	Science/Social Stuides	Science/Social Stuides	Science/Social Stuides	Science/Social Stuides	Science/Social Stuides	100
2:50–3:20	Work/Activity Time	Work/Activity Time	Work/Activity Time	Work/Activity Time	Work/Activity Time	0–125 (Depends on child)

FIGURE 4.1
Weekly Schedule

understanding is key to their and our success. If we don't know our children inside out and upside down, we won't know for certain where they are, where they need to go, and how best to help them get there. Allowing any child to slide by, for any reason, is never okay. We all know it's not okay, but sometimes we're just not sure what to do. Having a clear plan, and clearly communicating it to children in kid-friendly language, puts both teachers and children in the know—a very powerful place to be.

Understanding where children need to be and what they need to know by the *end of the year* creates a sense of urgency in our monthly planning; intentionally building each month on the one that has come before helps ensure that every child gets there. The Common Core State Standards advise us about where children need to be and what they need to know—we're the ones who get to plan and decide how children will best get there.

When students self-reflect, track, and share their learning, long-term retention and motivation increase (Chappuis 2009, 13). These student actions help children see their growth over time, and instill what Peter Johnston calls agency—the sense that if children act, and act strategically, they can accomplish their goals (Johnston 2004). Keeping a notebook for tracking and reflecting on learning is an easy way to keep everything together.

Trusting children and giving them access to a wide range of interesting books and materials that are worthy of what we're asking them to do says, "I trust you. I believe that each one of you is the kind of kid who can work hard and figure things out, and I want to give you everything you need to do that. I can't wait to see what you'll do and learn." And remember the Guthrie and Humenick (2004) research from Chapter 3? Here I'm doing my best to ensure that children have access to a wide range of interesting texts and materials.

Authenticity Matters

I can't fake it. My questions, inferences, or images—whatever the strategy focus happens to be—must be genuine. That's why book selection is key; choosing well-written picture books, beautifully illustrated informational texts, and poetry you love and can use over the course of a year to model a variety of thinking strategies is essential. No matter how perfect someone else may tell you a book is, or how great a lesson they taught using it, it won't be perfect for you unless you can connect with it and put your personal stamp on it in some way. Shopping for books is akin to shopping for clothes—if we don't take the time to try them on to see how they fit, they are destined to remain in our closets and on our shelves.

This is part of planning with the end in mind. We need to do our own assignments—we need to do just what it is we're asking children to do. That way, whether it's thinking aloud about what we're wondering and finding the answers in the text, inferring theme by paying close attention to what characters say and do, or describing why reading matters, we can anticipate where some learners might get stuck and even think ahead about potential small-group mini-lessons.

Use Precise Language

Be precise when you share your thinking. Say what you need to say as clearly and concisely as you can, then move on. Use real language and standard terminology when talking with children; nothing says *inferring* quite like *inferring*. Once you've decided on how you'll define a strategy and how you'll format your responses to the reading, keep your language the same. Remember, you're the model. What you say and how you say it very quickly becomes what they say and how they say it.

When I begin to teach children how to think out loud, I have the same expectations for them as I do for myself. I want their think-alouds to be genuine, their language precise, their responses text based and thoughtful. I start by showing them how to make their thinking and learning visible. My goal is to give them a framework for speaking and listening, as well as to help them build a common language for talking about books and ideas. For example, when children share their connections, I ask them to begin this way: "When I read [or heard] these words in the text . . . it reminded me of . . ." or "When I saw the picture of . . . in the text, it made me think about . . ."

Asking children to recall the words or point out the picture keeps their connection text based and gives the rest of us a point of reference as we listen and learn from their thinking. If a child says only, "My neighbor brings us flowers," I might say, "What were the words in the story that made you think about your neighbor?" If the child doesn't know, I'll reread the page and ask him to listen carefully. When he identifies the appropriate section, I say, "So when you heard the words about the lady growing and sharing flowers with her neighbors, it reminded you of your neighbor who shares his huge sunflowers with you? Is that right? If the child answers yes, I might ask, "So how does that feel, when your neighbor shares those huge sunflowers with you? How do you think the character in the story feels? Why does making connections to another person's feelings matter? How might that lead us to inferring the big ideas?"

When the children and I share our connections (or mental images, inferences, questions, and so on) to enhance understanding and construct meaning, I call it *thinking through the text together* (Anderson et al. 1992). This early phase of "having at it" is essential both now and throughout the year, because here readers have opportunities for activating, building, changing, and revising their schema as they engage in conversation with their peers and their teacher. Early in the year, thinking through text together helps children become aware of what's going on inside their heads as I read, learn how to articulate their thinking for themselves and others, and think aloud about their learning and thinking. Later in the year, as read-alouds and children's thinking grows in sophistication, thinking through text together also allows authentic opportunities for constructing meaning, reflection, and insight in the whole group, in small groups, and with partners.

Articulation is key for twenty-first-century learners, and in the "note on range and content of student speaking and listening" in the Common Core State Standards, the authors write that "students must have ample opportunities to talk in a variety of rich, structured conversations—as part of a whole class, in small groups, and with a partner" (2010, 22).

Asking children to get eye-to-eye and knee-to-knee, or turn and talk, is another early and important way to put speaking and listening (and comprehension!) into play in powerful ways, and allows every voice to be heard. When

I say, "One, two, three, eye-to-eye and knee-to-knee," children turn to someone sitting close to them and think out loud about something I ask them to discuss from the read-aloud or mini-lesson. They might share connections to a specific character and how it leads to deeper understanding, predict outcomes and refer to evidence in the text to back it up, or explain new content learning—anything that gives children practice listening and speaking about big ideas. Turning and talking is also useful when many children want to share, or when you want to encourage children who are shy or reluctant to share in the large group.

But what do we do with all this great thinking? How can we "hold thinking"—making it both permanent and visible? When planning, I need to think through not only what I want kids to know, do, and understand, but also how *both* of us will know what they know. What will students make or do during work time to show how they're growing today, and over time?

The trick here is to not overdo it. We want to make sure that there's a balance between letting children read and get "in the zone," and making and doing (Atwell 2007). Three times a week is just about right. Assessment for learning doesn't have to be time consuming—in the target/assessment part of the planning document, you'll see examples of some of the quick ways we can collect evidence.

Maybe it's a quick exit ticket at the end of work time, where children respond in their notebooks, on a sticky note, or in a conference to questions like "What do I understand about my topic today that I didn't understand before?" and "What did I do today that helped me grow stronger as a reader?" Maybe it's turning and talking with a partner about their book (this could be a "catch" during the work time, or at the end of work time and before the share), conferring with their teacher, or tallying how many times they reread a book, and what they noticed and learned about themselves as readers after all that rereading.

Responding in these ways engages children in their learning processes—it's energizing and intellectually satisfying to record or talk with someone about how and why you're getting smarter! Creating anchor charts is one of my favorite ways to capture thinking and make it visible, public, and permanent. Co-constructed, authentic, and ongoing, anchor charts are perfect for helping children and me see how we're all growing and getting smarter over time.

■ OCTOBER PLAN ■
Digging into the Thinking Strategies; Focus on Schema

Big Ideas About Schema	Demonstration of Understanding
What do I want students to walk away with at the end of this study and remember ten years from now and beyond?	*What kind of summative, end-of-study assessment can we create that exists in the world and has a real purpose and audience?*
Active readers use their schema to construct meaning, enhance understanding, and engage with the text. Active readers make connections between reading and their lives, between and across texts, and from their reading to the world. Active readers distinguish between connections that are meaningful and relevant, and those that are not. Active readers build, change, and revise their schema when they encounter new information in their reading, engage in conversations with others, and gain personal experience.	"How Do We Know What We Know?" exhibition focusing on the deeper structure systems: How do readers think? How does making connections make us smarter? Children will host second graders ("Would you like cookies and punch?") *and* pairs will lead a small-group discussion explaining what they've learned about how readers think, how making connections makes them smarter, and how making connections helps them grow as readers. (Smart is something that you get.) They'll share their personal work, anchor charts, and a short think-aloud about an important connection in a book of their choosing, either from a book they've read themselves or one they've heard during a read-aloud.

(continued)

■ OCTOBER PLAN ■ *(continued)*

Possible Guiding Questions

What compelling questions will foster inquiry, understanding, and transfer of learning?
- How do I know what I know?
- How do readers think?
- How do active readers use their schema to make connections and get smarter?

Possible Supporting Targets	Possible Assessments for Learning
Long-term targets are in bold, and daily targets are listed below them.	*These formative assessments match the daily targets and let kids and me know where we are and where we need to go.*
I can use my schema to help me make meaning and engage with the text. • I can switch on my schema before I read to help me make meaningful connections. • I can make connections between what I know and what I read. • I can explain how making connections makes me smarter.	• Children practice with a partner; I listen in and take notes • Conferring, sticky notes (Figure 4.5) • Conferring and discussions during reflection and share time
I can explain how and why readers make connections. • I can make connections across texts to help me figure out the big ideas. • I can make connections to characters in stories to help me become a better human being. • I can make connections between the books I/we read and what is happening in the world.	• Whole-class and small-group discussions; conferring • Book lineup, exit tickets (page 87), and Venn diagrams (page 88) • Anchor chart: "We can make connections from our reading list to the world!"; list text and connections
I can describe the difference between connections that are meaningful and those that are not. • I can explain why some connections help me make meaning and why some don't. • I can explain how the connections I make in my independent reading help me make meaning.	• Whole-group discussion and anchor chart (pages 82–84) • Conferring and small-group discussion
I can build, activate, and revise my schema through reading, writing, listening, and speaking. • I can tell what I already know about a topic before I read. • I can make connections between what I already know and my new learning to help me remember and understand. • I can delete misconceptions from my mental files.	• Whole group, small group, partner work, and conferring • Anchor chart: "Activating, Building, and Revising Schema" (page 90)

■ OCTOBER CALENDAR ■

By the end of October I want students to host a "How Do We Know What We Know?" exhibition with second graders. The students will offer cookies and punch, and pairs will lead a small-group discussion explaining what they've learned about how readers think, how making connections makes them smarter, and how making connections helps them grow as readers. Smart is something that you *get*.

They'll share their personal work, anchor charts, and a short think-aloud about an important connection in a book of their choosing, either from a book they've read themselves or one they've heard during a read-aloud.

Guiding questions for the month: How do readers think? How do readers get smarter? How do I know what I know?

■ Weeks 1 and 2
- Reading-content focus on thinking strategies—general overview and going deeper with schema
- Big-idea content focus on the following: How do my family, my friends, my home, my school, my environment, my experiences, and books help me know about the world and build my schema?
- Possible mini-lessons:
  - Analyzing content of "How I Know What I Know" with a variety of mentor texts. (See Tried-and-True Texts below.)
  - What is schema?
  - How we use schema to make sense of the world
  - How we grow our schema over time
  - With each read-aloud: How do I use my schema to make meaning? What *new* schema did this book help me build? How did this book change or revise the schema I already have?
  - Making meaningful connections

■ Weeks 3 and 4
- Explicit instruction, practice, and reflection on activating, building, and revising schema as we learn and grow, and what we'll share with second graders at our "How Do We Know What We Know?" exhibition of individual work, anchor charts, books, and documentation/talk about meaningful connections.
- Figure out our roles and responsibilities for the exhibition: How will the small groups work? Who will lead? What questions might we ask our guests? When is the best time for treats?

Tried-and-True Texts for Focusing on Schema
Walk On! by Marla Frazee
Those Shoes by Maribeth Boelts
Stand Tall, Molly Lou Melon by Patty Lovell
Hazel's Amazing Mother by Rosemary Wells
What You Know First by Patricia McLachlan
Another Important Book by Margaret Wise Brown
The Falling Raindrop by Neil Johnston
Now One Foot, Now Another by Tomie dePaola
The Little Yellow Leaf by Carin Berger
Chrysanthemum and *Lilly's Purple Plastic Purse* by Kevin Henkes

Songs of Myself compiled by Georgia Heard
Oliver Button Is a Sissy by Tomie dePaola
Ira Sleeps Over by Bernard Waber
The Two of Them by Aliki
Without You by Sarah Weeks
Why Do Leaves Change Color? by Betsy Maestro

Active Readers Make Connections to Construct Meaning

"Girls and boys, you know how we've been learning about what readers do when they come to a word they don't know? Today we are going to begin learning about what active readers do to make meaning when they read. Do you know that readers think and read at the same time? You do? I love that you know that already! Teachers know that, too, and we've learned that one of the most important things readers do when they read is make connections from what they already know to information in the text—that helps them understand and remember what they're reading, and grow what they know.

"Thinking about what you already know is called *using your schema*, or using your background knowledge. Schema is all the stuff that's already inside your head, like places you've been, things you've done, the books you've read—all the experiences you've had that make up who you are and what you know and believe to be true. When you use your schema, it helps you use what you know to better understand and interact with the text."

I look out at Whit and notice his socks still require attention. Kenta's hands are outside his Broncos shirt, but now they're picking rocks out of the soles of his orange and blue Nikes, making little piles. Bret's braiding appears to be nearing completion.

"There are many ways readers use their schema—we're going to spend some time over the next few weeks to learn how, why, when, and where readers make connections between what they already know and what they're reading and learning."

Twenty-seven blank faces stare up at me. Two parents have joined us; make that twenty-nine. I forge ahead. "Let me show you what I mean. I'm going to read a story to you; its title is *The Relatives Came* by Cynthia Rylant. I'll read for a while, and then I'll stop and think out loud to show you how I use my schema, or what I already know, to make connections from my own life to the story. I'm going to let you know what's going on inside my head while I'm reading the story out loud to you."

To avoid confusion between reading and thinking, I tell them, "When I'm holding the book up like this, I'll be reading. When the book is down on my lap like this, I'll be thinking out loud. Are you ready?"

I begin to read. "This page makes me laugh. You see right here, where I read to you, 'It was different, going to sleep with all that new breathing in the house'? I understand exactly what Cynthia Rylant meant. That's because *at the same time I was reading*, I was making a connection to when I was a little girl, remembering how my family and all my cousins and aunts and uncles would visit my grandparents in their farmhouse on old Route 92 near Oskaloosa, Iowa.

"Sometimes it was so hot and sticky at night that we'd all pile down to the living room—just like in this picture—because it was the only air-conditioned place in the house. We'd sleep together on the black carpet with the pink and red roses intertwined, listening to Aunt Rosie's scary Melvin stories and dreaming of Shetland pony rides, the midway at the state fair, and Grandma's gingerbread boy or girl pancakes."

As soon as I've shared my connection to the text, I say, "Did you notice how much fun I was having just thinking about being with my cousins and sleeping downstairs on those hot Iowa nights? I'll probably always remember *The Relatives Came* because of all the connections I make while I'm reading it."

When I get to the page where the relatives are heading back to Virginia and everyone is waving good-bye, I read it, then put the book in my lap.

"I love this part. When I saw the picture of the people standing in their pajamas and waving the relatives off in the dark, right away I began to think about a good-bye game my grandma and I used to play. It was called 'Kissed You Last.' When we'd get up so early in the morning to drive back to Colorado, my grandma and I would always see who would get to kiss the other one last. I would always win, because I kept blowing kisses all the way down the lane and onto the highway. I loved playing that game. Do you see how using my schema helped me understand just how the people in the book feel?"

As the story ends, I notice I have everyone's attention. The two parents are smiling. Encouraged, I can't wait to talk about what the children are thinking. "So what did you notice?" I ask.

Only Cory raises his hand. "Can we go read now?" he asks.

Oh, brother, I'm thinking, but I say with a smile, "Absolutely. Happy reading, everyone!"

Over the next two weeks there will be similar lessons. I think aloud on consecutive days—Julie Brinkloe's *Fireflies* and Gloria Houston's *My Great-Aunt Arizona* are two favorites. By this time children are usually itching to have their say, and although I continue to model my connections, I encourage them to share theirs, too. This is when we begin thinking through the text together and getting eye-to-eye and knee-to-knee. *Koala Lou* by Mem Fox, *The Snowy Day* by Ezra Jack Keats, and *Chrysanthemum* by Kevin Henkes never fail to engage kids and get them connecting in real ways. Why? They've lived these stories!

At this point I begin scripting and charting their responses. Kids love to see their connections (and their name) in print, and it shows them how much

I value what they have to say. Charting holds thinking—it makes our thinking public and permanent, and traces our work together.

Making Meaningful Connections

When I first began teaching children about using their schema to help them make connections to text, they connected to everything! I remember children waving their hands wildly, making the dreaded "Uunh! Uunh! Uunh!" sound, barely able to contain themselves. When I'd call on them, they might say something like, "I have a connection! You know the author of the book?"

And I'd say, "You mean Eve Bunting?"

"Yeah. Well my cousin's name is Eve."

"Really?" I'd say, and on we'd go.

And there'd be other comments, like, "I have a red dress, too," or, in response to a picture of a tiny bird in the upper corner of an illustration, "I once had a bird."

Then another child would say, "You had a bird? I have a bird right now! His name is Sal."

And then, "Sal? That's a girl's name!" Giggles ensue. By this time, neither Eve Bunting nor I could get the kids back.

It's not that I now get only brilliant, meaningful connections from children—every year someone knows an Eve or has a red dress, too, or even once had a bird. But I've learned it's up to me to teach through these kinds of connections. Now I know it's up to me to gently redirect the children's tangential responses right away before they become the norm.

Thinking Through Text Together: An Anchor Chart in the Making

I begin a mini-lesson several days later this way: "You know how we've been talking about the difference between connections that help us understand our reading and the ones that don't? I have an idea that might help us. Today when I'm reading aloud to you, I'm going to record your connections in my notebook, and after school I'll write them on a chart so you can see them. Tomorrow we'll talk about them and figure out which kinds of connections help us most."

After school I transfer all the children's responses to a chart, which reads as follows:

We have been learning that active readers make connections between what they know and what's in the book to better understand their reading. When we read Hazel's Amazing Mother *by Rosemary Wells, children made these connections:*

> *I helped the mailman once.*
> *I have a calico cat.*
> *I once got lost in the mall and I was so scared!*
> *My grandma made me a doll.*
> *I have new shoes, too.*
> *My neighbor's name is Hazel.*
> *Once my sister was playing and the big kids took her ball. My dad came out and told them to go home.*
> *Belle's story about her mom and "the power of love."*

The next day we decide to put a *1* next to each response that helped us understand more about the story, and a *2* next to responses that didn't help us or maybe led us astray. I tell the children that as I reread the story, they need to be thinking about the connections we made yesterday and try to figure out which ones help us understand and figure out the story best.

"Let's look at the first one," I say when I finish reading. "'I helped the mailman once.' Does that help us learn more about the story?" A chorus of no's. (I put a 2 there.)

"And this one: 'I have a calico cat.' Do you think that connection will help us?" More no's. (Another 2.)

"What about this? 'I once got lost in the mall and I was so scared!' Does this one help us?"

Olivia answers, "It could help. Put a 1 there."

I think to myself, *A 1? What's meaningful about the mall?* But I say, "Keep talking, Olivia. Tell us why you think there should be a 1 there."

"Well, if you had really ever been lost in the mall, it would help you understand how Hazel felt when she got lost. You would get it." *Wow*, I think, *she's right!* And I wonder: How many times have I missed opportunities like this one? How many times have I not pursued a child's thinking simply because it didn't fit with mine? Olivia's thinking—*"it would help you understand how Hazel felt when she got lost"* is all about developing empathy—the depth of understanding we are looking for. One of Wiggins and McTighe's (2005) six facets of understanding, empathy as a way to insight, involves the ability to put oneself in the shoes of another.

I think, *Thank you, Olivia!* but I say, "What are the rest of you thinking? Put a thumb up if you agree with Olivia." Twenty-six thumbs come up, and though I understand they all don't empathize in quite the way Olivia has, I know that some of them learned something big from her just now, and there will be more opportunities just like this one.

We go on down the chart, marking 1s and 2s as we go. When we finish, I ask, "What can we learn from all this great thinking we just did?"

Taylor, who up to now has just been listening, says, "I think that when something is only on one page, and you make a connection to it, and then it just gets, umm, well, it just kinda gets swept out of the story, that connection isn't going to help you much."

Justin looks at Taylor and says, "Yeah, 'cause it's not so much about the story—it's not a very big connection."

"Yeah," Taylor nods. "A tiny little connection isn't going to help you much."

"Taylor and Justin," I say, "I loved the way you two just had a conversation, and I think I see what you mean. Boys and girls, how do you think we might write that on our chart?"

Kendal answers, "How about if we connect to a word, like *mailman* or *cat* or *soccer ball*, that doesn't really help us, but if we connect to a bigger thing, like if it's on almost all the pages and it's what the book is really about, like an idea or something, then it can help you."

"Let's see if I've got it," I say. "Do you mean that if we make a connection to a word, like *mailman*, or maybe someone's *name*, it probably won't be as helpful as connecting to something the book keeps coming back to, like a big idea? Taylor, Justin, Kendal, everybody, do we have it?" Heads nod, and I record it on the *Hazel's Amazing Mother* chart.

"So what are you noticing about us as readers?" I ask next.

They say, "We're getting smarter every day!" My husband was right. It's not even November, and not only do I know children are getting smarter, but they know it, too.

Small-Group Work: Early Opportunities for Focused, Student-Led Conversation and Collaboration

It's ten o'clock and children are sprawled every which way on the worn, warehouse-issue carpet. They are in groups of threes and fours, clustered around three-foot-square pieces of white butcher paper. Arms and legs, markers and crayons are everywhere.

Before reading aloud *Ira Sleeps Over* by Bernard Waber, I tell children, "Today while I'm reading, I want you to keep your connections *inside* your heads." I explain that once the story is over, they will go to one of the big pieces of paper on the floor (one child to a side, four to a group), talk together about their thoughtful connections to the story, and record their most important one using pictures, words, or both.

"Then we'll come together and talk about the reasons for our connections—how do they help us as readers? What did you learn from each other? What big ideas does Bernard Waber want us to understand?"

There is a copy of the book for each group (this isn't essential, but the multiple copies help focus and support young readers).

As the children work in their groups, I talk with a few, but mostly I listen. Now, and during share time, I do some informal assessment. I want to know the following:

- Are children making meaningful connections that enhance understanding?
- Are they listening to each other and responding in appropriate ways?
- Do they understand how making connections helps them grow as readers?
- Are children making connections when the text is causing them difficulty?

I stand back and watch Whit, Ana, Maggie, and Cory. They are busy arranging the paper just so, deciding who will sit where, and arguing about where the exact middle of the paper is so they can place the markers there. Whit turns his back to the group and at least begins to flip through the book, but the conversation for Maggie, Cory, and Ana turns to crayons.

I'm groaning inside. Where's that great talk I know they're capable of? But I resist getting in the middle of it. I glance around the room to see how the other groups are doing and decide to stay where I am. I listen in. Ana is talking. "Remember the part of the story when he wanted his teddy bear but it was at home? Well, that part reminded me of when I didn't have my teddy bear and I really wanted it. Remember when everyone had lice in our class? My mom made me put all my stuffed animals in a big trash bag, and I couldn't sleep with anything for a whole week! It was terrible." (Empathy again!) "That's what I'm going to write about. Then I'll make a big trash bag right here . . ."

I start itching again (how long do lice live, anyway?), but Cory, Maggie, and Whit are writing and drawing. Relieved, I remember that it often takes adults a while to get focused—why should it be any different for children? I check in with the other groups and notice Jake has drawn a picture of a little boy in a bed (Jake) and a little boy in the doorway waving good-bye (Keenan). He writes, "The first time I went to Keenan's house for a sleepover, I wasn't homesick. But when he came to my house, he was. He's coming again, and I really hope he'll make it." Many children have drawn pictures of teddy bears, best friends, and beds.

About thirty minutes later, the big papers are stacked in the middle of our meeting area, the children seated in a large circle around them. "Let's have the group whose paper is on top tell us about their connections first, and then we can set about answering these big questions on the board here," I say. "Sit on the side of the paper that shows your work."

As the small groups share, I discover that many children are making connections to the story and are able to share them with others. I recognize that fewer are able to think aloud about how making connections helps them grow as readers, and most of those who are use my words ("It helps me understand how Ira feels"). I remind myself (again) that children can use a strategy without fully understanding it, and that they will gradually gain control of it through continued modeling and authentic practice.

This is one way, in addition to extensive time spent reading, that we can address text complexity in the primary grades. Here, children are responsible for the thinking, not the reading. With time and practice, the two will merge.

Connecting to Characters: What Can They Teach Us?

Because trusting yourself and working hard are central to my goals for children, my choices for early read-alouds highlight characters who demonstrate these characteristics. Now it's time for children to make connections to characters within, between, and among texts and contemplate what they might learn from them. The Common Core State Standards ask children in grade one to "Describe characters, settings, and major events in a story, using key details" (2010). We've begun this process already, but I want more for them. I also want children to go deeper into character studies by learning to

- make connections to characters within, between, and among texts to help them make predictions and better understand universal character behaviors and traits;
- infer big ideas by paying attention to what characters say and do;
- consider how they can become better human beings—better citizens of the world—by studying closely what characters say and do when they encounter challenges or simply live their lives.

I begin by thinking aloud about two characters from books that children particularly love—Oliver Button from *Oliver Button Is a Sissy* and Grace from *Amazing Grace*. "Remember this page?" I ask. "Right here, where Raj tells Grace she can't be Peter Pan because she isn't a boy and Natalie whispers that Grace can't be Peter Pan because she's black?

"That makes me think about Oliver Button. Do you remember this page here?" I hold up both texts with the appropriate pages facing out for children to see. "This is the part of the story where the boys are making fun of him because he loves to dance. I'm thinking of Oliver Button at the same time I'm reading about Amazing Grace—I'm thinking they're alike in some important ways. When it says that Grace keeps her hand up to be Peter Pan, even when Natalie and Raj don't think she could be, and then when Oliver Button doesn't give up wanting to dance just because those boys are teasing him—they both stand strong. They don't give up, even though that would be the easy thing to do.

"Will you turn and talk about that? Think about this instance, and also try to remember other things that are the same about Oliver Button and Grace. What words might you use to describe them?"

Children respond with words like *strong, brave, smart, determined,* and *courageous.* Next, I ask, "So what can we learn from Oliver Button and Amazing Grace? How might they help us be better human beings?" Here are some of their responses:

- "We have to respect everyone, even if they like to do different things, or are different from us—like maybe what they wear or the color of their skin or if they talk a different language."
- "If I see my friend or someone teasing a kid, I'm going to say in a regular voice, 'Stop that, please. You're being mean and that's not nice.'"
- "I can be who I want to be, once I figure it out."
- "If I see someone who is lost or crying or sad, I'll help them."

So that children are clear about why we use strategies—they help us actively engage with the story or content, construct meaning, and grow understanding—I almost always link our strategy work to the big ideas, whether our work is in fiction, nonfiction, or poetry. In this instance, children decided that the following are some of the big ideas in these two stories:

Follow your heart.
The more you practice, the better you get.
Stand up for yourself.
Sometimes people change their thoughts.
Hard work will take you places.
Be true to you.

A few days later I line the long chalkboard ledge with many of the storybooks we've read aloud over the first six or so weeks of school. *Stand Tall, Molly Lou Melon; How to Heal a Broken Wing; Odd Velvet; Amber on the Mountain; Chrysanthemum; The Two of Them; Lilly's Purple Plastic Purse; Oliver Button Is a Sissy; Now One Foot, Now Another; Amazing Grace; The Royal Bee;* and *Ira Sleeps Over* stand tall, side by side, ready for scrutiny. These books are more complex than what most children would be able to read independently at this time of year, but they can access them in sophisticated ways because they've listened to them being read aloud and they've had multiple opportunities to talk together about them.

My plan is for children to get with a partner, select a book they'd like to work with, and find a quiet spot where they can study their book closely. I ask them to focus in on the main character: What words would they use to describe him or her, and what's the evidence in the text that supports their thinking? What does their character say and/or do when they have a problem? What can we learn from these characters? How can their experiences make us better human beings?

It's still early in the year, and these are big questions for children to answer, so once they're with a partner, I give them the questions to discuss one at a time. I'm listening in all the while, taking notes about who said what as well as I can. When they finish, I ask each child for an exit ticket—a short, half-page response that looks like this:

My name _____

The name of the character I studied closely _____

What words best describe the character you studied today? What's your evidence?	What can you learn from this character to help you be a better human being?

Next I do a "catch." We gather in a circle, and partners share their exit tickets. Children naturally make connections between and among their characters—they can't believe all the connections they have! You're probably inferring that it happens like this because I've set it up to happen. I know that the characters and the big ideas in the books that line that ledge all connect to each other in one way or another, but I don't want to do the thinking for them. I want them to discover it all on their own.

Creating Venn diagrams to compare characters or other features in pairs of books is another way to help children make connections between one character and another and enhance understanding. (Figure 4.2 shows my charting of connections between *Oliver Button* and *Amazing Grace*; Figure 4.3 shows Emily's Venn diagram of connections between *Now One Foot, Now the Other* by Tomie dePaola and *The Two of Them* by Aliki. You'll find that children also love to compare different versions of the same story, particularly fairy tales, stories by the same author, and like topics in informational texts.

FIGURE 4.2
A Venn diagram shows the class's connections between Amazing Grace *and* Oliver Button Is a Sissy.

FIGURE 4.3
Emily's connections between Now One Foot, Now the Other *and* The Two of Them

Building and Actively Using Schema Throughout the Year

Throughout the year I teach children to use and develop their schema for making connections between what they know and what's happening in the world through exploring individual authors, particular types of text, text features and characteristics, and topics of interest.

Connecting Our Readers to What's Happening in the World: Raising Social Consciousness

I used to think children as young as six, seven, and eight needn't wrestle with real-world issues such as war, homelessness, poverty, and prejudice. But when it's the buzz on the playground and in the lunchroom, when it's blaring from radios, televisions, and newspapers, it's time to talk.

I've learned that children love to grapple with complex social and moral issues, and that they often have clearer heads than some grown-ups I know! Sometimes I search for just the right book to help me launch the discussion; other times a read-aloud will spark a discussion about something I hadn't planned. Memorable text-to-world connections have included these:

> Kevan's connection between *Smoky Night* by Eve Bunting and the mini-riots the night the Broncos won the Super Bowl.
>
> Ailey's connection between *I Have a Dream* by Mike Francen and a swastika that was burned onto our school's playing field.
>
> Max's connection between *Miss Maggie* by Cynthia Rylant and his aunt who has Alzheimer's disease.
>
> Taylor and Keenan's connection between *How Many Days to America?* by Eve Bunting and the war in Kosovo.
>
> Lilli's connection between *Lifetimes* by Bryan Mellonie and Robert Ingpen and the rampage at Columbine High School.
>
> Edward's connection between a newspaper article about fighting in the Balkans and gang activity in his neighborhood.
>
> Children's connections between a *Time for Kids* magazine article about the September 11 tragedy and our classroom "Promise to Each Other."

Building Schema for Authors, Types of Text, and Text Elements

Because most early readers have limited background knowledge for individual authors, types of text, and text features and characteristics, I work in a deliberate way throughout the year to build background knowledge in these areas.

Teaching children key features of fiction, nonfiction, and poetry, and showing them how to recognize what to expect when they encounter particular types of texts, authors, and the like, helps them know what to expect and how best to go about reading and making sense of the texts they encounter. I have three charts displayed, and we add to them whenever we become familiar with an author, learn about a different type of text, or work with characteristics and features that are unique to poetry, narrative, or expository text.

Topic Study: Activating, Building, and Revising Schema

Whenever we begin a new topic of study, I begin by asking, "So what's our schema for this? What do we know about _____?" To help children activate what they already know, I sometimes liken the schema to opening mental files in their heads. I tell them that sometimes we have to stop and think about what we already know; we have to search our brains for that mental file, open it, and make connections between what we know and the new information to help us remember and understand it. I show the children some of my paper files, as well as those I've created on the classroom computer. I model how I make new files, add information to existing files, and revise and delete information.

FIGURE 4.4
A schema chart

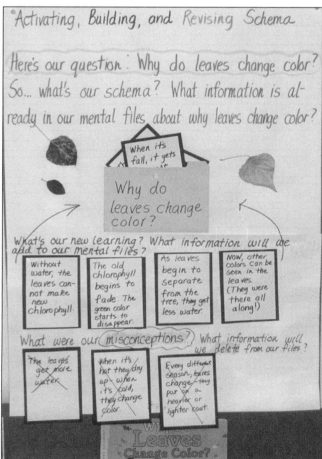

"The files in your brain are a lot like these files," I tell them. "You can work with them the same way. Let's try it. Remember yesterday when Maggie asked the question, 'Why do leaves change color?' Open your mental files right now—what information do you already have in your head that would help answer her question?" I record each response on a 5-by-7-inch sheet of paper and place the sheet in a paper file labeled "Why do leaves change color?"

The next day I read aloud a text on the subject and as we encounter new information, I write it down and add it to the file created the day before. When we finish, we open the file and look closely at our thinking and learning. We determine what information should be kept in the file and what information should be crossed out or deleted. Figure 4.4 shows a chart that records this process. (For an adaptation of this lesson, check out the color insert in *Teaching with Intention*, Miller 2008).

Evidence of Understanding and Independence

What you see in this section are examples of some of the ways in which children have demonstrated evidence of understanding and independence (see, for example, Figure 4.5). During the last week or so of each study, I take the time during individual conferences for students to look through their evidence—what they've made—and notice and name their growth during this study and throughout the year. They look through their notebooks for short entries, lists of books they've read and want to read, and so on, and they also spread out and study the work they've placed in their file folders. (Each child has an accordion file folder that holds his or her artifacts over the course of the study, as well as key artifacts from those that have come before.) It's really a celebration of learning, and a wonderful opportunity for children to do some self-assessing and teachers to gain insight into how children view themselves as readers and learners.

It gives both of us a chance to reflect on these questions:

Where are we going?
Where am I now?
What can I/we do to close the gap?

And, it also gives us a chance to ensure that no one falls through the cracks.

This is the perfect time to go back to the guiding questions—both those for this study and those for the year, asking children:

What are you learning about what readers do?
Why does reading matter?
How does reading make you bigger and stronger?
What can you do now that you couldn't do before? How do you get smarter?
How do you interact with other readers? How does this help you grow?

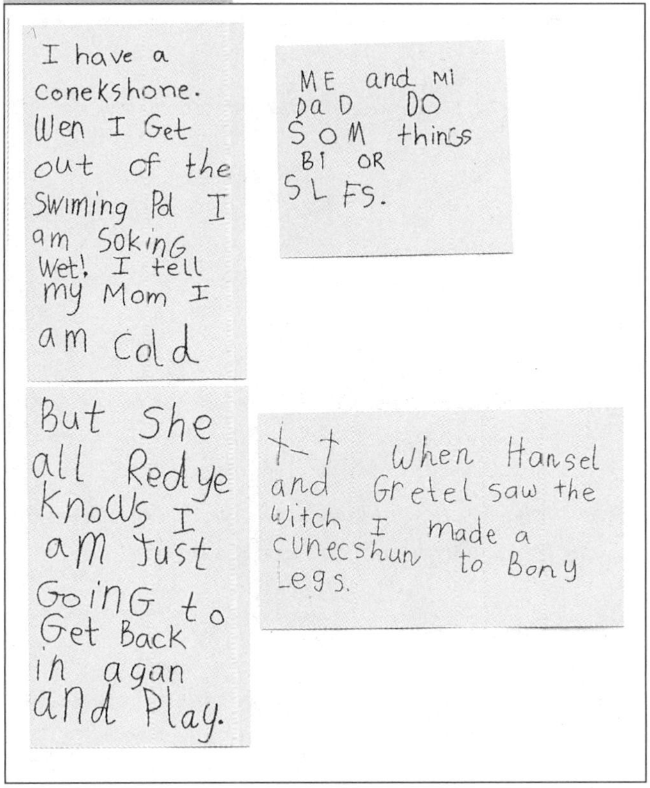

I have a
conekshone.
Wen I Get
out of the
swiming Pol I
am soking
wet! I tell
my Mom I
am cold
But she
all Redye
knows I
am Just
Going to
Get Back
in agan
and Play.

ME and MI
DaD DO
SOM things
BI OR
SLFS.

+ t When Hansel
and Gretel saw the
witch I made a
cunecshun to Bony
Legs.

FIGURE 4.5
(Left column) Emily's connection to Amelia Bedelia Goes Camping *by Peggy Parish; (upper right) Whit's connection to* Just Me and My Dad *by Mercer Mayer; (lower right) Chris's connection to* Hansel and Gretel

After children have been through this process once, I ask them to prepare for the rest of their end-of-study conferences the day before we meet. This is about children taking responsibility and ownership for their learning, and paves the way for goal setting and making plans.

In addition, I gather information for individual children through

anecdotal notes and running records from individual conferences;
small, needs-based groups, including both surface and deep structures;
listening in;
observation;
anchor chart contributions/exit tickets;
and of course the end-of-study summative assessment!

When you use schema, it's like adding things together. Say you see leaves falling. You think in your head, "Oh, it's fall now!" It's kind of like your old schema comes out of your head and grabs the new schema and pulls it back inside your head.
—Christopher

Schema is what you know; it's your thinking.
—Madi

When you change your thinking about something, you change your schema.
—Devon

Everything you hear and see and feel, everyplace you go and everything you do, puts more schema into your head.
—Grant

When you use your schema, it wakes up memories.
—Nina

It's impossible to have the same schema as someone else. People do different things, go different places, and read different books, so how could their schema be the same?
—Cory

So let's say you know about something, you have some schema for it. Then you hear something new about it. You add the new stuff and your schema just gets bigger and bigger.
—Ben

When you have schema for something, you have to open up that file in your brain and make connections to your reading or writing or math. You get smarter!
—Bret

Madison and Camille offer greetings and poems during Coffeehouse Poetry Day.

In November and December

Poetry Genre Study; Focus on Sensory Images

Matthew works hard to create mental images as he listens to *My Father's Dragon* by Ruth Stiles Gannet.

The muted trumpet of Miles Davis plays on the CD player, floating among the voices in the crowded classroom. Hot chocolate simmers in the PTA's relic of a coffeepot; a mountain of miniature marshmallows fills a bowl nearby. Long rolls of deep blue paper decorated with construction paper stars, coffee cups, planets, flowers, hearts, and crescent moons cover the windows and darken the room. Table lamps and tiny white lights draped from the ceiling provide the only light.

Freshly scrubbed tables are rearranged into cozy pairs. Handmade flowers in tiny clay pots, poetry books, bowls of pretzels, and small containers of words from magnetic poetry kits have replaced crayons, markers, scissors, sticky notes, pencils, and glue.

Parents and children sit together, munching pretzels and sipping steamy hot chocolate in mugs brought from home, reading poetry by the likes of Eloise Greenfield, Maya Angelou, Aileen Fisher, Jane Yolen, Valerie Worth, and Georgia Heard. But the poems receiving the most enthusiastic reviews? They're the ones written by the children themselves, published and spiral-bound into books, with enough copies for everyone.

Black is the clothing color of choice; berets adorn the heads of the truly hip. Starbucks, you say? No way! We've transported ourselves back to the 1960s (ancient history to everyone in the room but me), and it's Coffeehouse Poetry Day in Room 104.

It's time to begin. I know because the sixth child has just asked me when we're going to start, and I see numbers seven and eight approaching. I give Frank a wink and a nod. He walks to the makeshift stage—a table with two chairs taped on top, a red stepstool to get there, and a well-used microphone gleaned from an enterprising custodian. He climbs the steps and sings into the microphone, "Everybody listen!" The response is deafening: "Right now!" Startled parents look up, stunned at their children's silence. Finally, they, too, stop talking. This signals Madison to the stage.

Microphone in hand, she begins. "Welcome, parents, children, and friends, to our Coffeehouse Poetry Day. We've been learning how readers and writers create mental images when they read and write. When we read our poems, we want you to see if you can create some mental images, too. Listen and wait for the pictures to come alive in your minds."

Abby begins. "Hi, everyone! I'm Abby, and the title of my poem is 'Dolphins.' Dolphins dive / into the ocean. / Flippity flop! / Splishity splash! / Dolphins never stop. / Twisting, twirling / in the shining sunlight, / all day long." One by one, and sometimes in twos, children extend greetings and read their poems into the microphone. I'm at the ready, turning up the volume of Miles's muted trumpet between poems, turning it down as children read.

Icicles
Icicles drip in the morning light, and freeze in the darkness of the night.
Icicles scream as if they were talking to the wind.
Caroline

Trains
Trains rumble over tracks.
Big black tunnels wait. Dark metal zooms through the night.
> *Zach*

Henry
When I hold my Guinea Pig Henry
he makes me feel safe inside.
Warm fur
red eyes
chubby little body.
Henry is my buddy.
> *Olivia*

The Changes of the World
When winter falls,
it seems like years have passed.
Layers and layers of rock
lay silent
on the stiff, brown ground. I look out
my bedroom window.
It seems like things have changed
in the world,
and people have gotten older.
> *Zachary*

Hot Tubs
Hot tubs,
steamy bubbles,
powerful jets,
ZOOM like shallow waves
in the ocean.
San Diego hot tubs,
that's where I want to be!
> *Griffin*

Poppy
I remember my Grandpa.
I used to go everywhere he'd go.
He fixed me really good bacon.
I used to love to sleep next to him.
I really miss my Poppy.
> *Cory*

Space

In space stars twinkle
in the darkness of night.
Saturn's rings twirl
and planets swirl
as if they were dancing.
  Emily

Sunday Morning on CBS

Football people
race across the field,
leaping to tackle you
to the green and grassy ground.
  Devon

Leaves

The leaves tiptoe to the ground with only a soft, gentle sound. We hear
  the leaves go crinkle, crackle,
crunch, crunch
under our feet.
We rake them into a mountain
of red, orange,
yellow, brown and purple.
The leaves
tiptoe to the ground
with only a soft, gentle sound.
  Madison and Camille

  When you read about Coffeehouse Poetry Day just now, did you find yourself creating images in your head? Maybe you visualized a classroom (yours?) with tiny white lights overhead, or pictured twenty-seven children and their parents dressed in black. Maybe you caught a whiff of the hot chocolate and heard the notes of a trumpet, or the children's boisterous "Right now!" And just maybe you noticed a lump in your throat when you read Cory's poem about his Poppy.

  When readers create mental images, they engage with text in ways that make it personal and memorable to them alone. Anchored in prior knowledge, images come from the emotions and all five senses, enhancing understanding and immersing the reader in rich detail (Keene and Zimmermann 2007).

KATE
KYLE
LEANNA
PRESTON
MORIA
KISSA
Adam
JOEY

Our Promise to Each Other

When we care about each other and our classroom, we share what we have, listen carefully, help each other learn, work hard, and have fun together. We understand that everyone makes mistakes, that we stand up for ourselves and others, and when someone asks us to stop, we stop. This is who we are, even when no one is watching!

A BOOK OF Promises

Oliver Button Is a Sissy

Collaborating to compose "Our Promise to Each Other" sets the tone for learning and cooperation early in the year.

Giving children a framework for thinking and talking about appropriate ways to ask someone to stop helps build respectful, caring communities.

What can I do when someone is annoying or hurting me? Look the person in the eye and say nicely,

I don't like it when _____

I feel _____ when you _____

I want _____

When someone tells you this, what can you say back? Look the person in the eye and say nicely,

I heard you say _____

I won't _____

I am sorry.

Creating classroom environments that are literate, organized, purposeful, and accessible nurtures literacy and fosters independence.

Children need comfortable, quiet spaces for working in small groups, pairs, and independently.

Scissors, markers, glue, crayons, pencils, and sticky notes should always be handy.

Why are some tornadoes tall and others short?

Source: Wolrd Book tornadoes 1999.

Bigger winds makes tornadoes taller. Small winds make tornadoes smaller.

Models constructed from clay and paper illustrate a child's learning and demonstrate understanding.

Creating environments that nurture literacy and foster independence requires thoughtful planning.

Asking children to respond to a read-aloud allows them to focus on the content of the story without being responsible for reading it, too.

Reading and thinking aloud gives teachers opportunities to model the cognitive processes used to construct meaning.

Knowing ourselves as readers and recording what we've learned about books in the classroom helps readers make good choices.

Ben's definition of synthesis.

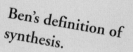

Hollis and Olivia work to better understand Sherry Garland's *The Lotus Seed* by recording and organizing their questions, mental images, connections, and inferences.

NOVEMBER AND DECEMBER PLAN

Poetry Genre Study; Focus on Sensory Images

Poetry Genre Study; Focus on Creating Sensory Images	Demonstration of Understanding
What big ideas do I want students to walk away with at the end of this year and remember ten years from now and beyond?	*What kind of summative, end-of-study assessment can we create that exists in the world and has a real purpose and audience?*
Active readers and writers of poetry understand how and why creating images enhances comprehension.	Coffeehouse Poetry Day focusing on children's original poems and the images they create in the readers' (and listeners') minds
Active readers and writers of poetry understand that images come from all five senses and the emotions, and are anchored in prior knowledge.	Children will host their parents and read aloud their poems from our newly bound poetry anthology.
Active readers use their images to draw conclusions, create unique interpretations, recall significant details, and remember a text after it has been read.	Parents are encouraged to bring and read a favorite poem, too.
Poets create images in their poems to help their readers draw conclusions, create unique interpretations, recall significant details, and remember their poem once it has been read.	
Active readers use their images to help them infer the big ideas in their reading.	
Images are fluid—readers adapt them when they encounter new information.	
Poets trust the reader to infer big ideas—they don't *tell* the reader everything.	
Active readers build, revise, and adapt their images when they encounter new information from the text, from others, and from personal experiences.	
Poets revise and rework their poems until they sound and feel just right.	

(continued)

■ NOVEMBER AND DECEMBER PLAN ■ *(continued)*

Possible Guiding Questions

What compelling questions will foster inquiry, understanding, and transfer of learning?
- What do poets do?
- How do poets think?
- What do readers do?
- How do readers think?
- How does creating sensory images in our reading and writing help us grow as readers and writers?
- Why do readers read poetry?
- Why do writers write poetry?

Possible Supporting Targets	Possible Assessments
Long-term targets are in bold, and daily targets are listed below them.	*These formative assessments match the daily targets and let kids and me know where we are and where we need to go.*
I can explain what poetry is. • I can get ready to read poetry. • I can explain what to expect when reading poetry. • I can memorize a poem.	• Anchor chart: What is poetry? How do we read it? How does it sound?
I can read words and create images at the same time. • I can notice when my mental "movie camera" shuts off and can use a fix-up strategy to get it turned back on. • I can name several fix-up strategies that readers use to make meaning. • I can create images when I read independently.	• A sticky note to mark the spot, with fix-up strategy recorded on it • Exit ticket on ongoing anchor chart: "What are fix-up strategies, and how do they make us stronger readers?" • A sketch of a mental image along with the words that sparked the image
I can use mental/sensory images to help me remember what I read. • I can illustrate a memorable image from a story. • I can create images to help me retell stories and infer big ideas.	• Artistic response • Thinking strip/*The Magic Fish*—children use their images to retell and infer big ideas with a partner
I can build, change, and revise my images when I learn new information from the text, from others, and from my experience. • I can explain/show how I revise my images when I learn something new. • I can use drawings and models to explain ideas, thoughts, and feelings when I read.	• Artistic representation/partner work • Readers' choice (see examples of this in the "Evidence of Understanding and Independence" section at the end of this chapter)
I can describe my images in detail to help another person understand the text better. • I can dramatize a poem to help me and others better understand it. • I can explain how a poem makes me feel. • I can explain how using my schema, making images, and inferring work together.	• Small-group performance • Two-column notes: words/feelings • Whole-class discussions, conferring, making thinking visible

◼ NOVEMBER AND DECEMBER CALENDARS ◼

By the end of December, the students will host their families at our Coffeehouse Poetry Day and read aloud their poems from our newly bound poetry anthology.

Parents are encouraged to bring and read a favorite poem, too.

◼ November

- Guiding questions: What do readers do? How do readers think? How does creating mental/sensory images help us as readers?
- Reading-content focus on thinking strategies—schema continued, going deeper with making mental images/making mention/name inferring
- Big-idea content focus on how creating mental/sensory images helps us recall important details in our reading, remember a text after it has been read, and infer big ideas
- Possible mini-lessons:
  - Practicing making mental images with rich text: *Night Sounds, Morning Colors* by Rosemary Wells
  - How images are created from the readers' schema and words in the text; how images help us retell
  - How images help us remember what we've learned
  - How images can help us draw conclusions and infer big ideas
  - How creating mental images while we read gives us ideas for writing

◼ December

- Guiding questions: What do poets do? How do poets think? How do poets use sensory images to help their readers grow?
- Reading and writing content focus: thinking strategies—schema continued, going deeper with creating mental/sensory images, continuing to make mention/name inferring
- Big-idea content focus on how poets see the world and the ways in which they help others see the world
- Possible mini-lessons:
  - Poetry exploration in reading and writing
    + What is a poem?
    + What do poets do?
    + Where do poets get their ideas?
    + What can we learn from poets in the world to help us write our poems?
    + How can we help each other?
  - Explicit instruction, practice, and reflection on the power of poetry, along with the following:
    + How images can help readers and writers construct meaning and enhance understanding
    + What poems will we share on Coffeehouse Poetry Day?
    + How will we illustrate them?
    + Will we want a table of contents?
    + How will we arrange the room? What will we serve? What about music?
  - Roles: Announcer. How will we greet our guests? How will we introduce each other when we read our poems? Who will invite parents to share their poems? Who/how will we decorate the tables/windows/door?

Tried-and-True Texts for Teaching Poetry and Sensory Images
Night Sounds, Morning Colors by Rosemary Wells
Ruby in Her Own Time by Jonathan Emmett
Wolf's Coming! by Joe Kulka
The Chipmunk Song (and others) by Joanne Ryder
Growing Frogs by Vivian French
Without You by Sarah Weeks
Night in the Country by Cynthia Rylant
The Magic Fish by Freya Littledale
Duck! Rabbit! by Amy Krouse Rosenthal
The Quiet Book by Deborah Underwood
The Napping House by Audrey Wood
City Dog and Country Frog by Mo Willems
Twilight Comes Twice by Ralph Fletcher

Poetry
Songs of Myself: An Anthology of Poems and Art compiled by Georgia
    Heard
all the small poems and fourteen more by Valerie Worth
Honey, I Love and Other Love Poems by Eloise Greenfield
Here's a Little Poem compiled by Jane Yolen and Andrew Fusek Peters
The Big Book of Poetry by Bill Martin Jr.
Color Me a Rhyme by Jane Yolen
Creatures of the Earth, Sea, and Sky by Georgia Heard
The Random House Book of Poetry for Children compiled by Jack
    Prelutsky
Farmer's Dog Goes to the Forest: Rhymes for Two Voices by David Harrison
A Child's Garden of Verses by Robert Louis Stevenson, pictures by Gyo
    Fujikawa
Mother Goose, pictures by Gyo Fujikawa

Favorite Poetry Websites
American Academy of Poets, www.poets.org
    "Poetry is the liveliest use of language, and nobody knows more
    instinctively how to take delight in that playfulness than children."
The Poetry Foundation, www.poetryfoundation.org
Poems 180—Library of Congress Poem a Day Project, www.loc.gov/
    poetry/180/
Poetry Out Loud—National Recitation Contest, www.poetryoutloud.com
Three-year-old recites Billy Collins's "Litany," www.youtube.com/
    watch?v=uVu4Me_n91Y

Thinking Aloud: In the Beginning

A favorite book for thinking aloud about creating mental images is *Night Sounds, Morning Colors* by Rosemary Wells. The inside flap issues an invitation: "Look. Listen. Open all your senses." Who could resist? Violets laugh and sing in Mama's garden, a father hums "Danny Boy" as he tucks his little boy into bed, a train whistles through the darkness of the night.

"Listen again to the words about the faraway train and its whistle," I say to the children during the read-aloud. "When I read those words, vivid images, or pictures, come into my mind. I have an image of my mother, brother, and me streaking across the flatlands of Kansas on a train called the *El Capitán.* I see us looking up at the night sky through the skylights above us, my brother and I thinking we could count the stars. I hear the rumble of the wheels on the tracks, and the porters in their fancy red and black outfits talking in whispers outside our compartment.

"Even now I can feel the excitement of going to the dining car for breakfast. I have images of starched white tablecloths, deep red napkins the size of my mother's silk scarves, fragrant fresh flowers in silver vases, and more knives, forks, and spoons at each setting than one little girl could possibly use. And the cinnamon rolls! My image of them fills an entire plate, with yummy white frosting slowly oozing down into little puddles at the bottom.

"Girls and boys, did you notice how creating mental images seemed to make the text come alive for me? It's like I was back on the *El Capitán,* streaking across the countryside, looking up at the stars, sitting down in that fancy dining car, and eating those yummy cinnamon rolls all over again. The page about the train will always be important to me—I'll always remember it—because of my connections to it and the images they create in my mind. Someone else reading the book would have different images, because that person's schema is different. No one else, not even my mother or brother, would remember those train rides the same way I do."

I take a couple of days with the Wells book, sharing one or two pages each day and talking about how the images I create enhance my reading and understanding of the text. On day three, I say to the children, "Lie down, close your eyes, and listen to the words as I read. Pay attention to the images that come alive in your mind. Put your thumb up when an image comes into your head."

They're into it. Flat on the floor, eyes scrunched shut, they wait with anticipation. I read the fish page, and one tiny thumb after another shoots up, vying for attention. Not only do they see fish weaving in and out of pagodas, as in the book, but they become fish right before my eyes! Big fish with bulging eyes, puckered lips, and swishing tails squirm (swim?) around the meeting area.

A fish named Frank stops midstream and says, "Wait a minute, guys. What's a pagoda?" And before I know it, four children try to fashion one with their bodies. Emily says, "Look, Frank, see? It's one of those tall Chinese-like houses—you know, the ones with the curvy roofs? I have one in my fish tank, and the fish really do swim in and out of the windows and the doors. Swim through this door right here!" Frank swishes right through.

I think, *Well, Debbie, this isn't quite what you expected, but what's happening is a good thing, right? Uh . . . right.* I'm grateful it wasn't a page full of tigers.

The page with the birthday cake sends thumbs flying once again.

They can see that birthday cake! "How many candles are on your cake?" I ask. "Seven! And they're burning hot and bright! Ouch! I just touched one!"

"My cake has just one candle, but it's a big red number three right in the middle. It's my baby brother's cake."

"The cake in my head is big and round and it has a soccer player on it. There are words. Let's see . . . They say [eyes closing tight]—oh! I see them now! They say, 'Happy Birthday, Paige' and 'You're Number One!'"

Next I ask, "What kind of cake is in your image?"

"Chocolate!"

"No! Mine's white with lemon filling, my favorite!"

"Wait! Listen to this! I see an angel food cake with white frosting and pink and red hearts all over it, and seven purple candles, and it tastes delicious!"

"Oohs" and "aahs" and "Are we going to have snack?" and "When's lunch?" (two long hours from now) let me know it's time for a change of pace.

"Wow, you created some very vivid mental images—I loved all the details you included," I tell them. "What did you notice about your images of the birthday cakes?"

"Everybody saw a different kind of birthday cake!"

"You're right. They were all different. Why do you suppose that is?"

Several of them say, "Because our schema is different!"

"Good thinking. I can tell you're going to be really good at this. One last thing. Before you go to read, I'm interested in knowing what you're thinking about creating mental images so far. Any thoughts? Ideas? Questions?"

My pencil and notebook are ready. "It's so much fun!" and "I love making mental images!" and "Can we practice again tomorrow?" are typical responses, but Kenta's thoughts take my breath away. "Well, here's what I'm thinking. I'm thinking mental images are sort of like connections, only a lot bigger. Say a connection is like a kernel of corn. But when you put it in the microwave and it pops up big and hot, now *that's* a mental image. You hear it and see it and smell it and taste it and love it. That's what I'm thinking."

The room is silent; the only sound is that of my pencil furiously writing to catch every word. Madison asks, "Did you get that exactly, Mrs. Miller? We should put it up in the room somewhere." Kenta knows just the spot.

Focusing on just a snippet or two from a picture book or poem allows children time to practice developing an image completely. Asking questions like "How many candles are on your cake?" and "What kind is it?" gives children permission to add details that personalize their images and make them unique.

Books such as *Night in the Country* by Cynthia Rylant, *The Salamander Room* by Anne Mazer, *The Napping House* by Audrey Wood, *Creatures of Earth, Sea, and Sky* by Georgia Heard, and anything by Joanne Ryder also offer rich snippets of text for thinking aloud, thinking through text together, and getting eye-to-eye and knee-to-knee to talk about sensory images.

In addition to picture books, what type of text is best when children begin to become more adept at making mental images on their own? What type of text bridges whole-group work and independence? One answer is poetry. Short, thought-provoking, and full of images, poetry allows even early readers to navigate the text once it's been read aloud several times. I've learned that the best decoders aren't necessarily the most thoughtful readers, nor are the most thoughtful readers necessarily the best decoders. Asking children to read and respond to the same text creates additional opportunities for children with different strengths to listen and learn from each other.

Anchor Lessons

The lessons that follow show how I use a given text to deepen children's understanding of poetry and narrative text by showing them how creating mental images can help them access and understand these types of text. Using poetry and picture books, children practice creating and adapting images in their minds and make them concrete through artistic, dramatic, and written responses. Children explore how

> images are created from readers' schema and words in the text;
> readers create images to form unique interpretations, clarify thinking, draw conclusions, and enhance understanding;
> readers' images are influenced by the shared images of others;
> images are fluid and readers adapt them to incorporate new information as they read; and
> evoking vivid mental images helps readers create vivid images in their writing.

Images are created from readers' schema and words in the text (artistic response)

I make ten or so copies of three or four poems I know children will love—those written by children from previous years are perfect. I think about the content of the poems I choose. Do children have enough background knowledge for the topic? Is the text clear? Do the poems lend themselves to unique interpretations?

I read each poem aloud several times, asking children to listen carefully and think about which poem creates the most vivid mental images for them. Next I say, "Take a copy of the poem you've chosen and a piece of drawing paper, and find a place you can work well. Read the poem to yourself a couple of times, and then capture the image that's in your head the best you can on paper. Take about ten minutes, and then we'll share our work."

When children gather to share, I ask those who have chosen the same poem to sit together, share their images, and talk about what they notice. After the small groups have shared, I ask children to tell the large group what they've learned. Their words may not change ("Our images are different because our schema is different"), but the experience of this kind of activity helps children anchor their words and give them meaning. (Figure 5.1 shows some responses as displayed in a classroom.)

FIGURE 5.1
One class's mental images

Readers create images to form unique interpretations, clarify thinking, draw conclusions, and enhance understanding (dramatic response)

Although the concepts in the heading above are inherent in all the lessons described in this chapter, dramatizing short pieces of text is another way to engage and teach young readers about mental images, as I learned from the fish with the puckered lips in the *Night Sounds, Morning Colors* experience.

I ask children to get together in groups of three or four and find a place where there is enough space for them to work together comfortably. I tell them, "Close your eyes and listen carefully to the poem I'm about to read. Pay special attention to the words in the poem and your schema to create vivid, detailed images."

I read the poem aloud three or four times and ask children to think aloud in their groups about the images they've created. Next I say, "Put your thinking together to create a dramatic interpretation of the poem. Think about things like this:

- What is most important?
- Why do you think that?
- How will you show that?
- How can everyone be included?"

Later, I ask children to share their dramatic interpretations. I ask each group to talk about why they chose to dramatize the poem the way they did, focusing on how each group chose to interpret the poem in a different way, based on their images and what they believed to be most important.

Children also love to choose their own poems or short pieces of text to dramatize and present to the group. Sometimes the audience tries to guess what the poem is about; other times one or two children will read the poem while others in the group act out their images. Later, when we learn how readers use dramatic responses to figure out a tricky word (like *pagoda*) or understand a puzzling piece of text, children will have had practice with this type of response.

Readers' images are influenced by the shared images of others (artistic response)

I choose Georgia Heard's poem "Ducks on a Winter Night" (1997) because I know it's a poem my children have some schema for, yet it's sophisticated enough to require thoughtful interpretation. It reads as follows:

Ducks asleep
on the banks of the pond
tuck their bills
into feathery quills,
making their own beds
to keep warm in.

I write the poem on chart paper, and the children and I read it together three or four times. We don't talk much about images or meaning; I ask children to go to their seats and draw the images they've created from the poem independently. Next, I ask them to share their images with the person sitting next to them and talk about not only their images, but also the bit of text that inspired that particular image.

When they finish, I say, "Let's read the poem again. As we read, pay attention to your images this time through. After learning about your partner's image and rereading the text, would you change the image you've drawn in any way? Did your partner's image change your understanding of the poem? Did rereading the text change the way you picture it?" After the children have listened to the poem again, I say, "Go to the other side of your paper and draw your image as you see it now."

At their tables, the children share their work. This was a great help for Nicole. She had originally thought the quills referred to in the poem were porcupine quills; after a conversation with her partner, Abby, she had a much better understanding of the poem.

Images are fluid and readers adapt them to incorporate new information as they read (artistic response)

Until now, most lessons I've described have focused on creating detailed images in response to a poem or a short piece of text. These types of images aren't the kind that change much once they've been created. But with Jane Yolen's book *Greyling*, I show children how readers' mental images can be fluid—that they can change to incorporate new information.

Greyling is the story of a fisherman and his wife who live in a moss-covered hut by the sea, longing for nothing more than a child of their own. One day the fisherman finds a small gray seal stranded on a sandbar. But this is no regular seal. . . .

The first day, without showing children the pictures, I read aloud the first half of the book, quickly sketching some of my most vivid images on sticky notes and thinking aloud about how they change as I continue to read and learn more about the story. When I finish, I place them on the dry erase board.

"Let's take another look at my images," I say. "Do you see how they changed as I kept reading? Here I have an image of a seal in the fisherman's arms, and in this sketch my image of the seal has changed into a little boy. As I continue to read, the images in my head continue to change, too. Do you see?"

"Is it kind of like a movie going on inside your head?" Madison asks.

I tell her it's exactly like that. "Tomorrow," I tell the children, "I'll read the rest of the story and you'll have a chance to see what it's like to have a movie going on inside your head, and do some sketching, too."

The next day, the children bring a clipboard and a pencil to the meeting area. I give them a record sheet divided into fourths and headed "Adapting Mental Images During Reading." I reread the first half of the book, showing children the pictures this time through. When we get to where we left off the day before, I say, "Now I'm going to read you the rest of the story. I'm not going to show you the pictures right now; I want you to listen to the words and keep track of how the images in your mind change as I continue to read. I'll read a while, then stop, giving you time to sketch your images. When we finish, we'll take a look to see how you've adapted your images to include new information in the text. Are you ready?"

Figure 5.2 shows one child's response to this exercise. Other great books for this lesson are *City Dog and Country Frog, The Chipmunk Song, The Librarian of Basra, Growing Frogs,* and *The Magic Fish.*

FIGURE 5.2
Whitney's changing mental images for Greyling *by Jane Yolen*

Evoking vivid mental images helps readers create vivid images in their writing (artistic/written response)

A wonderful consequence of teaching mental images in reading is the effect it has on children's writing. I learn this the day I ask children to draw their images as they listen to a nature CD called *Mountain Streams*. The peaceful sounds fill every corner of the room, and the rich details in the children's drawings catch me by surprise. Orange and pink sunsets, rushing waterfalls, meandering streams, and black-sky thunderstorms cover their sheets of paper.

Just as I'm about to ask children to come up front to share their images, Kenta skips over and whispers in my ear, "My table thinks we should *write* about our mental images, too. Can we? Please?" I tell him it's a brilliant idea and ask him to make an announcement to find out what the rest of the class thinks. They're with him! (And to think I almost missed the boat on this one.)

Children who couldn't seem to get past writing about loving Mom, Dad, brothers, sisters, grandmas, grandpas, dogs, cats, me, trips to the park, and birthday parties at McDonald's are now writing about cool summer breezes, cabins off in the distance, and swooshing waterfalls splashing their faces with tears. Shawnda writes, "The rushing wind rolls across the Rocky Mountain heights. The stream squiggles down the mountain." And Mitchell, whose topic of choice usually has something to do with monsters, writes, "The golden sun sets behind the purple mountains in flashes of pink and red." As more and more children share, I say, "Guys, your writing is unbelievable today! Your images are so clear, and your words—they sound like poetry! Do you hear what I hear?" Their beaming faces and exuberant nods tell me they do. "So what do you think happened? What made the difference today?"

They attribute their brilliance to the peacefulness, to the beautiful sounds that helped them get ideas, and to the images they created in their minds. I attribute their brilliance to all those things, too, but I know there's more to it. They're writing beautifully because the stage has been set for them. They've been creating images in different contexts for about a week now; I've taught them about detail. They've been listening to and reading poems and stories with beautiful language, too; I've taught them about rich words. And now they're putting all that learning into yet another context: writing. It's probably no surprise that we launch into poetry during this study—or that music is now a ritual in our writing workshop.

Children continue writing poetry in writing workshop over the next few weeks—we've got Coffeehouse Poetry Day to get ready for!

Evidence of Understanding and Independence

Following are examples of some of the ways in which children have demonstrated evidence of understanding and independence. See page 91 for a more detailed explanation of what you'll find in this section.

My dad always says I'm daydreaming, but that's not the right word. I'm making mental images and connecting them together. I'm not daydreaming, I tell him, I'm thinking.
    —Cory

When my mom reads me Harry Potter, it's like I have a paint set inside my brain. And I never run out of paint!
    —Ben

Yesterday I was skiing so fast, I just knew I was in for a major wipeout, and then I made a mental image of what I should do. I could see me curving to slow down in my head, and then I just did it in real life! My feet started curving. It really helped me!
    —Andrew

One day I was telling children how I sometimes listen to Broncos games on the radio when I'm driving. I told them about how I create images in my mind as the announcer describes the action on the field and how it makes the game a lot more interesting and memorable for me. At the end of the story, Nina raised her hand. "Mrs. Miller, there's just one thing I don't get. How do you drive with your eyes closed?"

Dear Debbie,
I started reading Whit The Lion, the Witch, and the Wardrobe *several nights ago because he had gotten a little sample of a chapter of it from an annotated youth version with Carol in the doctor's office waiting room. We borrowed Thad's paperback copy and read the first chapter, which he seemed to soak up well. The only illustrations in the book, however, are very small and simple pen-and-ink sketches covering maybe one-fourth of the first page of each chapter. After we finished the first chapter, Whit hungrily thumbed through the pages until he came to the start of each chapter, looked at the sketch, and asked me to read him the name of the chapter so he could try and figure out what was going to happen in the story. Since this was the first chapter book with minimal illustrations I'd ever read to Whit, I apologized for the lack of illustrations and suggested maybe we could look in the library for a version of the book that had more pictures. Whit*

kind of gave a sigh, and then said in a slightly condescending tone, "No, Dad. Don't you think we can make mental images as we read the story?"

Thanks for the great year Whit is having!

Hunt Walker

Conferring is often the best window into children's thinking. The things they say and the creative ways they find to apply their learning leave me shaking my head and smiling in amazement, as in the following conferences with Frank and Grace, Daniel, and Kenta.

"Hey, Frank," I say, "how's Little Bear *going for you today?"*

"It's great!" he answers. "And you know what? When I am reading Little Bear*, I can just put me right in the story. I'm doing what Little Bear is doing. When I turn the page, it's like someone else is turning the page. See right here? When Little Bear says, 'I'm cold,' I'm cold, too—freezing cold! I'm really shivering, see?"*

"You do look cold!" I say as I wonder to myself, Those couldn't be real goose bumps on his arms, could they?

At this point Grace, who sits across from Frank, overhears us. "Frank, listen to this," she says. "My mental images are sort of like that, but not exactly. It's like I'm inside the book, like you say, but the book characters don't notice me. I'm part of what's happening, but I'm invisible. Are you invisible, too, or does Little Bear see you?"

"Oh, he definitely sees me, and I see him. It's kind of like Little Bear and I are brothers. When Mother Bear made snow pants for Little Bear, she gave them to me, too! And you know what else? I can pop out of one character and into another if I want. Little Bear's image just pulls me in, and I'm not at school anymore. I'm in his life."

"Hi, Daniel," I say. "Tell me about what you're doing over here in the corner." It looks to me like he's covering entire pages with sticky notes, but I'm willing to listen.

"I'm covering up all the pictures with sticky notes because I want to make my own mental images. These aren't very good. I know that's not what billy goats really look like, and see this troll? Trolls only have one eye and wouldn't wear clothes like that!"

"So you're saying your schema about billy goats and trolls is different from the illustrator's?" I ask him.

Daniel nods yes. "I have lots more schema for billy goats and trolls. See my images?"

"I see what you mean about the one big eye," I say, "and the clothes, too. Your images really are different."

"Oh," he says, "remember when Ben brought in that picture of Hagrid from Harry Potter *and had a big fit because Hagrid didn't look like Ben's image? It's kind of like the same thing!"*

Kenta wildly motions to me across the room, jumping in and out of his seat. "Look at this!" he says as he points to a picture in the book Stars and Planets *edited by David Levy, a small diagram illustrating how Earth's seasons change. "I really get what you mean about making mental images now. I kept looking at this picture and I didn't get it at all. But then I saw these arrows, and I made it move in my mind! The earth is turning around the sun, and I can see leaves for fall, and snow coming in the winter, and beautiful-smelling flowers in spring, and the hot sun in summer, with people in shorts, all happy and stuff. Here's my mental image of it! See how the sun hits different parts of the earth at different times of the year?" (Figure 5.3 shows Kenta's drawing.)*

FIGURE 5.3
Kenta created this mental image from Stars and Planets *edited by David Levy.*

Sharing ideas in book clubs engages young readers.

In January and February

Book Clubs; Focus on Asking Questions and Inferring

Im PrdCting Rhoda is not going to cleanUp her room. Whi? Bekos I DONt like To clen UP MY room EVr.

C

Personal connections help drive a book club discussion.

A pples, carrots, and yogurt are back in our lunches. Holiday cookies, cakes, and candies are, thankfully, long gone, along with the mugs that sing while you sip, the very large reindeer pins with blinking noses, and the lovely red sweatshirts with every child's name written in glitter. It's time to get down to business.

"Can you believe it's January already?" we ask each other in the halls.

"How can that be," we wonder, "when we have so much left to teach?"

We're afraid we'll never get to everything. And we're right—there's a good chance we won't.

We stop to remind ourselves of conversations in faculty meetings, on the stairs, and in the parking lot. We remind ourselves that we believe in depth over breadth; we believe that teaching a few things well makes more sense than teaching many things superficially. And we resolve to continue to do what we believe is best for our kids, our school, and ourselves.

So what's next? By now children know all about thinking about their thinking. They're ready to learn how to engage in deeper, more thoughtful conversations with others and respond to text in ways that increase their capacity for understanding. Now is the time to build on what has come before.

Over the past few months, children have come to know each other well. They know about each other's interests, special talents, and little idiosyncrasies. They know that Adam is the dinosaur expert, Thad is fascinated with JFK, and Paige is a standout soccer player. They've been outraged by the bullies in *Oliver Button Is a Sissy*, sipped hot chocolate together on Coffeehouse Poetry Day, and had experiences working in a variety of large and small groups. They have history.

And because they do, the time is right for increasing the sophistication of the read-alouds, dedicating time every week for children to engage in book club conversations and discussions about books and big ideas, and continuing to increase the complexity of the texts they are reading independently.

Taking the Conversation Deeper

It's one thing to share thinking and listen respectfully, and quite another to *listen actively* and *respond thoughtfully* to others in order to understand another's point of view or inform one's own. All year children have had practice getting eye-to-eye and knee-to-knee, talking through the text together, and sharing their learning and thinking during reflection and share time. Now is the time to have them assume more responsibility for making meaning by introducing book clubs into the reading workshop.

I explain to the children that because they've gotten so good at thinking out loud and listening to each other, they're ready to learn how to listen and learn together in new ways. "When readers talk together about books, they make connections from the thinking of others to their own thinking to get smarter," I say. "Whether it's to better understand a tricky part of a text or talk about a favorite page, thoughtful readers engage in dialogue to better understand books, each other, and the world."

The strategies of questioning and inferring are particularly helpful in teaching children how to take the conversation deeper. Asking children to choose a burning question from a chart we've created together, or posing an open-ended question myself and working with them to infer meaning, is a perfect way to get started. The question serves to focus the dialogue; showing children how to collaborate to infer answers, solve problems, and construct meaning comes next. And where best to practice? Book clubs, of course!

Modeling, naming what I do and what I notice the children doing, and guiding them as needed gets us started. Children aren't raising their hands now. I want them to learn how real conversation flows; I want them to learn how to get it going, keep it going, and take it deeper. Book clubs give children the perfect opportunity to practice these actions in an authentic way and consolidate all the skills and strategies we're learning.

I teach children to ask themselves the following questions before jumping into conversation:

- Does what I have to say connect to the question or topic?
- Can I connect what I have to say to what someone else has said?
- Can I support what I have to say? What evidence in the text supports my thinking?
- Has someone else already said what I am about to say?
- If I am speaking to disagree, can I repeat what I heard the other person say, and explain in a nice way how and why my thinking is different?
- Does what I want to say take the conversation deeper?

I admit it sounds a bit daunting, but year after year I've listened and watched as children work and learn together in ways that exceeded my expectations. So . . . expect brilliance. Model well and model often. Pay attention to detail. Trust yourself and your kids. You won't be disappointed!

Book Clubs for Primary Kids?

It was a speaker at a literacy conference in Denver who inspired me to introduce book clubs to six- and seven-year-olds. She spoke about the rich discussions that were possible for children in the intermediate grades.

What about primary kids? I asked her (in my head). *Just because children aren't yet fluent readers doesn't mean they can't think and talk about books and big ideas in meaningful ways.*

I knew then and there that book clubs would soon be coming to my classroom. I'd always wondered how children would talk about books if I weren't there. Would they respond in the same ways they did in the large group? Would they remember what to consider before jumping into the conversation? What words would they use to make their thinking visible? Would they talk about their questions and inferences? Might they even synthesize information? Maybe book clubs could help me find out.

Over the next few weeks I hatched a plan. I realized that more than anything else, I wanted to provide a time and place for children to engage in active, lively conversation about books and ideas in a natural, real-world kind of way, without an agenda. Giving children ongoing opportunities to get together *by themselves* to enjoy books, share ideas, and engage in the social nature of learning became my primary goal.

I thought about the book clubs I'd been in over the years. There were the professional ones, where we read only work-related texts. There was the neighborhood one, where we read best sellers. And there was the one where women's angst reigned supreme.

I thought about my current book club, now in its fifth year. What was it about this one that kept us coming back? I thought it had to do with the diversity of the group and the diversity of the books we read. The group includes men and women, teachers and stonecutters, journalists, accountants, businesspeople, brokers, and more. Our reading reflects our individual and collective interests. We keep coming back because although we mostly talk about books, we talk about other things, too. We gain new insights, challenge old perspectives, and sometimes feel we've solved the problems of the world. (And then there's the food . . .)

How can I transport this same kind of spirit into the classroom? I wondered. First, I knew that the kids needed to see and hear what I was talking about. They needed to see a book club like mine in action. To that end, I recruited four parents I knew well—two moms and two dads—and explained what I was after. With only a little arm twisting, they agreed to model a book club with me. I gave them each a copy of *Where the Wild Things Are* along with some sticky notes, and we set a date. It worked so well that I now convene a model book club each year.

On the specified day, we sit in a circle on the floor, with the children sitting in a bigger circle around us. We chat a bit, pass around animal crackers, and begin talking about the book. (Don't worry—parents never lack for words. One time they went on for thirty minutes, just talking about connections! By then the children had themselves become wild things, and I was ready to set sail myself.)

I ask the kids to watch and listen carefully to what the adults do and say. Afterward I write down their observations on chart paper and hang it on the wall near where their own book clubs will meet. The children observe the adults

working together to figure out answers to questions,
taking turns talking,
asking questions,
laughing,
rereading parts of the book,
making text-based connections from the book to their lives and other
    books,
inferring, and
working together to understand.

These skills are specifically referenced in the Common Core State Standards under speaking and listening—skills that will help students become better human beings and have richer, more powerful, connected, and meaningful lives.

Children choose books for their book clubs from those we've read aloud and discussed previously. That way, they all can discuss books that are sophisticated enough to warrant thoughtful conversation. Although some children can read them, knowing how to read the book is not a requirement. Multiple copies of these titles are kept together in a small bookshelf.

At first I wondered if having heard and discussed a book before might dampen the children's enthusiasm, but it seems to have just the opposite effect. Their familiarity with the text seems to jump-start the conversation, giving them the confidence they need when the focus of the talk shifts to new thinking and ideas.

I meet briefly with each group *the day before* their book club meets (usually during work activity time) and we read aloud some or all of the text again; children follow along in individual copies. I ask them to bring sticky notes or their notebooks with them to the read-aloud so they can prepare for the next day's discussion by marking the text with a sticky note (using pictures or words) or otherwise making notes. Because I want to ensure a mix of boys, girls, interests, and reading abilities, I group children accordingly, four or five per group. They switch book groups in time, but during this study, they essentially remain the same.

During this study, book clubs meet every Friday during work time in the reading workshop and last fifteen to twenty minutes. They don't all end at the same time—when they're finished, they're finished. After children finish, and before moving to independent reading, they reflect on how things went (see reflection sheet), choose their next book, and rejoin their classmates in reading workshop.

What am I doing when children are in their book clubs? Mostly roaming. Listening in. Taking notes. Learning. Considering upcoming mini-lessons. And feeling, in general, pretty proud! I make a point of staying on the periphery of children's book clubs as much as I can—I want to find out just where children are and where they need to go.

You might be wondering whether children are able to talk together about books and ideas independently and in meaningful ways. Do they talk about connections that help them remember and understand, questions that matter, and inferences that make sense? Can they point to evidence in the text that supports their thinking? Yes! And I think I know why. The books they choose, and their knowledge of the language and strategies that readers use, propels them into lively conversations as they discuss issues and ideas, gain new insights, and challenge old perspectives.

■ JANUARY AND FEBRUARY PLAN ■
Book Clubs; Focus on Asking Questions and Inferring

Book Clubs; Strategy Focus; Inferring and Asking Questions	Demonstration of Understanding
What do I want students to walk away with at the end of this year and remember ten years from now and beyond?	*What kind of summative, end-of-study assessment can we create that exists in the real world and has a real purpose and audience?*
Book Clubs • Talking is thinking. • We are smarter together—conversation is an art that broadens our horizons, helps us connect to other people and the world, and makes our lives richer. • Reasons to be in a book club: You meet interesting people! You read books you might not otherwise read. Listening and being open to different perspectives make us smarter and help us grow. Humans thrive with connections, relationships, and lasting friendships. • Talking about books and big ideas makes you a more interesting and interested human being. **Asking Questions** • Active readers spontaneously and purposefully ask questions before, during, and after reading. • Active readers determine whether the answers to their questions can be found in the text or whether they will need to infer and/or consider another source.	Book Club Jamboree at The Bookies! (The Bookies is our local, independent bookstore.) Children will have their weekly book club here; parents and interested others will be invited to join them.

(continued)

- Active readers understand that hearing others' questions inspires new questions of their own; likewise, listening to others' answers can inspire new thinking.
- Active readers understand that the process of questioning is used in other areas of their lives, both personal and academic.
- Active readers understand that asking questions deepens their comprehension.

Inferring
- Active readers determine meanings of unknown words by using their schema, paying attention to textual and picture clues, rereading, and engaging in conversations with others.
- Active readers use their prior knowledge and textual clues to draw conclusions, determine themes and big ideas, and form unique interpretations of text.
- Active readers know to infer when the answers to their questions are not explicitly stated in the text.
- Active readers make predictions about text and confirm or contradict them as they read on.
- Active readers understand that inferring deepens their comprehension.

■ JANUARY AND FEBRUARY PLAN ■ (continued)

Possible Guiding Questions

What compelling questions will foster inquiry, understanding, and transfer of learning?
- What's so great about book clubs? Why do book clubs matter?
- How do readers think?
- How do readers get smarter?
- What makes a great question? Why do questions matter? How does asking questions make us smarter?
- How does inferring help me get smarter/read better?

Possible Supporting Targets	Possible Assessments
Long-term targets are in bold, and daily targets are listed below them.	*These formative assessments match the daily targets and let kids and me know where we are and where we need to go.*
I can figure out new words and build my vocabulary with lots of different strategies.	
• I can explain how rereading and using clues in the pictures and the text help me figure out what words mean.	• Anchor chart (Figure 6.2)
• I can share new vocabulary and word meanings with my book group.	• Individual sticky notes (Figure 6.3)
• We (our book group) can share our learning with everyone!	• Teacher note taking during reflection and sharing
I can participate in collaborative conversations and book clubs to better understand a text and the world around me.	
• I can build on what others say in conversation to help us all get smarter about our reading and the world.	• Student reflection, teacher observation
• I can support my inferences with details from the text.	• Two-column notes: my inference/supporting details in text
• I can ask questions to isolate my confusion and get smarter.	• Questions on sticky notes/include book title
• I can reflect on what worked well in book group and how we can make it better next time.	• Reflection sheet (page 123)
I can infer the big ideas when I read.	
• I can pay attention to what the characters say and do.	• Anchor chart: "Inferring Big Ideas in Our Reading"
• I can recognize repeated words and phrases.	• Same as above. Will connect to determining importance in March
• I can talk with my book group about my big ideas and listen carefully to theirs.	• Teacher observation/note taking/brainstorming upcoming mini-lessons
I can explain how asking questions deepens my comprehension.	
• I can ask questions that help me dig deeper into a topic or a text.	• Exit ticket: My biggest question from my reading today . . .
• I can share my questions about my book club book with my book group to see what they think.	• Teacher observation/note taking/ brainstorming upcoming mini-lessons
• I can respond thoughtfully to the questions of others to deepen our comprehension.	• Think sheet
• I can focus on a burning question in my reading and answer it.	• Questioning web (page 141)

■ JANUARY AND FEBRUARY CALENDARS ■

SUNDAYMONDAYTUESDAYWEDNESDAYTHURSDAYFRIDAYSATURDAY

During January and February the children will meet in book clubs each week, adding context for the importance of questioning and inferring to comprehend text and having great conversations about books. They will work toward hosting a Book Club Jamboree at the end of February with local adult book clubs in the area.

■ Weeks 1 and 2

Guiding questions: How does inferring make me smarter? How does it help me read better? What is a book club? Why does it matter?

- Reading-content focus on inferring
- Big-idea content focus on connections to other humans through talk that makes us smarter
- Possible mini-lessons:
  - Fishbowl model: what book clubs do
  - What a great book club conversation looks like, sounds like, feels like
  - How readers figure out the "unknown"—word level, plot level, idea level, character level, and so on
  - Predictions with text support, how readers use prior knowledge plus text to get smarter, how "the reader writes the book"

■ Weeks 3–5

Guiding questions: What makes a great question? Why do questions matter?

- Reading-content focus on questioning
- Possible mini-lessons:
  - How do questions help us read better?
  - What types of questions help us understand?
  - What different purposes do questions serve?
  - How do I get my questions answered? Where can readers go to find answers?
  - Does every question have an answer?
  - What makes a great question?
  - What do the "most interesting" questions help us do, see, and learn?

■ Weeks 6–7

Guiding questions: How does inferring make me smarter? How does inferring help me read better?

- Reading-content focus on inferring
- Possible mini-lessons:
  - How to track/pay attention to what the characters say and do to infer big ideas
  - How to support my inferences with details from the text
  - How to make predictions about text and confirm or contradict predictions as you read
  - How to infer when answers to questions aren't directly in the text
  - How to create interpretations to enrich and deepen experience in a text
  - How to use prior knowledge and textual clues to draw conclusions and form unique interpretations of text
- Other: Start planning jamboree—contact local bookstores and book clubs, create invitations, determine purposes. What information should we share? How will we share it?

■ Week 8

Prep for Book Club Jamboree! Finalize documents to share, groups, texts; practice flow of the day, and so forth.

Tried-and-True Texts for Primary Book Clubs, Questioning, and Inferring

How to Heal a Broken Wing by Bob Graham (almost wordless)
Amazing Grace by Mary Hoffman
Now One Foot, Now the Other by Tomie dePaola
City Dog and Country Frog by Mo Willems
A Circle of Friends by Giora Carmi (wordless)
Oliver Button Is a Sissy by Tomie dePaola
The Lion and the Mouse by Jerry Pinkney
Odd Velvet by Mary E. Whitcomb
The Tin Forest by Helen Ward
Grandfather Twilight by Barbara Berger
An Angel for Solomon Singer by Cynthia Rylant
The Royal Bee by Francis Park and Ginger Park
Where Are You Going, Manyoni? by Catherine Stock
How Many Days to America? by Eve Bunting
Amelia's Road by Linda Jacobs Altman
Are You a Snail? (and others) by Judy Allen
Tut's Mummy Lost and Found (and others) by Judy Donnelly
Inside the Titanic by Hugh Brewster
Actual Size (and others) by Steve Jenkins
Monarch Butterfly (and others) by Gail Gibbons
A Mama for Myzee by Isabel Hatkoff
One Tiny Turtle (and others) by Nicola Davies
Without You by Sarah Weeks

Also appropriate are any other well-written, well-illustrated texts that connect to your social studies and science units of study.

Book club choices that come from children's independent reading might include the titles listed below, depending on where children are as readers. Each book has individual stories—one story is perfect for book club conversation and discussion, *and* they all have big ideas!

The Little Bear Series by Else Holmelund Minarik
Little Bear
A Kiss for Little Bear
Little Bear's Friend
Father Bear Comes Home
Little Bear's Visit

The Frog and Toad Series by Arnold Lobel
Frog and Toad
Frog and Toad Together

Frog and Toad All Year
Days with Frog and Toad
Frog and Toad Are Friends

And then there are wordless books! Great titles for book clubs, questioning, and inferring include the following:

A Circle of Friends by Giora Carmi
The Umbrella by Ingrid and Dieter Schubert
The Lion and the Mouse by Jerry Pinkney
Why? by Nicolai Popov
Chalk by Bill Thompson
Looking Down by Steve Jenkins
Wave by Suzy Lee

For this reflection sheet, I would use a half sheet—5 by 7 inch would be best for early readers. I would never ask children to reflect on all of these questions at once. Each week I would pick a few, depending on what I know they need in order to grow as learners or our learning targets for that week.

Book Club Reflection

My name _____

Book title _____

What did I learn in my book group that I didn't know before? How did I get smarter today?

Did everybody get smarter in book club today? Yes? No? Why?

Did I participate in the conversation?

Did everybody have a chance to talk?

What is my goal for the next book club?

What will our group read next?

Inferring

Cory and Whit rush into the classroom minutes before the bell. They scurry over to a corner, where Cory plunks down his backpack and takes out what looks to be an ancient cell phone. "See, Whit? Here it is. My mom says it's broken, but I'm inferring we can fix it!" Out of the corner of my eye I watch them turn it over and over, furiously pushing buttons, pulling the antenna out and pushing it back in, checking the batteries, listening for a dial tone.

To their surprise (and mine), the phone begins to make a strange beeping sound. "See? I just knew it!" Cory says. "It just needs a little something. Go get a magnifying glass, quick!" They methodically examine every inch (centimeter?) of the phone. But no amount of close examination renders them a dial tone. The beeping stops. "Well, Whit," Cory says softly, "at least we tried."

"Cory," Whit pleads, "we can't give up yet. Oh—wait! I know!" He races over to the basket of two-column note forms and grabs one. "We can infer what's wrong with it," he says. "Let's put our thinking together. I'll draw the phone on this side, and you write our thinking over here. This is going to be a huge infer! When we figure it out, let's show Mrs. Miller! She'll go crazy for this!" (They were right—see Figure 6.1.)

The children have been learning about the ways readers (and telephone repairmen) infer for a few weeks. When I think about how far the kids have

FIGURE 6.1
Cory and Whit's two-column notes on the phone

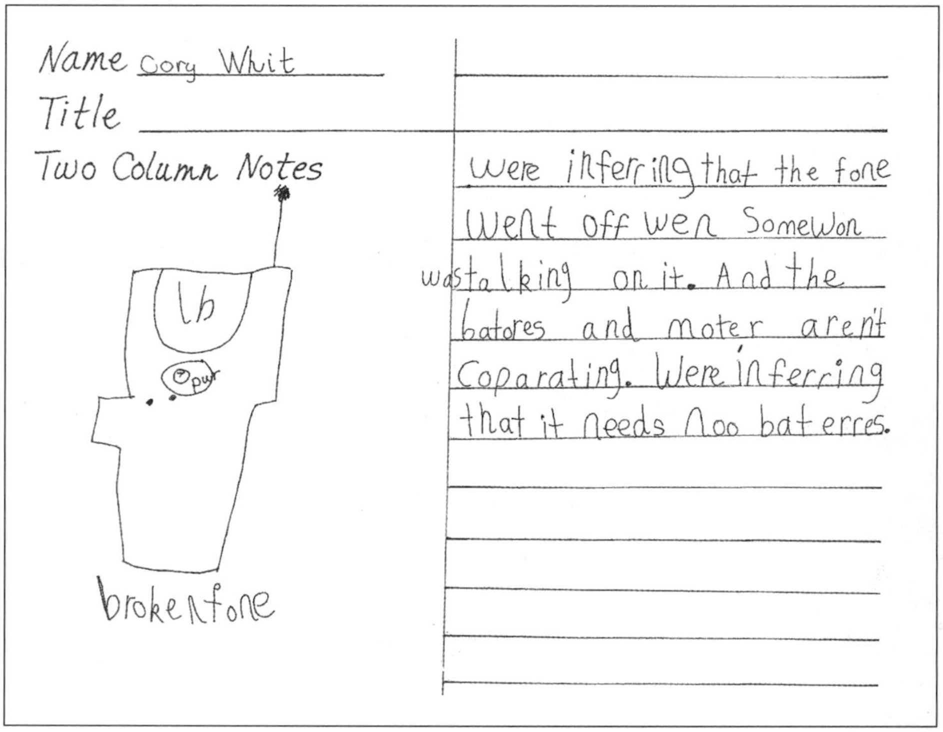

come, I realize it's because I've come a long way, too. I remember when I wasn't even sure what inferring was, let alone how to go about teaching it.

I think back to the day when ten of us were scrunched into the old book room at University Park Elementary, where Chryse Hutchins, staff developer at the Public Education and Business Coalition, was leading an after-school discussion on teaching inferring to our first and second graders. "So what's everybody thinking?" she asks us. We love Chryse, but the room is freezing. We think those might be snowflakes outside the window. And we don't really feel like thinking. Chryse knows all about wait time, but so do we. Undeterred, she asks, "So how is inferring going in your classrooms? Who would like to share what you've been doing?" Kristin and I exchange glances. Should we tell?

Kristin gives me a silent kick. I take the cue. I'll tell. "Well, Chryse, I'm confused, actually. Kristin and I have been having this ongoing discussion about inferring, and we've been wondering things like, well, what does it mean to infer? At first we thought it was about predicting, but if a child makes a prediction and confirms it a page later, is that really an inference, or just a simple prediction?" We think inferring is bigger than predicting, but we're not sure.

This conversation took place early in our work with Chryse, and we were surprised to learn that she wasn't sure about the difference either. And she was smart enough to admit it to us. As with the best staff developers, Chryse was one of the first to engage us in conversations in which we all participated in the learning. So what is inferring? Prediction is a piece of it, but our hunches were right: there is more to it. Inferring, according to Anderson and Pearson (1984), is the heart of meaning construction for learners of all ages.

It's no accident that our strategy work focuses on inferring and questioning as we launch into book clubs. When you think of your book groups, what kind of thinking do you do most?

What follows are some key considerations and anchor lessons on inferring that put theory into practice. When readers infer, they use their prior knowledge and textual clues to draw conclusions and form unique interpretations of text.

Anchor Lessons

Readers determine meanings of unknown words by using their schema, paying attention to textual and picture clues, rereading, and engaging in conversations with others

A book like *Where Are You Going, Manyoni?* by Catherine Stock is perfect for teaching children about inferring at the word level. Set on the Limpopo River in a dry, sparsely settled area in Zimbabwe, it's the story of a little girl who passes through the veld on her way to school. Along the way, she skips past shady kloofs, red sandstone koppies, acacia and baobab trees, foraging bush-pigs, and malala palms, all of which offer opportunities for authentic modeling of how to infer meanings of unknown words.

On the first day, I read aloud the first few pages, thinking aloud about the meanings of words like *baobab, Limpopo,* and *bushpig.* On the page with the baobab tree, I say, "Hmm. Baobab tree? What kind of tree is that? I think I've heard the word *baobab,* but I'm pretty sure I've never seen a tree by that name. I'm going to reread this page. Let's see, it talks about the *great, gray* baobab tree. I think *great* means *big* in this sentence. When I look at the picture, there's a huge tree that is grayish. See this one? I'm inferring that it is the baobab tree."

After modeling several other words in much the same way, I say, "Think a minute about what you just saw and heard me doing to infer the meanings of words I didn't understand. What did you notice?" Children noticed I was

> rereading,
> paying attention to the words,
> looking closely at the pictures,
> using my schema,
> taking my time, and
> thinking really hard.

"Good noticing!" I tell them. "Now it's your turn. Listen carefully as I read, and if you hear a word you don't understand, raise your hand and we'll work together to infer its meaning." I read about halfway through the book, and along the way we infer the meaning of *forages, pan,* and *kloof.* We record our thinking on a chart labeled "What can you do to help yourself figure out the meaning of an unknown word?" The chart is divided into three sections, headed "Word," "What we infer it means," and "What helped us?"

The next day we talk about what we remember and what we learned from our work the day before. I reread the book, and when we get to the part where we left off, I again ask children to raise their hands if they hear a word they don't understand, adding that day's words and our thinking to the chart. At the end of the book we find a glossary of unfamiliar words and their meanings, which gives us an opportunity to confirm or correct some of our definitions on the chart. We decide to mark each with either a *C* when our thinking is confirmed, or a *C* with an *X* on top when our definition is contradicted by the book's glossary.

When we finish, I ask the children what they've learned, and I record their thinking on the chart (see Figure 6.2). Before I send them off to reading workshop, I say, "In your reading today, if you come across a word and you don't understand what it means, think about what we've learned and give it a try. Happy reading!"

Postscript: Check out the sticky notes shown in Figure 6.3. A group of kids at one table came up with the format, and after they shared it with the rest of the class that day, it caught on. Thereafter, children brought their books and sticky notes to share. This allowed us to talk about the meaning of the unknown words together, which gave several children at once a chance to learn new words, and gave me an opportunity to clear up any misconceptions.

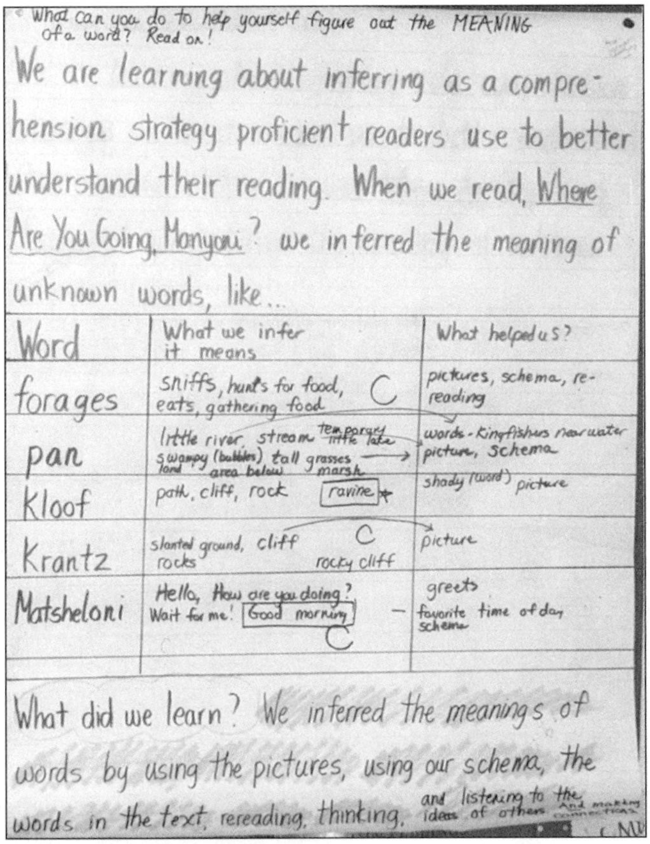

Readers make predictions about text and confirm or contradict their predictions as they read on

Books with opportunities for making clear-cut predictions that can be confirmed or contradicted in the text are useful for teaching children about prediction. One such book is *The Royal Bee* by Frances and Ginger Park, the story of a young boy in Korea named Song-ho,

FIGURE 6.2
Inferring meanings of words from Where Are You Going, Manyoni? *by Catherine Stock*

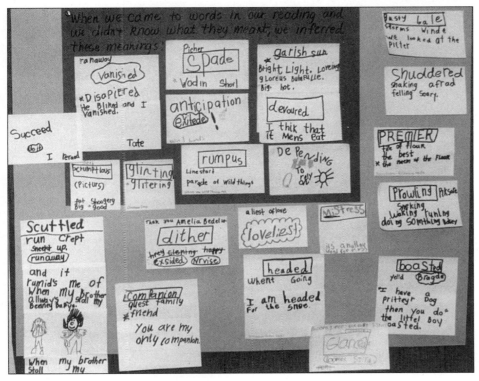

FIGURE 6.3
Children brought their sticky notes to share.

who wants desperately to learn how to read and write. But back then, only the privileged *yangban* children are allowed to go to school, and Song-ho is very poor.

I read aloud the first few pages, stopping to infer meanings for such unknown terms as *yangban, sangmin,* and *Royal Bee*, and giving children a bit of background knowledge about the culture of Korea at the time of the story. When we pick up the story again, Song-ho hears the ringing of the school bell off in the distance and follows its sweet sound deep into the valley.

Once there, he looks through the rice-paper doors of the Sodang School and sees the shadows of the yangban pupils and their master. When Master Min slides open the door, Song-ho asks if he can be his pupil. The master admires Song-ho's bravery, but he knows that "rules are rules, and sangmins were not allowed to attend the Sodang School." With a lump in his throat, he tells Song-ho to go home.

I put the book down. "So what are you thinking? What do you predict will happen next?" Grant raises his hand. "I predict Song-ho is going to get into that school, and he's going to learn to read and write poetry."

I record his prediction on a two-column chart labeled "Our predictions—and the thinking behind them" and ask, "What's the thinking behind your prediction, Grant? What made you predict that Song-ho will get to go to the Sodang School, even though Master Min tells him to go home?"

"Well, you know how the star of the book always gets the really good stuff? That's why I think he'll get to go."

"That's smart, Grant. You're using your schema for stories like this one to predict what might happen.

"Does anybody have a *different* prediction?" I ask, hoping to see at least one raised hand. But it's not to be. This day everyone predicts that Song-ho is going to the Sodang School, and that he's going to learn to read and write.

"Let's go back into the text," I say. "Listen as I reread and see if you hear anything else that might have helped you predict he'd get to go to school and learn to read and write." I add the children's thinking and mine to the chart, right under Grant's. As we read on, the children confirm their prediction when Master Min says, "Welcome to the Sodang School, Song-ho." I put a C for "confirmed" under their prediction.

The second day I read the rest of the story. Just as we predicted, Song-ho learns to read and write. We learn about the Royal Bee, a contest of knowledge held every spring in the Great Hall at the governor's palace. Only one pupil will be chosen to represent the Sodang School.

I close the book and give children the two-column note form, asking them to predict who will go to the Royal Bee on one side and to record the thinking behind their prediction on the other. (An example of their responses is shown in Figure 6.4.) We share, and then I read the rest of the story aloud. Guess who gets a big cheer when I finish the story? Could it be Song-ho?

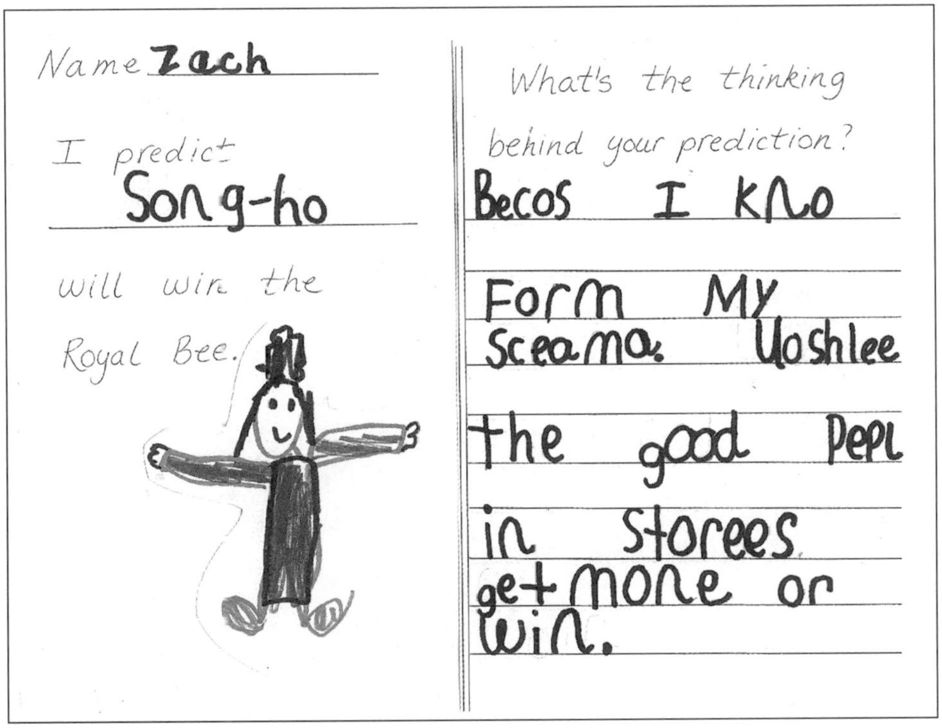

Name **Zach**

I predict **Song-ho**

will win the Royal Bee.

What's the thinking behind your prediction?

Becos I kno form my sceama. Uoshlee the good pepl in storees get more or win.

FIGURE 6.4
Zach's predictions about Song-ho

Readers use their prior knowledge and textual clues to draw conclusions and form unique interpretations of text

Once I saw the glee on the faces of those "fish" flailing around the meeting area (see Chapter 5), I knew I needed to provide children regular opportunities for dramatic expression. But it was Frank's question about the pagoda that kept me thinking. With practice, could dramatic responses really help kids draw conclusions and form unique interpretations of text? Could acting out a tricky word or a puzzling piece of text really serve as a means to understanding? Could one child's images build or strengthen the images of another, thereby enhancing their learning?

Frank and the pagoda experience showed me that these activities could help kids—but I had to figure out how I could involve everyone in a manageable way. Again I took up Georgia Heard's book of poems, *Creatures of Earth, Sea, and Sky.* The poems are short, I know children have at least some schema for most entries, and the content is just difficult enough for children to have to think through each poem carefully to understand it.

I choose six poems I think lend themselves best to dramatic interpretation and copy them onto chart paper. The children and I read each of them aloud several times. Then I say, "Think carefully about the poems we just read. Which one of them is most interesting to you? Which one makes you think, 'Hmm, what is this poem really about?' Choose one you'd like to understand better.

"Once you've decided, go to the poem you want to learn more about. Take it with you and find a place in the room where you can work well. You have about fifteen minutes to build on each other's ideas and figure out how your group can best interpret the poem you've chosen. Good luck!"

I observe Mitchell, Geoffrey, and Allan. They've chosen the poem "Dressing Like a Snake":

> A snake changes its clothes
> only twice a year.
> Beginning with its nose,
> peeling down to its toes:
> new clothes suddenly appear.
> Wouldn't it be nice
> to dress only twice
> instead of each day of the year?

What will they do with this one? I wonder. *Do they get the fact that it's about a snake shedding its skin? What conclusions will they draw? And how in the world will they create an interpretation that mirrors those conclusions?*

I tell myself to stay out of it, and once again, it's a wise decision. Figure 6.5 shows the three boys acting out the snake's shedding its skin.

Children love to use a two-column format to help them organize their thinking as they practice inferring (Figure 6.6). They mark up the text, record their thinking as it evolves, and in the end come up with what they think the poem or text is about.

Postscript: Children saw these exercises as riddles, and spontaneously began writing their own during writing workshop. We decided to write a poem

FIGURE 6.5
Mitchell, Geoffrey, and Allan "Dressing Like a Snake"

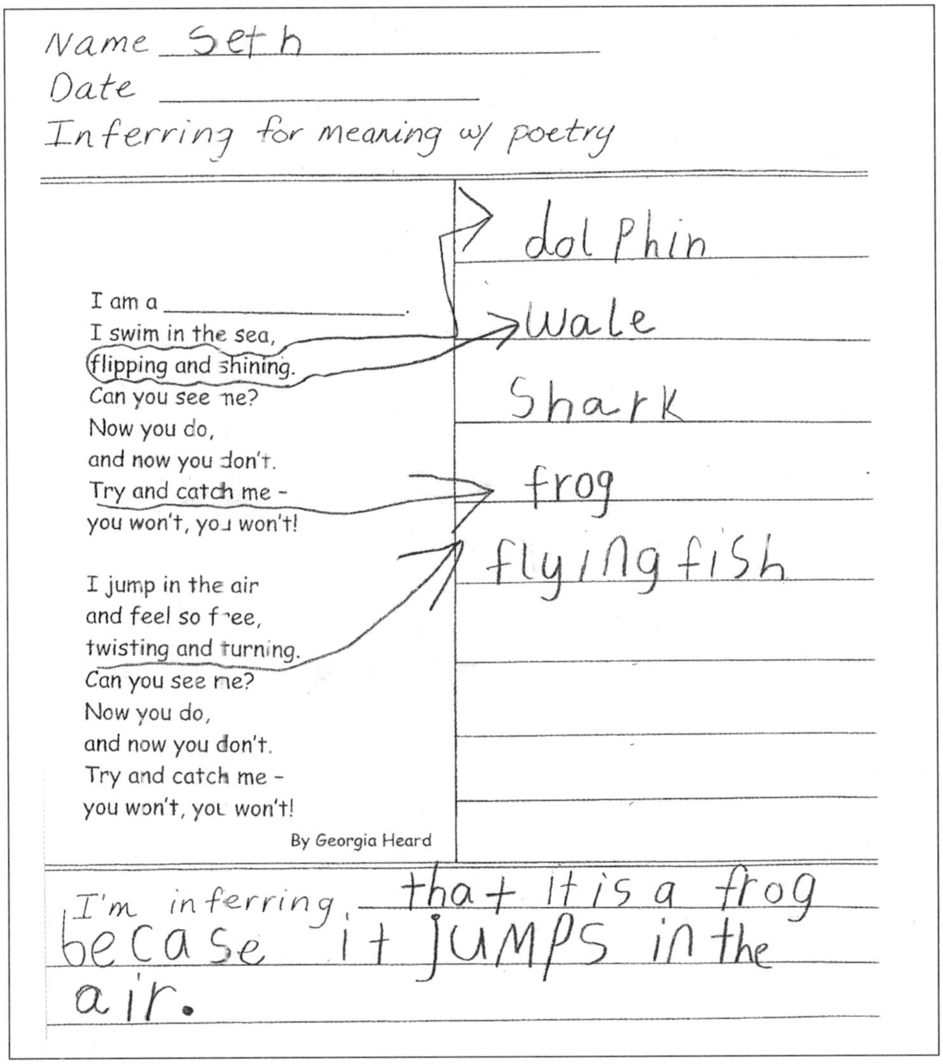

Name Seth
Date
Inferring for meaning w/ poetry

dolPhin
wale
Shark
frog
flyingfish

I am a ___________.
I swim in the sea,
flipping and shining.
Can you see me?
Now you do,
and now you don't.
Try and catch me -
you won't, you won't!

I jump in the air
and feel so free,
twisting and turning.
Can you see me?
Now you do,
and now you don't.
Try and catch me -
you won't, you won't!
By Georgia Heard

I'm inferring that It is a frog becase it jumPs in the air.

FIGURE 6.6
Children used a two-column format for inferring.

together and send it home to see if their parents could figure out what we were describing. This was such a hit that I began to post the children's riddles out in the hall, with spaces for passersby to write what they inferred the poems were about. After a week or so, children wrote in the titles of their poems, giving those same passersby a chance to confirm or change their thinking.

Readers know to infer when the answers to their questions are not explicitly stated in the text

How Many Days to America? by Eve Bunting is the story of a family forced by soldiers to flee the village they love. They board a small fishing boat in the middle of the night, taking with them only a change of clothing and some jewelry to buy their way to America. The trip is a dangerous one; the motors of the little boat stop, the passengers run out of food and water, and thieves come aboard, demanding money and jewels. Will they ever reach America safely?

I choose a book like this one because I know the story will provoke lots of questions, most of them requiring readers to infer answers by using clues in the text and their prior knowledge. I know, too, that because the content is difficult, there will be opportunities for teaching children to actively listen and learn from each other.

I begin by reading aloud and modeling my questions. Three or four pages in, I invite children to share their questions; I add them to mine in my notebook. By the end of the story, we've asked many questions:

> Why did the soldiers make them leave?
> Why did she have to give him her wedding ring? And garnets?
> Why are the soldiers shooting at them instead of helping?
> Did they go to our America? We don't have trees like that.
> Where are they from?
> Why did the thieves steal from them? They were so nice.
> Will they ever get to America?
> Did they get to go back to their village?

After school I write the questions on a chart, and we take a couple of days to go back into the text to work together to figure out the answers. I think aloud about how I'm using my schema, the pictures, and the words in the text to help me infer answers; gradually I invite children to do the same, recording our thinking on the chart. Focusing on one question at a time allows me to show children how to extend dialogue by building on the conversation of others.

Readers create interpretations to enrich and deepen their experience in a text

Have you ever read a book that changed the way you thought or felt about something? Have you ever read a book that made you feel you were a better person for having read it? Maybe you learned something about yourself that you never knew before, looked at an issue from another point of view, or changed your thinking about something you once believed to be true.

Growing up in the small town of Lamar, Colorado, I would sometimes explore with my family the crumbling ruins of nearby Camp Amache, a Japanese internment camp set in the sand and sage of the southeastern part of the state. Sitting under the lone cottonwood tree, I'd listen to stories of how this land had once held hundreds of Japanese Americans against their will during World War II. I learned that the fear that they might in some way contribute to the Japanese war effort was the sole reason for their confinement. *This happened in America?* I wondered. I couldn't believe it. But when I read

James Bradley's *Flags of Our Fathers*, I gained a new perspective. Though the story was still hard to believe, I was at least able to understand the motivation and fears of those who believed that confinement of these U.S. citizens was necessary.

Before I begin reading, I talk to children about how authors often want their readers to take something away from their books—that authors want to leave their readers with something to think about and remember. "Books," I tell them, "can help you think about important things in new ways. As I read *Miss Maggie*, be thinking about what Cynthia Rylant might want you to think about and remember." Devon's written response to this book is shown in Figure 6.7.

Books like *Something Beautiful* by Sharon Dennis Wyeth, *If You Listen* by Charlotte Zolotow, *Those Shoes* by Maribeth Boelts, and *Tight Times* by Barbara Hazen also have characters who experience the ups and downs of childhood, and just might help children gain new perspectives.

miss maggie

I think She was triing to say alwas lisin to your heart. Becase She Sayed if he Lisened to his head he Wud Be out of there in a flash. But his feet wasn't lisening to his head. His feet was lisning to his hrart.

Devon

FIGURE 6.7
Devon's written response to Miss Maggie *by Cynthia Rylant*

Asking Questions

Rothstein and Santana (2011) consider a child's ability to formulate his or her own questions to be the most important learning skill. Questioning is an essential thinking skill, learning skill, and democratic skill. There is no one set of "right questions," but rather, everyone needs the opportunity to figure out the questions that are the right ones for them to ask. Questioning is at the heart of becoming an independent thinker and a self-directed learner (Rothstein and Santana 2011). That's why I'm including the scenario that follows: when we want children to understand that questioning is at the heart of becoming an independent thinker and a self-directed learner, we teachers need to take the time to think about the questions that are "just right" for us.

> *Yikes! This is one weird book,* I think as I read *The Stranger* by Chris Van Allsburg late one night. *What's it about?* I wonder, and *What's the deal with the guy?*

"How many times are you going to read that?" my husband asks, sleepily rolling over and pulling a pillow over his head.

"Come on," I say. "I know it's late, but just listen to a little of it—there's this one part I want to talk with you about." I take his silence to mean "I'd love to listen and share my thinking with you," so I begin reading aloud. When I finish, I realize he hasn't heard a word.

Mesmerized would be how I describe the children as they listen to the story the next day. (At least *they* know a good story when they hear one!) And the questions! "Who is the stranger?" many wonder as they sit eye-to-eye and knee-to-knee. "Do you think he's part of nature? Is he magic? Why would Farmer Bailey let a stranger into his house? How could the thermometer break like that?" Their questions seem endless.

In the midst of the hubbub, Grace plops herself into my lap and asks, "Mrs. Miller, what are you wondering?"

"Well, you know the part where the stranger is dressed in his old clothes and he's getting ready to leave? I'm wondering what made him decide to go."

"I know why!" she says, opening the book to the page where the stranger is holding the red leaf. "He had to go because he got his memory back. See the red leaf? Remember how it was green? When he blew on it and it turned red, he got his memory back. See his face? The red leaf made him remember who he was."

How did I miss that? I wonder. *And how did Grace figure it out so quickly?* I've always told children that our class is a community of learners and that I have much to learn from them, but have I really believed it? I am good at listening to children to inform my teaching, but have I ever really considered that a child, and an emergent reader at that, can help me understand a picture book?

I don't think so. Grace taught me I don't have to know all the answers to teach well. Understanding that I can be both teacher and learner has broadened my definition of my role in the classroom and increased my capacity to teach and learn.

It used to be that the books I deemed weird, or the ones that kept me a little off balance, remained on the shelves of libraries and bookstores. But now they're on my shelves, too. They've become the vehicle that propels my teaching (and learning) forward.

I learned that as my questions became less literal and more sophisticated, the children's did, too; as I began to think more deeply about my reading and learning, so did they; and as I began to ask questions that truly mattered to me, they did, too.

Coincidence? Not a chance. The connection is absolute. The children I teach are limited only when I choose to limit myself. And that hardback copy of *The Stranger* propped up on the ledge behind my desk? Call it a reminder.

Anchor Lessons

Readers purposefully and spontaneously ask questions before, during, and after reading

Grandfather Twilight is one of my favorite books for teaching children about asking questions. Beautifully written and illustrated by Barbara Berger, it's the story of Grandfather Twilight and how he puts the world to sleep night after night.

Before reading the book, I explain to the children that thoughtful readers ask questions not only as they read, but also before and after reading. "Like right now," I say, "I'm thinking some of you might have a question or two in your head about this book, *Grandfather Twilight*. Is that true? You *all* do? I really love how hard you work to make sense of the books we read."

I record our questions, and the children help me code them as we go, putting a *B* for questions we asked *before* we read, a *D* for those we asked *during* reading, and an *A* for those we asked *after* reading the book.

At the end of the read-aloud, our chart looks like this:

We are learning that readers ask questions before, during, and after reading. As we read *Grandfather Twilight*, we wondered:

B   What is twilight?
B   Is that Grandfather Twilight on the cover?
B   I wonder if he's magic.
D   What does *among* mean?
D   Is this about God?
D   How could the strands of pearls be endless?
D   How does the pearl get bigger and bigger?
A   Why would this author write a book about stuff she doesn't
        understand?
A   Could this be true?

Children notice right away that we'd asked questions before, during, and after reading, but I'm after more. "Here's something else I want you to think about," I say. "*Why* do you think readers ask questions before, during, and after reading? How does asking questions help you become a better reader?" Then I wait. And wait. And wait.

Finally, Madison raises her hand. "I'm thinking it keeps your head in the book. You don't want to stop reading because when you ask questions, you want to find out about them and you just can't stop. It keeps your mind awake."

Postscript: To keep track of the children's thinking and learning throughout this study, I begin a chart labeled "Thinking about Questioning." I divide the chart into thirds, with these headings:

What do we know about asking questions?
How does asking questions help the reader?
How do readers figure out the answers to their questions?

We add to our knowledge during subsequent lessons when I ask, "What did we learn about asking questions today? What new learning could we add to our chart?" Asking children questions like these gives them opportunities to process their learning and gives me a chance to mention what I notice, too. We record our new learning on sticky notes and place them under the appropriate category. See Figure 6.8.

FIGURE 6.8
The "Thinking about Questioning" chart

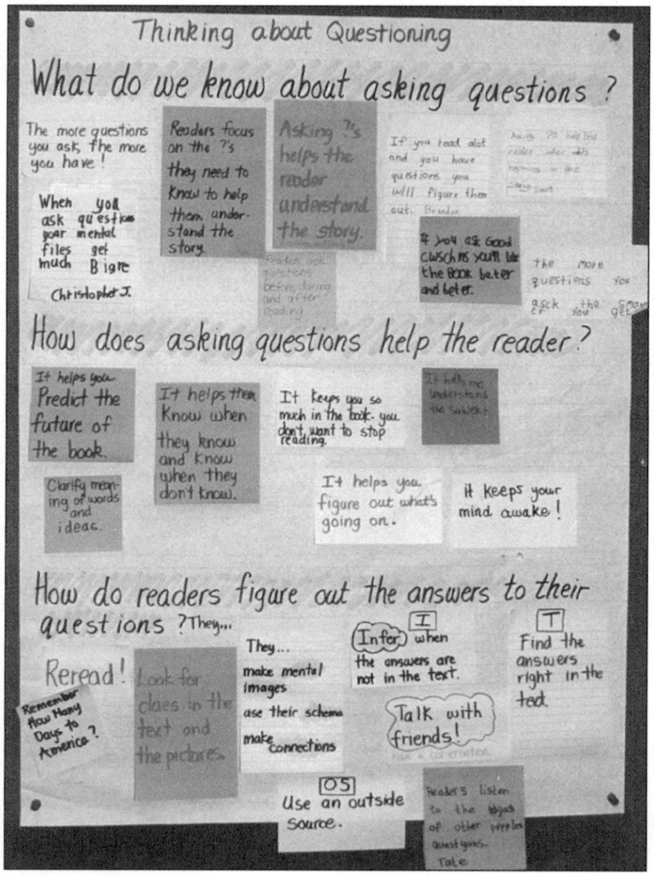

Readers ask questions for many reasons

Readers ask questions to

clarify meaning;
wonder about text yet to be read;
determine an author's style, intent, content, or format;
focus attention on specific components/features of the text; and
locate a specific answer in the text or consider rhetorical questions inspired in the text.

Because it's difficult to predict the kinds of questions children might ask, and it seems at odds with good teaching to limit their questions to a certain kind or category, I don't go down this list and focus on the reasons readers ask questions one by one. But I do want children to understand that readers ask different kinds of questions for a variety of purposes. How do I go about it?

Throughout our study of questioning, I pay attention to the kinds of questions the children and I ask, pointing out their specific purposes in the moment. We make note of them and add our findings to the chart, right under "How does asking questions help the reader?"

For example, when Meghan says, "I wonder if this book by Jonathan London is going to be like the other Froggy books," I point out that Meghan is asking a question to determine the story's content; she's wondering if her book will be like the others she's read by this author. Or when Maddy asks, "What does 'it is the flower of hope' mean?" I point out that smart readers also ask questions when the meaning of the text is unclear.

Readers determine whether the answers to their questions can be found in the text or whether they will need to infer the answer from the text, their background knowledge, and/or an outside source

The Lotus Seed by Sherry Garland is the story of a Vietnamese family forced to flee their homeland when a devastating civil war breaks out in their country. With soldiers clamoring at their door, they're allowed only a few possessions before scrambling onto a crowded boat and setting sail in stormy seas for America.

Sound familiar? I knew the children, too, would make connections between Eve Bunting's *How Many Days to America?* and *The Lotus Seed.* And I knew they'd have many questions about the content of the story, which would give me a chance to demonstrate that although some answers would require us to infer or to consult an outside source, others could be found right in the text.

I record the children's questions on a chart before, during, and after reading. Over the next several days we work through them, rereading the text (it's short) and thinking aloud about how we answered many of them. Coding answers with a *T* for those found in the text, an *I* for those we needed to infer, and an *OS* for those requiring an outside source helps make the process visible and increases children's awareness of how and why readers use a variety of strategies to find answers to their questions.

I'm in no hurry for us to get through the questions, nor is recording the answers my primary goal. I want to show kids that thoughtful readers, readers like themselves, not only take the time to ask questions, but also are compelled to seek the answers, even (especially?) when it takes a bit of doing.

At the end of the third day, our chart looks like this:

Where does this take place? **T**
What's a lotus seed? **OS** (Hollis brought one in!)
What is a dragon throne? **T** (author's note)
Who stole it? How did he lose it? **T** (author's note)
What's an altar? **T** (picture in text)
Why did her parents choose her husband for her? **OS** (Mrs. Miller's
      schema)
Why did he march off to war? Did he die? **I**
Why did she take the lotus seed, but not her mother-of-pearl hair
      comb? **I**
What does *scrambled* mean? **OS** (Brendan)
What will happen to them? **T**
Who's throwing the bombs? What war is this? **T/OS** (author's note and
      Mrs. Miller)
Where are they going? **T**
What city is this? **I**
Why did they all live together? **I**
Who is Ba'? Why did she cry and cry? **I**
What does "it is the flower of hope" mean? **I**
Why doesn't the author give us more information? **I**
Where is Vietnam? **OS** (globe, pull-down map)

Postscript: One would think that after three days of delving into a book, children would be ready to move on. Most are, but there are always some who can't seem to get enough of one book or another. Four days later, Hollis, Tate, Olivia, and Emily were still poring over *The Lotus Seed*.

They fashioned a response sheet by connecting five pieces of 12-by-18-inch construction paper lengthwise with tape; then they covered it with sticky notes that recorded their thinking. Labeled "Our Thinking About *The Lotus Seed*," the sheet bore evidence that these four were using strategies flexibly—they were on their way to learning how readers purposefully use a variety of strategies *when they need them* to construct meaning.

They had asked questions such as these:

Why did her parents get to choose her husband? We still don't get that.
Why didn't the little boy just ask to see the lotus seed?
How could he forget where he hid it? It was REALLY important.
When Mrs. Miller was reading us *The Lotus Seed*, we didn't know what
      the River of Perfumes meant, and we still don't.
Who is the new emperor?
Where did they go in America?
How many kids did she have?

They had created mental images, such as drawing pictures of these:

the lotus flower
red bombs exploding everywhere
an *ao dai*
grandmother shouting (her mouth one big circle) when she couldn't
　　find the lotus seed
an altar

They had drawn inferences, such as these:

We are inferring she ended up in New York because of all the tall build-
　　ings and the twinkling blinking lights.
We're thinking she has two or four other kids because in the picture
　　there might be some in front of her and some in the back of her
　　holding on to her hands.

They made connections, such as these:

When I feel lonely or sad, I cuddle up with my blanket or pillow, and
　　then I feel safe.
These soldiers are just like the ones in *How Many Days to America?*

They gave opinions, such as these:

We don't ever want our parents to pick our husbands! That's not right.
We think *The Lotus Seed* is the best book we've ever read!

So what do we do when children—in this instance Hollis, Tate, Olivia,
and Emily—are so enamored with a text that they just can't seem to let it go?
I empower them to hang on and hold tight. Why? Because it's in their best
interests! Learning situations like these don't come around every day. Or
week. So I'm flexible. I want children to take advantage of situations like
these—it's not something I can "make happen" when I want it to. But then
there's the question of the calendar. It's really all about balance, and knowing
kids well.

I ask these questions:

Are kids getting smarter?
Do they know how and why?
Are they sincere in their efforts?

Are they working hard to figure things out?
Is what they're doing moving them forward as learners?
What can I, and other children, learn from them?

Readers understand that many of the most intriguing questions are not answered explicitly in the text, but are left to the reader's interpretation

All I See by Cynthia Rylant is the story of a man named Gregory, who spends his days painting whales. He paints them by the side of a beautiful lake, sometimes whistling a theme from Beethoven's Fifth Symphony, his cat curled up at his feet. When he tires, he lies flat in his canoe and drifts down the lake, smiling up at the sky. A little boy named Charlie watches him from a distance, and the two become great friends.

Experience tells me that the answers to children's questions about stories like this one are not likely to be found in the text. Nor will they be easy to infer. We'll never know for sure why whales are all Gregory sees, whether this is his "real job," or what Charlie's passion will be. But thoughtful readers don't just shake their heads in confusion and keep on reading. Thoughtful readers know how intriguing it is to take the time to speculate about these kinds of questions and create their own unique explanations, or interpretations.

"Remember when we created dramatic interpretations of poems?" I ask. "Interpreting answers to questions that are hard to figure out is a lot like that. Readers create their own unique interpretations by using their schema, creating mental images, and talking with others to figure out what makes the most sense to them.

"Let's choose a question from our list," I continue, "one that we really want to figure out, and think out loud about how we might make sense of it."

I've made a questioning web—a circle with lines fanning out from all sides—and I write the question the children choose ("Why are whales all he sees?") inside the circle. I record their interpretations on the lines around it. They think that maybe . . .

he doesn't want to forget about whales, and he doesn't want the rest of the world to either.
he has so much schema about whales, he just has to let some of it out.
he's like a machine full of mental images, and they are all of whales.
he's passionate about whales.
the music is an invisible net for mental images—it traps them and helps him see whales.
if you care about something a lot, you see it everywhere.

he knows the blue whale is endangered—maybe he wants other people to know it, too, so somebody can do something.

he's an illustrator for books about whales. Maybe he's friends with Seymour Simon.

Here are some other books that work well in a lesson like this one:

How to Heal a Broken Wing by Bob Graham (Why is everyone so busy that they can't see that a little bird needs help? Why is the little boy the only one who notices?)

The Tin Forest by Helen Ward (Can this be real? Does his imagination come from books? Is the man still dreaming? Is he *in* his dream?)

When we finish, we talk about all the different ways we've come to think about, or interpret, the question. Sometimes we consider all our different ways of thinking to create a class interpretation; other times we focus on a single one.

Questioning webs are also useful with poetry and nonfiction text (our web in response to *Monarch Butterfly* by Gail Gibbons is shown at the start of Chapter 7). Children use questioning webs independently, too. For example, Matthew's response to his question "Why is Amelia Bedelia so weird?" is shown in Figure 6.9.

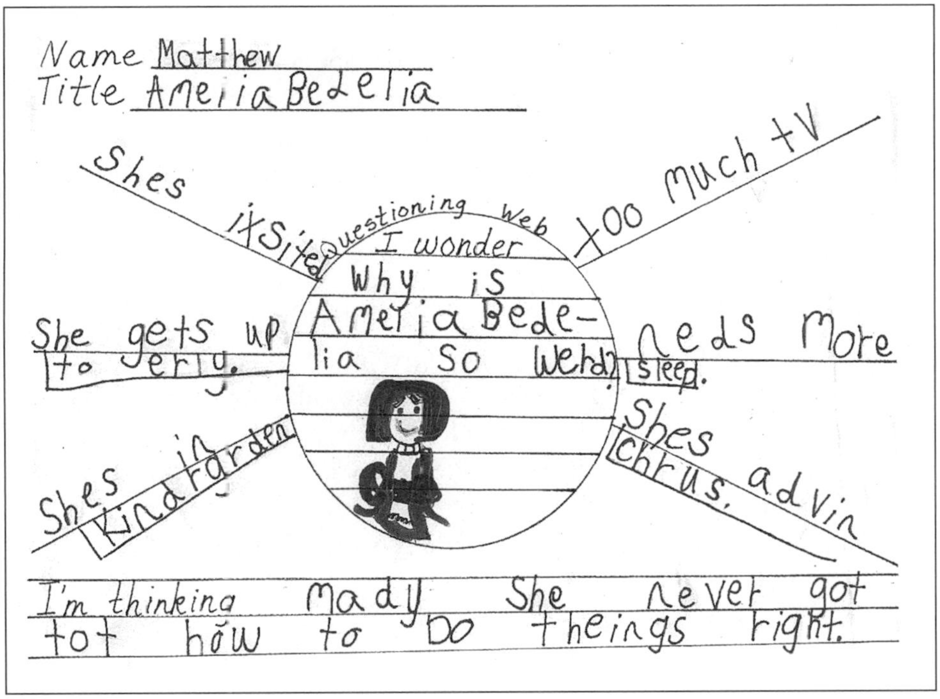

FIGURE 6.9
Matthew's questioning web for Amelia Bedelia Goes Camping *by Peggy Parish*

Readers understand that hearing others' questions inspires new ones of their own; likewise, listening to others' answers can inspire new thinking

What do you do when you have questions in your reading that you just can't figure out? I usually talk with somebody who's read the book (though that usually results in even more questions!) or try to force my best friend to listen to me read aloud at eleven thirty at night (with limited results).

In the classroom, inviting children to choose a question that is particularly puzzling and get together with a few others who are likewise intrigued provides opportunities for them to think and learn together. This type of activity promotes the social nature of learning in authentic ways and permits children to gain control of a strategy with the support of their peers. We've been thinking about structured book clubs, but in instances like this one—think about the Lotus Seed Girls as an example—children also come together spontaneously because of a shared interest.

As I listen in on the conversations, sometimes their thinking seems off the mark, and sometimes I think they're right on. But what I believe to be true isn't important at that point; it's the process of children working together to actively construct meaning for themselves that is key. Reminding myself that there usually isn't just one right answer keeps me from trying to influence the children's thinking. My advice? Resist the temptation to jump in and lead the kids to what you believe—you may be surprised at what you learn!

I've chosen Cynthia Rylant's *An Angel for Solomon Singer*, the story of a lonely man who lives in a hotel for men in New York City. Solomon Singer wanders the city streets, longing for his boyhood home in Indiana and dreaming of the things he loves: fireplaces, purple walls, porch swings, and balconies. One night he happens into the Westway Café, a place known for making dreams come true. A friendly waiter named Angel tells him to come back, and night after night he does. Soon Solomon Singer's life begins to change . . .

Children wonder:

Will there really be an angel in this story?
Why doesn't Solomon Singer move back with his parents in Indiana?
How could Indiana be mixed into his blood?
Why doesn't he come to Colorado? We have hotels here with balconies
    and purple walls.
Why does he keep coming back to the Westway Café?
Is the waiter really an angel?
Did his dreams come true?

We talk about the questions a bit, and I ask the children to think about which ones seem the most intriguing: "Which one would you most like to talk about with someone else?" I record their choices, pointing out that this might be something that would make sense for them to do in their book clubs, too.

"Listen again to the story," I say to them the next day, "and when I finish, get together with the children who are interested in discussing the same question as you are. I've written the questions and the names of the children who have chosen them on construction paper envelopes like this one. The paper inside is for you to record your thinking and anything new you wonder about. Be ready to share your work in about twenty minutes."

Sometimes I ask the children to record their answers first, share them with their group, then record their thinking again, noting how or whether their answers have changed, and why. I also encourage children who are reading the same book independently to get together in small groups to share their questions and think together about what they think the big ideas in the book are.

I design lessons like the one that follows to provide one last scaffold before I ask children to apply a strategy independently. The lesson also helps me assess which children may need extra support in small-group work and/or individual conferences—it's just the kind of "evidence of understanding" I need. See the planning documents at the beginning of the chapter to put this lesson in context.

I choose *Amelia's Road* by Linda Jacobs Altman because I know that although children will identify with Amelia, her parents, and her teacher, they'll also have questions about migrant farmworkers, labor camps, and why a little girl cries every time her father takes out a road map.

I've prepared a chart and a record sheet for children that are almost identical. Over the span of two or three days, everything we do together in the large group I ask children to do in their own reading as well. For example, on the first day, we

read the story aloud,
record our questions on sticky notes,
place them on the chart, and
choose a burning question we want to focus on the next day.

After the lesson, children do the same things. They

read independently,
record their questions on sticky notes,
place them on their record sheets, and
choose a burning question each wants to focus on the next day.

The next day we reread the story, focusing on our burning question. We work together to answer the question and spend time reflecting on what helped us most. The children then respond in writing to their individual questions during independent reading time and reflect on what helped them most. (See the class chart of *Amelia's Road* and Cory's corresponding response to *Tut's Mummy Lost and Found* by Judy Donnelly at the start of the "Frequently Asked Questions" section of this book.)

Evidence of Understanding and Independence

What you see in this section are examples of some of the ways children have demonstrated evidence of understanding and independence. See page 91 for a more detailed explanation of what you will find in this section.

Inferring is thinking in your head to help you understand, when the story doesn't let you in on it.
　　—Colin

When we infer together, it's like a wire that connects from my head to someone else's head, on and on and on, all around the circle.
　　—Riley

Inferring is something I always keep with me—wherever I go, it follows me around. I carry it with me to figure out things in my life.
　　—Frank

You know when you wonder why? If the book doesn't tell you, you can use your schema and the clues in the text to help you. That's inferring.
　　—Nina

Inferring is thinking about what's going to happen in the future.
　　—Madison

I'm thinking inferring is the biggest strategy so far, 'cause you see it's about using your schema and making connections and even mental images, too, and putting them all together to figure out what is happening.
　　—Justin

I'm inferring my dog is really good at it, like last night when I went to get his leash, he ran to the door! He was inferring I was going to take him for a walk. And whenever he hears the garage door opening, he starts jumping all around because he's inferring my dad's home.
  —Camille

When you have lots of questions about a book, that's good. Then you know there's going to be a lot of learning coming to you.
  —Daniel

I think that sometimes kids can learn stuff that grown-ups can't. A kid's brain isn't as stuffed with things they have to do, room to think and see and ask questions about things they don't already know the answers to.
  —Lilli

When you ask questions, it makes you want to keep reading so you can figure them out. It keeps your head in the book.
  —Madison

Asking questions is smart. It means you don't understand something and you know you don't understand it.
  —Bret

Sometimes you never get the answer to your really strong questions, but you should still keep working to figure them out, because the answer can come to you another day.
  —Whit

FIGURE 6.10
Daniel's question about Strega Nona *by Tomie dePaola*

Who is saying tailypo tailypo?

- are the Blak skrachis from the tailypo?

Wot hapined to the old man?

If the tailypo onlea ripet the coveres, howcome the hol house is gone?

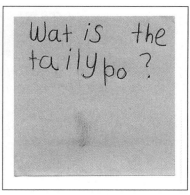

FIGURE 6.11A AND B
Chris's questions before, during, and after reading The Taileypo *by Paul Galdone*

The Magic Fish
When I read these Words I don't Want togo Siad the fishermen go! Siad his Wife. I'm Wondering Why the wife Wants So meny things? Why dosint go her silf. She shodint make the fishermen go?
                                    Bret

FIGURE 6.12
Bret's response to The Magic Fish *by Freya Littledale*

Ben and his Wonder Box

7

In March and April

Nonfiction Genre Study; Focus on Questioning (Continued) and Determining Importance

Questioning webs help children activate and organize their thinking and learning in order to answer a specific question.

Questioning Web

Do C. have teeth?

How long will it live?

How can it eat up out falling off?

Why isn't the mother w/ the egg? where is she?

Jaron + John
The C. turns black and grows wings and all its parts

Camilla + Olivia
There's memory created insi the egg.

Brandon + Allan
The chrysalis forms at a certain time; the body just knows how to form a butterfly

How does the butterfly form inside the chrysalis?

We think it has to do with DNA.

Madison
The caterpillar says "I want to be a butterfly."

Tate
Maybe it uses its DNA it maps out the future of the butterfly

Spencer, Holly, Camhm
until it finally totally forms.

Why does it turn green?

How does it hatch out?

How long is the chrysalis?

Why do they lay their eggs on the milkweed plant? ✓

How does the butterfly stick the egg onto the leaf?

Why do they eat their shell when they are first born

Can it grow longer than 2" long?

Why does it have to molt?

Why are his wings small at first?

How does a caterpillar turn into a butterfly?

How does the caterpillar stay on the leaf?

How can a tiny C. eat so much?

147

We continue with asking questions this month and next, for many reasons, especially this one:

> Young children are natural question-askers. They have to be to learn how to adapt to a complex and changing environment. But whether they continue to ask questions . . . depends in large part on how adults respond to them. (Robert Sternberg, as quoted in Rothstein and Santana 2011, 12)

I work to respond to children in ways that honor who they are now and who they will become. That means I respect their questions, encourage them to ask more, and work hard to show them how to go about figuring out the answers.

Asking questions drives our nonfiction genre study, and the thinking strategy of determining importance will help children as they work to figure out the answers to the questions that matter most. After all, "Learning is a consequence of thinking . . . Far from thinking coming after knowledge, knowledge comes on the coattails of thinking . . . knowledge does not just sit there. It functions richly in people's lives so they can learn about and deal with the world" (Perkins 1992, 8).

Wonder Boxes: I Can Ask Questions Anywhere, Anytime, About Anything!

Ben is balanced in the crook of a tree (as shown at the beginning of this chapter). Emily has a magnifying glass and is looking closely at a ladybug. Val's examining a leaf with curious lumpy growths, and Nina's on her back, hands behind her head, looking up at the sky. Ben, Emily, Val, Nina, and their twenty-three classmates are scattered across a section of the school's front lawn, wandering, wondering, and exploring the world around them.

Each child has a Wonder Box—a 3-by-5-inch file box they've decorated with small stick-on ladybugs, dinosaurs, birds, and flowers and filled with a stack of brightly colored index cards—Wonder Cards—on which to record their questions.

I've just read *The Wise Woman and Her Secret* by Eve Merriam, the story of a wise woman who knows the secret of wisdom and a little girl named Jenny, who learns that she knows the secret, too. (If you can't get your hands on this book, *The Looking Book* by PK Hallinan and *The Three Questions* by Jon Muth are also great titles to use when launching Wonder Boxes.)

As the children wander and wonder, they record their questions on their Wonder Cards:

How does a bird learn to sing?
Why do ladybugs have spots?
Are we right now out in space?
How does an ant find its way home?
How was the world born?
Why do trees have bark?
Why do dogs have wet noses?
Why do some leaves have lumps?
Who made God?
Why is the sky blue?
Why do bees sting?
Did dinosaurs ever walk on our playground?
How can it be so cold in springtime? (This one's easy: We live in Denver!)

Ever since the day the wise woman and her secret entered the children's lives, Wonder Boxes have been spotted in the lunchroom, on the playground, at home, and on field trips. Magnifying glasses have found their way into them, as well as shiny pebbles, feathers, dead bugs, "diamonds," flower petals, and "dinosaur fossils."

And I have begun to do some wondering of my own. When did I last look closely at a bustling anthill and wonder what goes on underneath? When did I last take the time to pick up a roly-poly and watch it curl into a little ball? And when did I last try to catch snowflakes on my coat sleeve, just to see if I'd be the first to find two that were the same?

Children everywhere know that the secret of wisdom is to be curious about the world, to open up their senses and see, hear, taste, touch, and smell life's treasures. Giving children time to explore their world, ask questions, and pursue the questions that matter most lets them know I value their curiosity outside the classroom as well as inside. My job is to continue to nurture their wonder, and work to awaken my own.

Tried-and-True Texts, Authors, and Resources for Determining Importance, Asking Questions, and Learning About Nonfiction/Informational Texts

Series
Dorling Kindersley Readers, DK Publishing, New York
I Can Read About . . . , Troll Associates, New York
First Discovery Books, Scholastic, New York
Eyewitness Books, Knopf/New York Zoo Books, New York
Let's Read and Find Out Science, HarperTrophy, New York
Read and Wonder Books, Candlewick Press, Cambridge, MA
Backyard Books by Judy Allen, Kingfisher, Boston

▩ MARCH AND APRIL PLAN ▩
Nonfiction Genre Study; Focus on Questioning (Continued) and Determining Importance

Nonfiction Genre Study; Focus on Questioning (Continued) and Determining Importance	Demonstration of Understanding
What big ideas do I want students to walk away with at the end of this study and remember ten years from now and beyond?	*What kind of summative, end-of-study assessment can we create that exists in the world and has a real purpose and audience?*

Research, informational/explanatory texts, and nonfiction
- "Actively using knowledge—putting knowledge to work—means learners apply what they've learned to experiences, situations and circumstances in their daily lives, expanding understanding and taking action" (Stephanie Harvey, as quoted in Daniels 2011, 118).
- "To build a foundation for college and career readiness, students must read widely and deeply from among a broad range of high-quality, increasingly challenging literary and informational text" (Common Core State Standards 2010).

Questioning and Determining Importance
- Readers distinguish the differences between fiction and nonfiction.
- Readers distinguish important from unimportant information in order to identify key ideas or themes as they read.
- Readers utilize text features to help them distinguish important from unimportant information.
- Readers use their knowledge of important and relevant parts of text to answer questions and synthesize text for themselves and others.
- Readers understand that the process of questioning is used in the whole of their lives, both personal and academic.
- Asking questions gives you power in the world—powerful thinkers have more questions than answers.
- "Inquisitiveness and thoughtfulness can lead to major contributions and big things in life" (Stephanie Harvey, as quoted in Daniels 2011, 112).

Party at the Museum of Nature and Science, where children will share with visitors a one-page spread (or other artifact) on a topic they are passionate about

Each child's project will include the following:

A key question about a topic they care about

Their answer ("Explain your learning in your own words, in a way that makes sense, without telling too much.")

Source citations ("Where did you get your information?")

At least two nonfiction conventions ("Which conventions will best help your reader better understand your content?")

■ MARCH AND APRIL PLAN ■ *(continued)*

Possible Guiding Questions

What compelling questions will foster inquiry, understanding, and transfer of learning?
- What is worth wondering about?
- What do I wonder?
- Why does asking questions matter?
- How do I share with others what's important to me?

Possible Supporting Targets	Possible Assessments
Long-term targets are in bold, and daily targets are listed below them.	*These formative assessments match the daily targets and let kids and me know where we are and where we need to go.*
I can ask questions anytime, anywhere, about anything.	
• I can ask questions about the world.	• Wonder Box cards
• I can ask and answer questions when I read informational text.	• Exit tickets; questions and answers from child's reading, including page numbers
I can explain the difference between fiction and nonfiction.	
• I know what to expect when I read fiction.	• Discussion, partner work, anchor chart
• I know what to expect when I read nonfiction.	• Discussion, partner work, anchor chart
• I can explain how fiction and nonfiction are the same and how they are different.	• Venn diagram (page 158)
I can identify informational text features and conventions to help me determine importance.	
• I can find labels in my reading and explain their purpose.	• Individual Convention Notebooks (pages 159 and 164) and whole-class anchor chart to explain purpose (page 160)
• I can find captions in my reading and explain their purpose.	
I can help another reader get smarter and more powerful by creating a text that teaches them about a topic that matters to me.	
• I can choose a question I care about.	• Children choose questions from their Wonder Boxes
• I know lots of ways to locate the specific information I need.	• Anchor chart: "How do we locate specific information?"
• I can put my learning in my own words, in a way that makes sense, without telling too much.	• Children's writer's notebook, one-page spread
• I can cite my sources.	• Children's writer's notebook, one-page spread
• I can present my learning in an interesting way.	• Children's one-page spread, museum party

■ MARCH AND APRIL CALENDARS ■

SUNDAYMONDAYTUESDAYWEDNESDAYTHURSDAYFRIDAYSATURDAY

March and April are usually broken up by state tests and spring break, but with spring in the air, it's a great time to dig into nonfiction—particularly any topic related to the natural world. Take your students outside for some research and observation to drive their reading and writing and nonfiction genre study. By the end of April, they should be producing beautiful nonfiction pages about a topic they care about, then taking their class-created books to the local museum of nature and science to wow the visitors who are lucky enough to meet your young scientists.

■ March

- Guiding questions: What is worth wondering about? Why does asking questions matter? How do I determine importance?
- Reading-content focus on questioning (continued) and determining importance
- Big-idea content focus on how readers learn and grow by reading widely and deeply from a broad range of high-quality, increasingly challenging informational texts
- Possible mini-lessons:
  - The differences between fiction and nonfiction
  - How to read selectively, depending on your purpose
  - How we name and hold on to new learning
  - What we can learn from comparisons, labels, photos, cutaways, maps, close-ups, tables of contents, lists, indexes, and glossaries

■ April

- Reading-content focus on questioning and determining importance, along with all the other strategies that have come before
- Big-idea content focus on what is worth wondering about and how I share what's important to me
- Possible mini-lessons:
  - How do I choose an important question from my Wonder Box?
  - How do I go about locating the information I need to answer a question?
  - How will I demonstrate my understanding? How will I share my learning in my own words, in a way that makes sense, without telling too much? (Paving the way for synthesis!)
- Explicit instruction, practice, and reflection on our work, and how we'll share our learning with visitors at the Museum of Nature and Science
- Contact the museum, and enlist a couple of parents to help us get our one-page spreads there intact. Should we make signs to let visitors know what we're up to and why we're there? Will we be open to answering questions about our content and what we did to figure out the answers to our big questions? Should we practice? (I'm thinking yes!)

Authors
Steve Jenkins
Gail Gibbons
Seymour Simon
Nicola Davies
Teruyuki Komiya

Newspapers
Your local paper
Weekly Reader, www.weeklyreader.com

More Resources
National Geographic Young Explorer,
    www.nationalgeographic.com/ngyoungexplorer
Time for Kids, Big Picture Edition, www.timeforkids.com
Click, www.clickmagkids.com
Kids Discover, www.kidsdiscover.com

Field Guides
Peterson Field Guides for Young Naturalists, including volumes on song-
    birds, backyard birds, caterpillars, and butterflies. Houghton Mifflin,
    Boston.
National Audubon Society First Field Guides, including volumes on rep-
    tiles, weather, trees, shells, amphibians, fishes, rocks and minerals,
    insects, and the night sky. Scholastic, New York.

Exploring and Learning About Nonfiction

"When are you going to teach us about those kinds of books?" Madi asks during share time, pointing to the red tubs of books labeled Dinosaurs, Flight, Reptiles, Biographies, Animals, Cars and Trucks, Magazines, Field Guides, First Discovery Books, Newspapers, Maps and Atlases, Big Cats, Disasters, and more.

"You mean the nonfiction?" I answer, surprised. The rest of the class is nodding, pointing, and bouncing up and down, letting me know they're interested in knowing more about those kinds of books, too. "We-ell," I say, "how about Monday?" Whoops of joy erupt from the troops, but I'm thinking, *What are you saying? Monday's only three days away!*

But now Maci had me thinking. I thought about her question and realized how smart of her it was to wonder about "those kind of books." I'd assumed that somehow children already knew that nonfiction books involved reading to learn new information—they'd been looking at and reading these books all year, hadn't they? And I'd assumed that if they could read and understand stories, they could read and understand informational books, too. I hadn't considered the importance of explicitly teaching them the difference.

I'd have taken a day or two to teach them about the table of contents, the index, maybe even the glossary in such books—and, of course, to explain that nonfiction is based on facts, real events, and real people. But Madi was after more than that. She'd learned how to determine importance in fiction. I suspected she was wondering how to go about doing that in nonfiction, and wanted to learn how to figure out the big ideas from those kinds of books, too.

That weekend I lugged home about twenty nonfiction books, vowing to make good on my word. As I read through them, I noted their distinguishing characteristics and features, determining which ones I thought were most important for children to learn. But by the time Sunday evening rolled around, it had become clear that before I could teach children how to use the features of nonfiction in purposeful ways, they needed to do some exploring. They needed to look at them closely and do some noticing.

It might be tempting to just "tell" kids about what to expect when they read nonfiction—it would certainly save time—but don't we want children to learn about big ideas firsthand whenever we can? All these years later, I still remember this quote by Piaget from my college days: "Each time one prematurely teaches a child something he could have discovered himself, that child is kept from inventing it and consequently from understanding it completely" (1970, 715).

Monday morning the meeting area is a sea of books about snakes, dolphins, gemstones, sharks, kittens, puppies, wolves, the ocean, shipwrecks, the human body, flowers, space, earthquakes, astronauts, cowboys, ballerinas, dinosaurs, soccer, volcanoes, bugs, and big trucks. My purpose? Just as we teach children to use math manipulatives by giving them time to "free explore" what they are and discover how they work, giving children time to explore nonfiction and make some discoveries on their own provides them with experiences to build on when more explicit teaching begins.

The children's eyes light up when they enter the room; it's almost as if I've laid out doughnuts and milk. They scurry over, devouring one book after another. "Oohs" and "Aahs" and "Check this out!" and "OHMYGOSH!" and "Can I have that shark one next?" let me know my plan is a good one. Their enthusiasm is contagious, and before long I'm down on the floor right along with them, oohing and aahing and learning myself.

Questions naturally arise, and out come the Wonder Boxes. Children begin recording questions like mad.

"How do wolves catch elk?" Devon wants to know. He's wondering how a wolf can capture an elk when the elk is so much bigger. (See Figure 7.1.)

"Why are some twisters big and others small?" Chris wonders.

"How do puppies come out of their mama's tummy?" Caroline asks. (See Figure 7.2.)

This is perfect, I think to myself. Children are loving the exploration of nonfiction, their interest in Wonder Boxes has been renewed, and they will have a wider variety of questions to choose from when it comes time to select their most important ones and read for specific information.

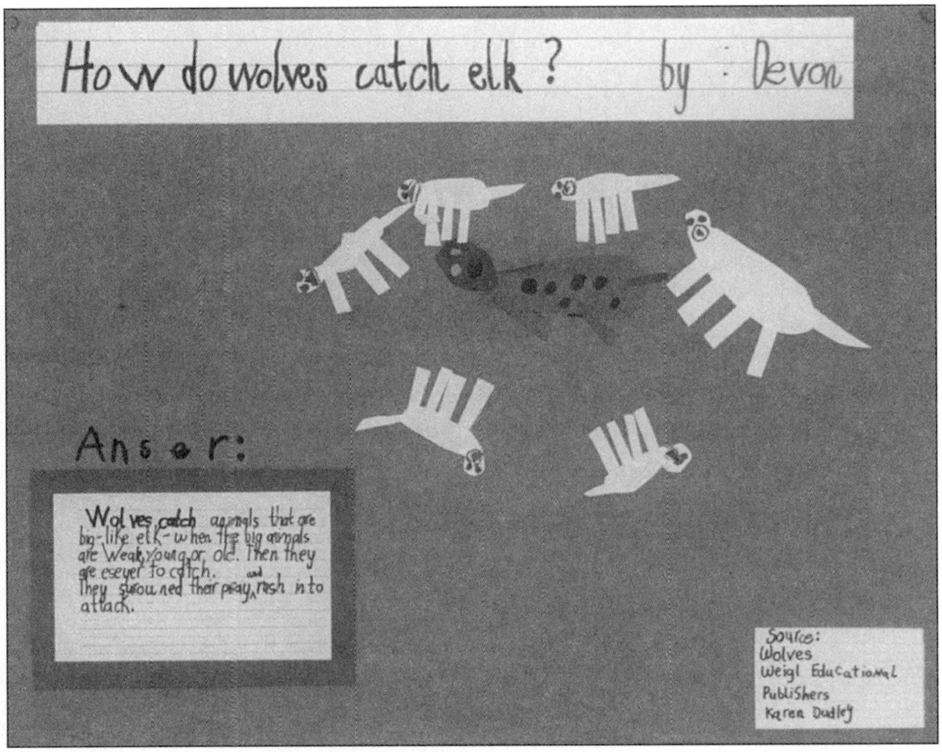

FIGURE 7.1
Devon's question

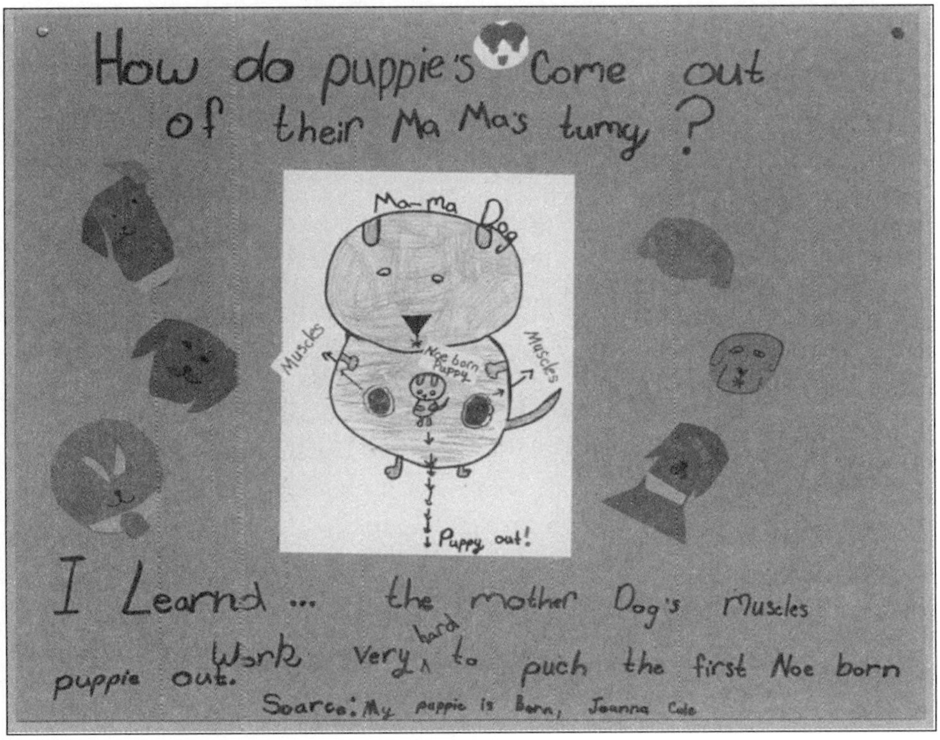

FIGURE 7.2
"How do puppies come out of their mama's tummy?" Caroline asks.

Modeling Differences Between Fiction and Nonfiction

I begin by holding up a copy of *Grandfather's Journey* by Allen Say. "What type of text do you predict this is?" I ask.

"Fiction!" the children reply.

"Knowing that it's fiction, how might you expect the story to be organized?"

Andrew predicts the story will have "a beginning, middle, and end." Others predict a setting, characters, a problem, some events that connect to the problem, and a resolution.

"Good thinking!" I tell them. "You remembered what we learned about fiction and how it is organized. Now can you predict what the story might be about?" Wyatt predicts it might be about somebody's grandpa who once went on a journey across the ocean to America. He thinks he's "probably going to have some trouble on the way, like maybe robbers or a war or something like that. But then he'll meet some nice people and make some new friends and get married and have kids and live happily ever after."

I want Wyatt and his classmates to be this confident and articulate when they make predictions about the organization and content of nonfiction text, too. Just as with narrative text, teaching children that informational text has predictable characteristics and features they can count on before they read allows them to construct meaning more easily as they read.

I hold up a book titled *Bugs! Bugs! Bugs!* by Jennifer Dussling. "What do you notice about this type of text?" I ask the children as I leaf through the book and read parts of it aloud.

"It's totally about bugs!" Cole answers.

"You're right!" I tell him. "It is all about bugs. You noticed right away that this kind of text is organized differently from fiction.

"You won't find a beginning, middle, or end in books like this. And you won't find characters, problems, or resolutions either. Instead, these kinds of books—you already know them as *nonfiction*—are organized around specific topics and main ideas, and they try to teach you something. When you read nonfiction, you can almost always count on learning something new. Let's read this book about bugs and find out what we can learn."

Another day I talk with the children about how they can use what they know about this type of text to make predictions about its content—what the text might teach them. I say, "Remember when Wyatt was able to predict what might happen in *Grandfather's Journey*? He was able to do that because he's learned, just like the rest of you, what to expect when you read fiction. When readers read nonfiction, they make predictions about the text, too. But they don't make predictions about the *kinds of things they expect will happen*. They make predictions about the *kinds of things they expect to learn*.

"When readers make predictions about what they'll learn, they activate their schema about the topic *and* what they know about the type of text they are about to read. Take a look at this book—*Nature Watch Spiders* by Barbara Taylor. Right away, because of its title and the photographs on the cover, I can tell it's a nonfiction text and it's going to be about spiders. See all the different kinds of spiders on the cover? I don't know a lot about spiders, but I do know they have eight legs, they spin intricate webs, and they're part of a group of small creatures called arachnids.

"I'm predicting this book will be about all the different kinds of spiders in the world, and that maybe I'll learn about where they live, what they eat, their life cycles, and even which ones are dangerous to humans." I flip through the book, checking the table of contents, the headings, and the index, and explain how these features help me make predictions about the text. I do the same with two or three other books.

The next day I ask the children to help me make predictions. I release responsibility by asking them to bring a nonfiction book they haven't read to the meeting area, get eye-to-eye and knee-to-knee with a partner, and make predictions about what they expect to learn.

I spread fiction and nonfiction materials out in the meeting area and ask children to get a partner, choose two or three items, and ask themselves, "Is this fiction or nonfiction? How do we know?"

I ask children to bring a nonfiction book and a fiction book to the meeting area, get into pairs, and create a Venn diagram that shows the two books' differences and similarities. We then create one large diagram that combines everyone's thinking (see Figure 7.3).

In his book *I See What You Mean*, Steve Moline writes about the skill of reading selectively:

> If we teach children that all reading is "reading for the story" we overlook many useful strategies that we employ when reading selectively. Some of these strategies include scanning, skimming, accessing the text through the index, using headings as signposts to the information we want, or just strolling through the pictures in order to orientate ourselves in the text. (2011, 18)

Children are surprised to learn that depending on their purposes for reading, they don't have to read the text in order. I model using various nonfiction strategies, showing the children what it looks like and what my thinking is as I skim and scan, access the index and the table of contents, use the headings to guide me, read the picture captions, and so on—all to find out what I need to know. I think aloud, too, about the information I want to remember, and show how I use sticky notes, highlighters, and my notebook to keep track of my learning.

FIGURE 7.3
*Venn diagram:
fiction and
nonfiction*

Name <u>All of us!</u>
Title <u>What have we come to expect when we read fiction and nonfiction?</u>
Venn Diagram

Fiction — beginning, middle, and end — setting characters problem events resolution — pictures — read from front to back — stories — themes

Title illustrations — they help you learn — they are fun to read words

Nonfiction — bold print — index — table of contents — read in any order — photographs captions headings cutaways — diagrams — information ideas — amazing facts

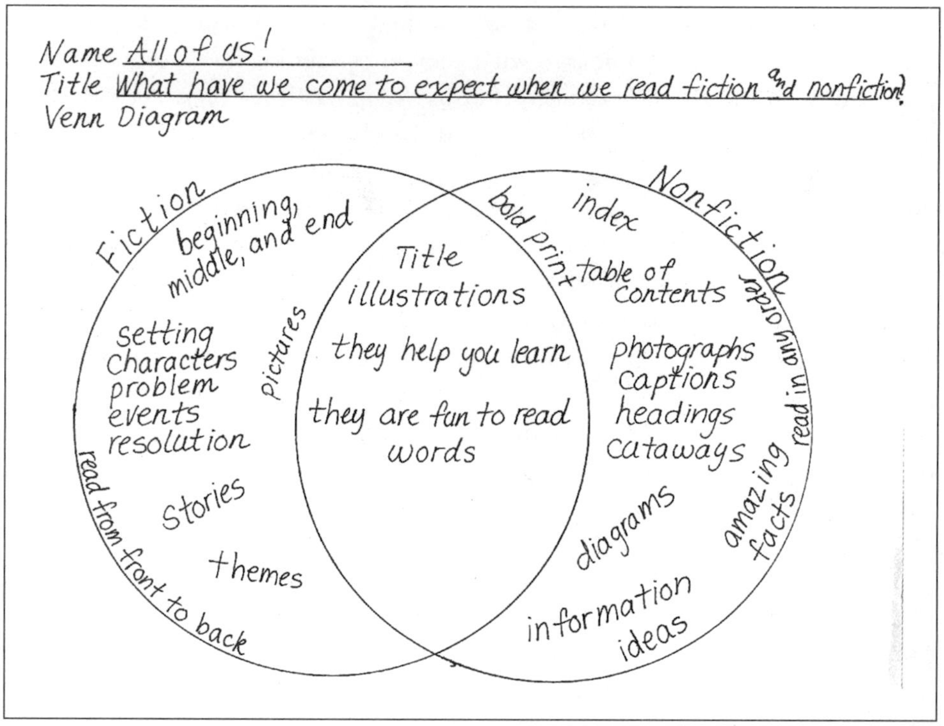

Noticing and Remembering When We Learn Something New

"Have you ever thought about the way you respond to new information?" Steph Harvey asks me one day as we sit, chatting away about nonfiction in her sunlit writing room. "Have you ever noticed what your inner voice says when you learn something new?"

"Not really," I answer, understanding the inner voice part but unsure about what it's supposed to be saying.

"It's something to think about," she replies, "and I have a hunch it's important.

"Here, take a look at this," she says, handing over a well-read *National Geographic*. "Think aloud as you read, and you'll see what I mean." I open the magazine's familiar yellow-bordered cover and land on an article called "Deadly Silk" by Richard Conniff.

"Wow, Steph, listen to this!" I say after a few minutes. "Did you know that some spiders eat their webs and reweave them up to five times a day? That's amazing! I never knew that. And get this: it's the female spider who does all that weaving. Once the males reach maturity, they wander around making love, not war. I didn't know that either!"

Steph's staring and smiling at me, for once silent. "What?" I say, throwing up my hands.

"Did you hear yourself?" she asks, rattling off "Wow!" "Listen to this!" "That's amazing!" "I never knew that!" and "Get this!" and adding, "See how those words signal you that you're learning something new?"

We go on to yak about something else, but Steph has me thinking.

"Boys and girls," I say the next day, "wait until you hear what I learned from my friend Steph yesterday." I tell them the whole story, and think aloud some more about the spider and its remarkable web to show them what I mean. They want to discover their inner voices, too, and record the words on chart paper that help them recognize that they're learning something new.

Soon I hear their cries:

"*Awesome!* Can you believe some ants squirt smelly acid when they're scared?"

"*Sweet!* It takes only eight and a half minutes for a space shuttle to reach space."

"*Cool!* Jumbo jets in the future will have two stories and carry more than five hundred people! I never knew that."

"*Whoa!* When Mount Vesuvius erupted, it buried the city of Pompeii under a layer of ash that was twenty feet thick. That's as high as our school."

"*Yikes!* I just learned that a meteor the size of Mount Everest hit our planet sixty-five million years ago and maybe caused the dinosaurs to be extinct."

"So how will you remember all the things you've learned?" I ask.

"I know," Meghan volunteers. "Let's put an *N* and an *L* on a sticky note for 'new learning,' and then just write the most important part—and the title of the book, and the page number, too, so we can find it and read it again if we need to."

Convention Notebooks

My teammate Michelle DuMoulin and I knew the importance of teaching our kids about the conventions, or features, of nonfiction. We knew this information would help focus and support young readers, and that even emergent readers could determine importance and construct meaning by paying close attention to features such as photographs, diagrams, captions, and comparisons. But we also knew we needed to build children's background knowledge and explicitly teach them what nonfiction conventions are, what kinds of information these conventions give us, and how they help us determine what is important in a text. We knew *what* we wanted to teach kids; it was the *how* that had us stymied. We vowed, as we sometimes do, that we wouldn't go home until we had a plan.

That evening Convention Notebooks were born. We finally figured out (hunger may have played a role) a way to teach kids how to recognize, remember, and begin to understand the purposes of the nonfiction features they found. Measuring nine inches square, Convention Notebooks contain twelve or so sheets of blank white paper and a construction paper cover and back. This is how they work:

Each day for two weeks Michelle and I focus on a different convention. Say our focus is on comparisons. Before class, we search our nonfiction libraries for at least five or six places where comparisons have been used and flag the pages with sticky notes. When it's time for the lesson, the children and I locate and name the comparisons we've found and read the surrounding text aloud. But noticing and naming nonfiction conventions is not enough. We also think aloud about how they help us as readers; we think aloud about the purpose of each one.

Next, Michelle and I ask children to find examples of that same convention in books from the classroom or the library and either record one example in their notebooks or create an example of their own. Children share their discoveries in small groups each day, and we record our learning on a two-column anchor chart (below) headed "What do we know about nonfiction conventions?"

Convention Notebooks not only build background knowledge for text features that children encounter in their reading, but also can be used as resources when children are asked to synthesize information to answer research questions. The notebooks help children think through which convention(s) will showcase their information best.

Convention	Purpose
Labels	help the reader identify a picture or photograph and/or its parts.
Photographs	help the reader understand exactly what something looks like.
Captions	help the reader better understand a picture or photograph.
Comparisons	help the reader understand the size of one thing by comparing it with the size of something familiar.
Cutaways	help the reader understand something by looking at it from the inside.
Maps	help the reader understand where places are in the world.
Types of print	help the reader by signaling, "Look at me! I'm important!"
Close-ups	help the reader see details in something small.
Tables of contents	help the reader identify key topics in the book in the order in which they are presented.
Indexes	help the reader find specific topics, words, and names in the book by listing them alphabetically with page numbers.
Glossaries	help the reader learn the meaning of words contained in the text.

Locating Specific Information

Throughout our study of nonfiction, determining importance, and questioning, I ask the children to place a Wonder Card or two into a basket. Two or three days a week we draw one out and search for its answer. First I model for children what I do when I want to find out specific information. I show them how to think aloud about certain questions:

What do I already know about the topic?

What type of book or other source will help me best?

How is the information organized in my sources? How will I go about locating what I need?

Then, after I've looked through the source of information: What did I learn? How can I synthesize my learning for myself and others? This sets the stage for children's final demonstration of understanding—their one-page spread about a topic of their choosing.

I gradually release responsibility to children by asking the same questions of the whole group. When (or if) we find the answer to our Wonder Card question, the child who asked the question records its answer on the back of the card and cites the source (author, title, date). Later I ask children to get into small groups or pairs; each group draws a question from the basket and works together to explore the answer. Questions we can't answer are posted outside the classroom, under a sign that reads "HELP! Can you help us with the answers to these questions? If you can, please write a note to us and put it on our teacher's desk. Thank you from all of us in Room 104."

Throughout this study I work closely with Jennifer Shouse, our talented librarian. She teaches the children about call numbers, where reference materials are in the library and the kinds of information they provide, how to access select sites on computers, and how we can get important information from words *and* pictures. When children need to print out information, Jennifer and I teach them to write and draw in the margins and highlight the key concepts that will help them with their research.

By now, the children have learned some of the characteristics of nonfiction. They've learned how to distinguish it from fiction, and how to make predictions about its organization and content. They've become familiar with the features of nonfiction books and their purposes, and how to locate specific information. They can identify the main topic and retell key details, and they can describe the connections between texts and big ideas. Most important, they've learned that reading nonfiction is all about asking questions and learning new things. I think they're ready to put all that learning to good use. *Bring on the Wonder Boxes,* I say to myself, *and let's find out!*

I ask children to find a spot in the room, spread out their Wonder Cards, and choose two or three that they care about most. "Which ones are you most passionate about?" I ask. "Which ones come from your heart?" Once they've decided, I ask them to put the questions they've selected in order of importance at the front of their Wonder Boxes.

They can't wait! The next day they arm themselves with their Wonder Boxes, sticky notes, bright yellow highlighters, pencils, and notebooks, and descend on the library and into the corners and spaces of the classroom, spreading their materials out on tables and floor. I'm struck by their independence. No one is asking me where the reptile books are or to read their book to them, and no one is wandering aimlessly about. And not one small soul is copying sentence after sentence into a notebook.

Children synthesize and share their learning in a variety of ways. These decisions are essentially theirs to make. I used to show the children examples of ways to share their learning, but I've come to believe that that limits their capacity to think creatively. I make sure materials are in ample supply, including posterboard for those who want it. I ask only that the children include their question; that they put their learning and answers in their own words in a way that makes sense, without telling too much; that they use at least one nonfiction convention; and that they cite their source(s) of information. The next section shows some of the ways children demonstrated their understanding of informational text, their strategies of questioning and determining importance, and a few examples of the ways in which they shared their learning at our end-of-study party at the Museum of Nature and Science.

Evidence of Understanding and Independence

What you see in this section are examples of some of the ways in which children have demonstrated evidence of understanding and independence. See page 91 for a more detailed explanation of what you will find in this section.

Bold print and headings tell you what the author thinks is important. The index and table of contents let you choose for yourself.
          —Wyatt

Themes go with fiction and learning goes with nonfiction.
          —Maddy

You know how when it rains? The grass and flowers and trees soak up all the water they need, and the rest just runs on down the street. We soak up what's important to us, too, and let the rest of it go away.
          —Christopher

The feelings that stories leave you with let you know what's most important.
          —Nina

Because our schema is different, the things that are important to us are different, too. Different things are important to different people.
          —Caroline

You learn and remember the things that are important to you. If you don't care about it, you won't remember it.
          —Andrew

The title gives you a big clue about what is going to be important.
          —Molly

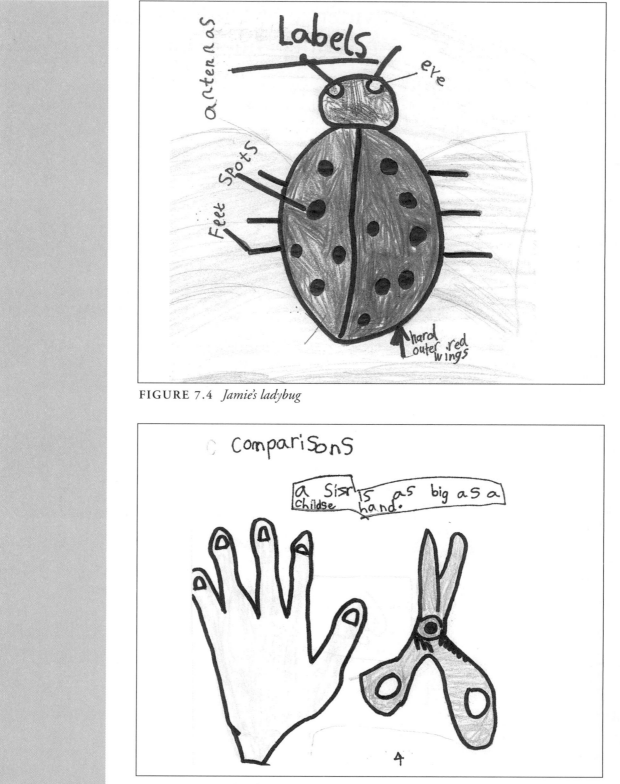

FIGURE 7.4 *Jamie's ladybug*

FIGURE 7.5 *Megan's comparison*

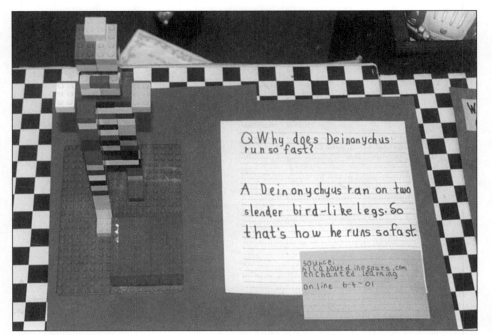

FIGURE 7.6
Mitch's project: "Why does deinonychus run so fast?"

FIGURE 7.7
Frank determines his own list of important rules.

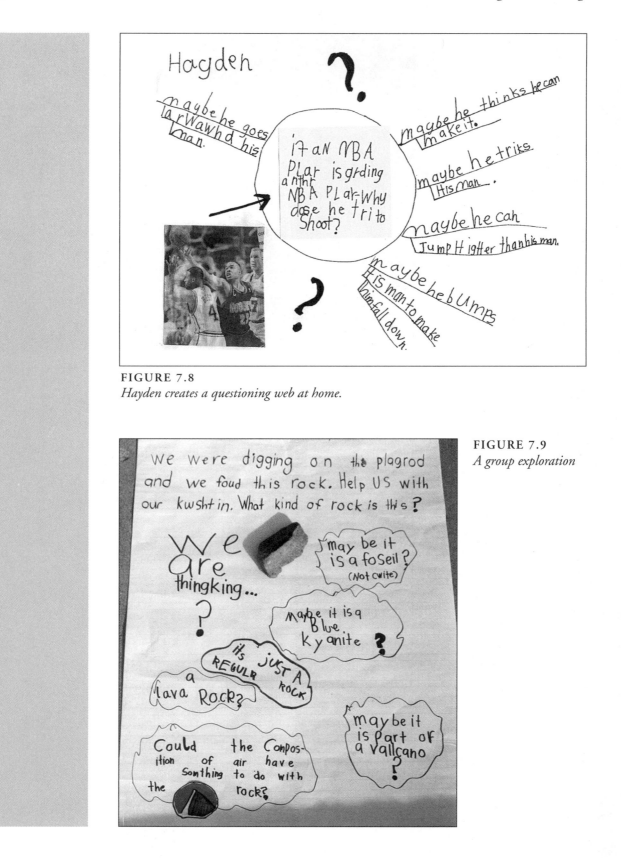

FIGURE 7.8
Hayden creates a questioning web at home.

FIGURE 7.9
A group exploration

The handwritten chart at top left:

Love a book? Recommend it to a buddy!

To	From	Title	Why?
Stephinie	Sarah	GOOD WORK AMELIA BEDELIA	you like the caracter!
Margret	Charlotte	The aniimal Rescue club	You Really Like Animals
Alben	Charles	Reb Wolf COUNTRY	You LICK WOlf and I THIC The bookis For You
Marin R	Marin W.	A mate For young Wolf	it is full of advenchers...
Emma	Tory	Cinderella	youn're a Farry tale gaul!
Margaret	Ellie	Dancing with Manatees	Becas you Lice Laerning
Kevin	Ben	NoISY Poems	you Like Sily poems
Marinn	Breanna	Just For you	It is Fany
cuLiet	Margaret	POCAHONTAS	You LIKE TO BE FREE TOO
Ian	Kate	THe YUCKY REPTILE	you Lick Lraening aBout Reptile
BeN	KEVIN w.	COLORFUL chameleoms	you Like nonfiction
David	Mrs. Miller	Mouse Soup	You Like stories like these!

8

In May

*Book Recommendation/
Opinion Piece for
Book Lovers' Festival;
Focus on Synthesis*

Asking children to think about why they're recommending a book to a friend encourages thoughtful recommendations.

Reflecting as you read enhances comprehension.

■ ■ ■ ■ Synthesizing Information

Frank pushes "play" and "Oh, What a Beautiful Morning" blasts out of the CD player. Whit quickly adjusts the volume, and the class and I sing our way over to the meeting area. Frank invites us to read the morning message they've written; he points to the words as we read, "Hi, everybody! Whit and Frank are going to teach a lesson on SYNTHESIS [all caps, bold print, red marker] today. Are you up for a challenge?"

A chart labeled "Whit and Frank synthesizing *Oliver Button Is a Sissy*" is pushpinned to the board. Below the heading they've drawn seven 3-by-5-inch rectangles, just the size of their sticky notes, with plus signs separating each one. After the seventh one, they've drawn a big equals sign with the words *Finl Sinthasis* written after it. I'm not sure exactly what they're up to, but I can't wait to find out. I'm pretty sure it's going to be good.

It's more than good. "You know how we've been learning about synthesis?" Whit begins. "Well, Frank and I had so much thinking about it that we want to share it with you. Frank is going to read *Oliver Button Is a Sissy* aloud, and I'm going to show you how we synthesized it. Are you ready?"

Frank reads the Tomie dePaola story aloud, and on the pages that have a sticky note, on which is written their synthesis of the story so far, Whit stops the story, reads the note, and places it in one of the squares (see Figure 8.1). When they get to the equals sign, Whit says, "So you see how we got to the final synthesis? We just kept adding on and adding on and adding on to our thinking. It got bigger and bigger and bigger, and now we totally know what the book is all about! You might want to try it in your reading today. Happy reading!"

Ahh, I think, *it really, really, really doesn't get better than this.* We've come full circle, and I'm feeling proud of them, and proud of myself, too. We did this together, and I can say with conviction, love, and happiness that each child has made a year of growth since that first day we came together and sang *Five Little Ducks, Little Rabbit Foo Foo,* and *Dr. Seuss's ABC.* I tell them what I'm thinking, and they can't help but reminisce with me.

FIGURE 8.1
Whit and Frank's synthesis

"Remember when we couldn't even *read*?" they say. "Remember Coffeehouse Poetry and reading our poems into the microphone? Remember work activity when Brody and Frankie's number scroll went all around the room? And remember the day Mrs. Miller cried when we sang her *This Little Light of Mine?*"

We talk about field trips, celebrations, parties, and the day our frog went missing. (Umm, he's still missing, but they still think he'll turn up any day now.) Then we talk books. Which ones do they say they'll remember forever? *An Angel for Solomon Singer. Odd Velvet. Pete the Cat. Oliver Button Is a Sissy. Amelia's Road. Brown Bear, Brown Bear, What Do You See? Wolf's Coming! Wangari's Trees of Peace. How to Heal a Broken Wing. Grandfather Twilight. The Royal Bee.* Then they move to nonfiction, and I do believe they name every book Steve Jenkins has ever written! I'm thinking my plan to have a Book Lovers' Festival is going to be perfect.

▦ MAY PLAN ▦
Book Recommendation/Opinion Piece for Book Lovers' Festival/Focus on Synthesis

Focus on Synthesis; Book Lovers' Festival; Opinion Piece	Demonstration of Understanding
What big ideas do I want students to walk away with at the end of this study and remember ten years from now and beyond?	*What kind of summative, end-of-study assessment can we create that exists in the world and has a real purpose and audience?*
Synthesis • Readers monitor overall meaning, important concepts, and themes as they read, understanding that their thinking evolves in the process. • Readers capitalize on opportunities to share, recommend, and criticize books they have read. • Readers extend their synthesis of the literal meaning of a text to the inferential level. • Readers synthesize to understand more clearly what they have read.	Book Lovers' Festival Small-group presentations of "You Must Read This!" opinion pieces to kindergartners

(continued)

■ MAY PLAN ■ *(continued)*

Possible Guiding Questions

What compelling questions will foster inquiry, understanding, and transfer of learning?
- What books and stories matter to me?
- What should I recommend?
- What do active readers do?
- How do readers grow? How did I grow as a reader this year?

Possible Supporting Targets	Possible Assessments
Long-term targets are in bold, and daily targets are listed below them.	*These formative assessments match the daily targets and let kids and me know where we are and where we need to go.*
I can describe *what* thoughtful readers do. • I can define synthesis. • I can synthesize when I read to make meaning and extend the meaning of a text.	• Scripting children's definitions, children's artistic representations • Conferring; thinking/synthesizing sheets (pages 174, 175, and 179)
I can describe *how* readers read and get better at reading over time. • I can describe how my thinking evolves when I read independently. • I can retell key details from my reading. • I can figure out new words and build my vocabulary with lots of different strategies. • I can participate in collaborative conversations to better understand the text and the world around me.	• Conferring, partner work, reflection and share sessions • Conferring, partner work • Anchor chart (ongoing) • Book clubs, partner work, reflection and share sessions
I can explain "Why read?" and how reading makes me stronger and more powerful in the world.	• Exit tickets, class discussions, conferring
I can persuade another reader to read my favorite book.	• Partner work, opinion piece, Book Lovers' Festival

◼ MAY CALENDAR ◼

SUNDAYMONDAYTUESDAYWEDNESDAYTHURSDAYFRIDAYSATURDAY

By the end of the year, we are ready for one last celebration of our year together as readers. What better way than to host a Book Lovers' Festival and help welcome the kindergartners into the first-grade reading club with a list of books and recommendations they can dig into over the summer?

- Guiding questions: What books matter to me? What do active readers do? How did I grow as a reader this year? What book will be my "You must read this!" book?
- Reading-content focus on synthesis
- Big-idea content focus on how I can spread the joy of reading
- Possible mini-lessons:
  - What is synthesis?
  - Why does synthesis matter for readers?
  - How to "not tell too much"; how to recommend a book
  - How to persuade someone else to read a book
  - What makes a good recommendation?
- Start planning our Book Lovers' Festival! How will we share with kindergartners? Should we have our books with us? Should we give them some browsing time afterward? Will we read our pieces, or should we know them so well that we can refer to them only when we need to? How can our voices and body language show our enthusiasm and excitement for the books we love?

Tried-and-True Texts for Synthesizing Information
Any well-written and accessible nonfiction texts that support social studies and science units of study will work well.

Narrative Nonfiction Titles
The Librarian of Basra by Jeannette Winter
Nasreen's Secret School by Jeannette Winter
Wangari's Trees of Peace by Jeannette Winter

Fiction Titles
City Dog and Country Frog by Mo Willems
The Alphabet Tree by Leo Lionni
Frederick's Fables by Leo Lionni
The Story of Jumping Mouse by John Steptoe
How Rocket Learned to Read by Tad Hills
The Little Hummingbird by Michael Nicoll
Fables by Arnold Lobel

What is synthesis? For a straightforward definition, *Merriam-Webster's Collegiate Dictionary* defines it as "the composition or combination of parts or elements so as to form a whole." So we could say that synthesis is the process through which readers bring together their background knowledge and their evolving understanding of the book to create a complete and original understanding of the text.

But what does this mean for our youngest readers? When I talk with children about synthesis, I explain that synthesizing information is all about how our thinking evolves as we read. In the beginning, it may seem like the book is going to be about one thing, but when we read more, and look closely at the illustrations, our thinking evolves—it gets bigger, and often changes in some way. I tell them the language of synthesis goes like this: "I used to think . . . Then I read or saw . . . Now I'm thinking . . ." So we think the book is about one thing; then we encounter new information in the text, and now we're thinking the book is about something more. We're synthesizing information—our thinking is evolving as we read.

For example, in our study of how one person can make a difference in the world, I read aloud *The Librarian of Basra*, the true story of Alia Muhammad Baker and her heroic struggle to save the books in her library. The story begins with what goes on in the library—it's a meeting place where book lovers come together to discuss "matters of the world and matters of the spirit." Then we find out—through the text and illustrations—that they're not talking about those things anymore. They're talking about the war that they're sure is coming, and now they're wondering things like, *Will our families survive? Will soldiers with guns fill the streets?* and *What can we do?*

A synthesis of the book right here might sound like this:

I used to think this book was going to be about people coming to the library to talk about matters of the world and matters of the spirit. *Then I read the words*, "Until now—now, they talk only of war." *Now I'm thinking* the book is about the library being a meeting place for people to come together to talk about the war and make plans about what to do.

Next we find out that Alia goes to the governor for help; she asks permission to move the books to a safe place. The governor refuses, but Alia doesn't let that stop her. Secretly she brings the books to her home each night after work. Because of this information, and my background knowledge about what happens in Iraq when a person defies the government, my thinking is changing yet again.

Now my synthesis might sound like this:

"*I used to think* this book was going to be about people coming together to figure out what to do about the war. *Then I read* the part about Alia asking for help, and how the governor refused to help her save the books. *Now I'm thinking* this is about a woman who loves books so much that she's willing to risk her life to save them."

Right about now, I ask children to share their synthesis with someone close to them, and ask them to use the words *I used to think . . . , then . . . , and now I'm thinking . . .* Does their thinking sound similar to mine? Yes. And that's good—they're dipping their toes into the water on the very first day.

Sometimes teachers ask, "But what about retelling? Isn't that enough? And really, doesn't it get at the same thing?" Retelling is important, but no, it doesn't get at the same thing. And it really isn't enough. Retelling is all about what happened in the story, including key details. A retelling of *The Librarian of Basra* would sound something like this:

"Alia Baker was the librarian of Basra, a city in Iraq. People came to the library to talk about books and ideas, but then the war came, and the people came to the library to talk about what they were going to do. Alia was worried about the books being destroyed and asked the governor for help. He refused, so she secretly took the books home night after night to keep them safe. Her friends and neighbors helped her. The library was burned down, but a lot of the books are safe in Alia's house until a new library is built."

Do you see the difference? Retelling is all about the facts at the surface level: this is what happened in the story. Synthesis is about what happened *and* the readers' evolving understanding of the big ideas in the book. Retelling can help with synthesis, but just because readers can retell a story doesn't mean they're thinking about or understanding the big ideas.

In a retelling, you don't hear things like, "I used to think this was about one woman risking her life to save the books, but I saw the pictures of Anis and his friends and neighbors helping, too, so now I'm thinking this is about lots of people who love books so much that they're willing to risk their lives to save them. They wish for peace just like we do."

What do you think? Is retelling enough?

Anchor Lessons

Readers monitor overall meaning, important concepts, and themes as they read, understanding that their thinking evolves in the process

I liken synthesis to throwing a rock into a pond: first there's a splash, and then the water ripples out, making waves that get bigger and bigger. Synthesis is kind of like that, too, I tell students. When you read, your thinking evolves when you encounter new information, and your understanding of the story gets bigger and bigger, just like the ripples in the pond. Next, I read and synthesize the book *Smoky Night* by Eve Bunting for them. That afternoon I transfer my synthesis word for word (or nearly) onto a chart labeled "Synthesizing *Smoky Night* (think aloud by Mrs. Miller)," pictured in Figure 8.2. I want the children to be able to take a closer look at how my thinking evolves as well as help them begin to track the language of synthesis.

Children catch on quickly—it seems as though we've been building up to this moment all year—and they're eager to have at it on their own. Ben asks me to make a record sheet "that has the ripple on it," and that night I'm happy to

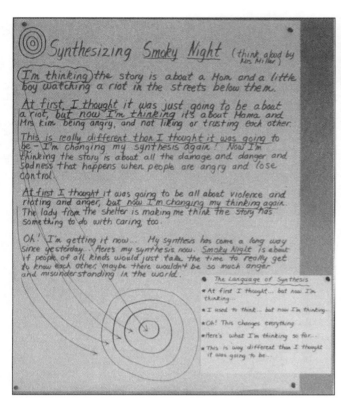

FIGURE 8.2
Synthesizing Smoky Night *by Eve Bunting*

comply. We use the sheet to record the evolution of our thinking as we read *The Alphabet Tree* by Leo Lionni, and many opt to use it to keep track of how their thinking evolves as they read independently. (See Bret and Maggie's written synthesis of a story by Leo Lionni in Figure 8.3.)

Not Ben. He pulls me to the side, thrusts the record sheet my way, and scrunches up his face. "This isn't really what I meant," he tells me, shaking his head. When I ask him what he really meant, he says, "Here, let me show you." He draws a small circle on the back of the sheet, then another, larger one around the first; I can tell now he's going for the *full* ripple effect. "I see what you mean, Ben, but won't it be hard to write in a circle?" I ask him.

"No," he answers. "It'll be *easy*."

It was. I drew the form to his specifications, and Ben tried it out the next day, requested a few minor adjustments, and was then ready to teach his classmates how it

FIGURE 8.3
Bret and Maggie's synthesis of A Color of His Own *by Leo Lionni*

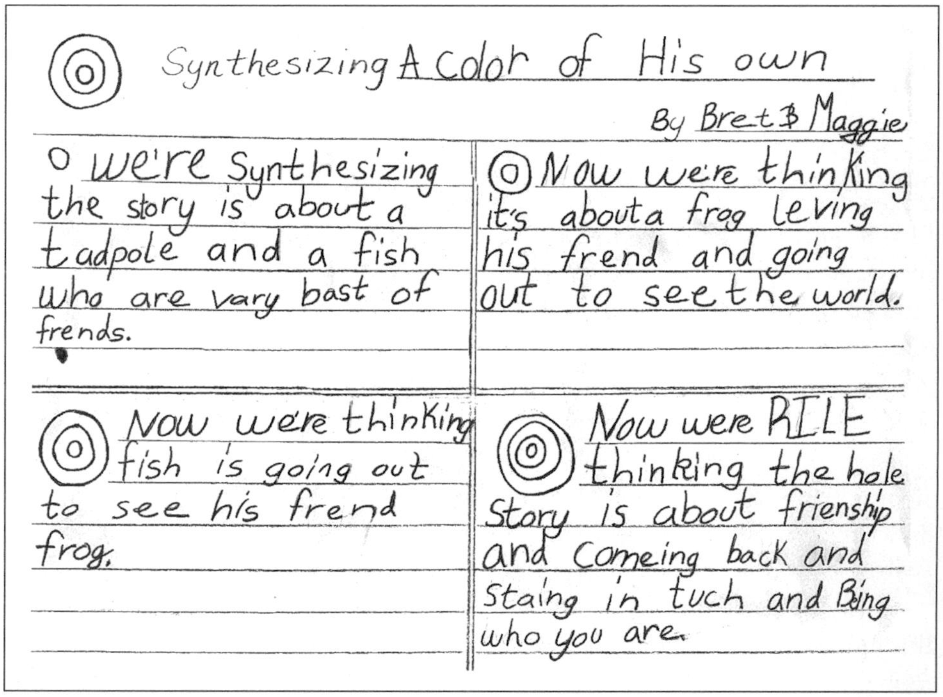

FIGURE 8.4
*Ben's synthesis wheel
as rendered by Rian
and Madi*

worked. It was a hit, of course, and not even one child got dizzy. (As for their teacher? Well . . . have you ever tried reading in a circle?) Rian and Madi's synthesis of *The Library* in Figure 8.4 uses the form that will forever be known as "Ben's synthesis wheel."

"So, Ben," I ask him several days later, "now that you are such an expert at synthesizing, how would you define it? How would you explain synthesis to somebody who didn't know what it means?"

He fumbles for the words he wants, and finally says, "Let me think about that."

Fifteen minutes later he seeks me out and hands me a construction paper circle. "Here—I figured it out," he tells me. "This is what synthesis is."

"It's beautiful, Ben," I say, admiring the brightly colored blue, orange, red, and green circles, "but how does this explain synthesis?"

"Let's sit down," he says, realizing this may take some time, "and I'll explain it to you. See the blue circle in the middle? That's what you're thinking first. Then see the next circle? The one that's mostly orange with just a little bit of blue? It shows how you still keep some of your beginning thinking, but when you learn more, you have even more thinking to add to it. Your thinking gets bigger. See the third circle? It's got some blue, and some orange, but it's mostly red, because now there's even more new thinking; you're going deeper and deeper into the text. And see the next one? It's mostly green. You see, the ripple isn't just a solid line; some of the best thinking leaks right on through." (See the last page of the color insert for Ben's drawing.)

I'm speechless. Ben, age six, has captured (synthesized?) the nature of synthesis. Where was he ten years ago when I needed him? (Oh, right—he wasn't even *born*.) I think his work is so brilliant that I stop the entire workshop so Ben can share what he's done with his classmates. They're not nearly as impressed. "We can draw synthesis, too!" they inform me, and they can—and do. (See the section called "Evidence of Understanding and Independence" at the end of this chapter for Rian and Madi's representations of synthesis.)

Readers retell what they have read as a way of synthesizing

I think of retelling as a fairly literal recounting of what children have read, learned, and remembered. To give the kids a framework for thinking about retelling as they synthesize what they've read, I teach them to

tell what's important,
in a way that makes sense,
without telling too much.

(Sound familiar? I laid the groundwork for this when children presented their learning on their one-page spreads last month.)

When teaching children how to retell as they synthesize fiction, I model the activity using familiar picture books and fairy tales. The children already know how stories are organized; their identifying the setting, characters, problem(s), an event or two, and the problem's resolution help focus and support their understanding of the book.

When teaching kids to retell details and information in nonfiction text, the framework for thinking remains the same, but the focus is on what they have learned rather than on the elements of story. I show them how to take notes by writing down only a few important words—just enough to help them remember what they've learned—and ask them to share their learning, sometimes orally, sometimes in writing, in their own words.

I gradually release responsibility by stopping now and then as I read aloud. I ask children to get eye-to-eye and knee-to-knee to synthesize the text so far, and then we collaborate and I chart their thoughts in the whole group. I ask them to read independently for five or ten minutes before I stop them to retell the story or what they have learned in their own words with a partner. I ask children who are reading the same text to synthesize it when they finish, then get together and compare their thinking.

I've learned that some of the best ways to give children practice and highlight some of the purposes of retelling occur in the moment. For example, when Maggie comes back after being absent, I might say, "Welcome back, Maggie! We read another chapter in *My Father's Dragon* while you were gone. Would you like someone to retell it for you?" Or "We read a book about the Underground Railroad while you were gone. Who will synthesize what we learned for Maggie?"

During share time, when a child is talking about a book most of the class is unfamiliar with, I might say, "Molly, could you synthesize your book for us? That will help us better understand your big idea."

When a child is going on and on about a story, a movie, a sleepover, or a playdate, I might say, "That sounds so cool [or fun, or interesting]! Take a minute and see if you can synthesize all that information. Remember, think about what's important, tell it in a way that makes sense, and try hard *not to tell too much*!"

And I often say at the end of the day, "When you go home today and your mom or dad says, 'What happened in school today? What did you learn?' what might you say? Let's synthesize our learning now so you'll be ready!"

Readers capitalize on opportunities to share, recommend, and criticize books they have read

Children recommend books to each other all year long (see the photo at the start of this chapter), and I give them opportunities to synthesize the books they recommend. I bring in several book reviews from the newspaper, and together the children and I decide on what information to include and what form their review will take. Whit's recommendation of *Oliver Button Is a Sissy* is shown in Figure 8.5. His review does a fine job of telling what's important in a way that makes sense without telling too much. This paves the way for our Book Lovers' Festival where readers recommend their "You Have to Read This!" book.

To get started, I ask children to get their notebooks, find a partner, and take a look at all the books they've recorded and read this year. Which ones are their favorites? Which ones have made the biggest difference to them as readers and thinkers? Which ones would cause them to tell a friend, "You *have* to read this book"?

Children decide we should invite the kindergartners to our Book Lovers' Party: "Then when they get to first grade, they'll know all the good books to read!" We decide that small groups of five or six will work best—that's three first graders and three kindergartners—and that the first graders will plan where their groups will meet ahead of time.

FIGURE 8.5
Whit's review of
Oliver Button Is a
Sissy *by Tomie*
dePaola

Readers extend their synthesis of the literal meaning of a text to the inferential level

I read John Steptoe's *The Story of Jumping Mouse* aloud, pausing at certain points for the children to write down their thoughts about the story. Lilli shares her synthesis in Figure 8.6. Figure 8.7 shows Max's perspective on the same story.

For this lesson, I tell children I will read a story aloud and that they'll be asked to synthesize during and then again after the reading. I tell them it doesn't matter how they choose to synthesize, only that they do it in a thoughtful, organized way. Once children have selected the supplies they need, we regroup in the meeting area and I begin the story. I read for a while, and then stop for them (and me) to synthesize the story up to that point. I repeat the procedure three or four more times, giving children time at the end to reflect and to connect their thinking into a larger, more meaningful whole.

The Story of Jumping Mouse isn't the first story we read this way. I begin with fables. I read several familiar fables aloud and do a basic retelling for the children, thinking aloud about how I infer the lesson, or moral, of each one. Fables are great here—they're short, and you can do two, three, or even four in a day, showing children how readers extend their literal synthesis (of the fable) to an inferential one (the moral or lesson).

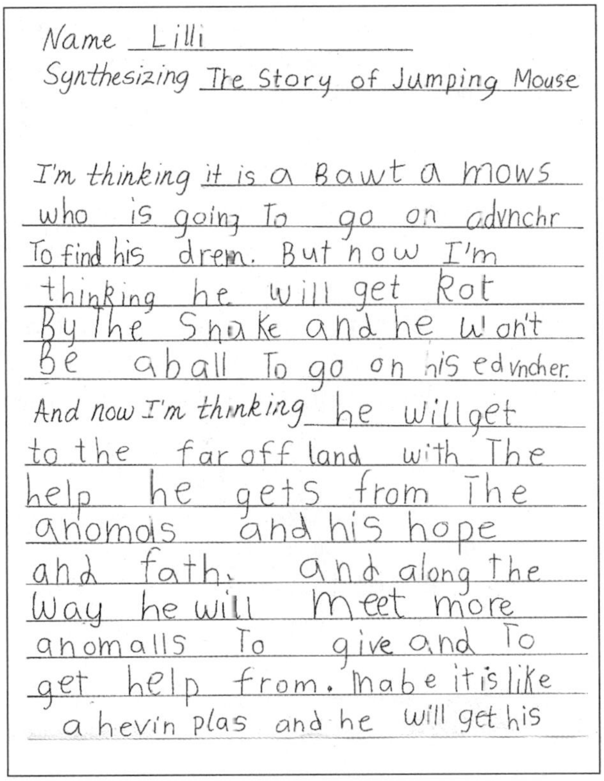

Name __Lilli__

Synthesizing __The Story of Jumping Mouse__

I'm thinking it is a Bawt a mows who is going To go on advnchr To find his drem. But now I'm thinking he will get Rot By The Snake and he won't Be aball To go on his edvncher.

And now I'm thinking he will get to the far off land with The help he gets from The anomals and his hope and fath. and along the way he will Meet more anomalls To give and To get help from. mabe it is like a hevin plas and he will get his

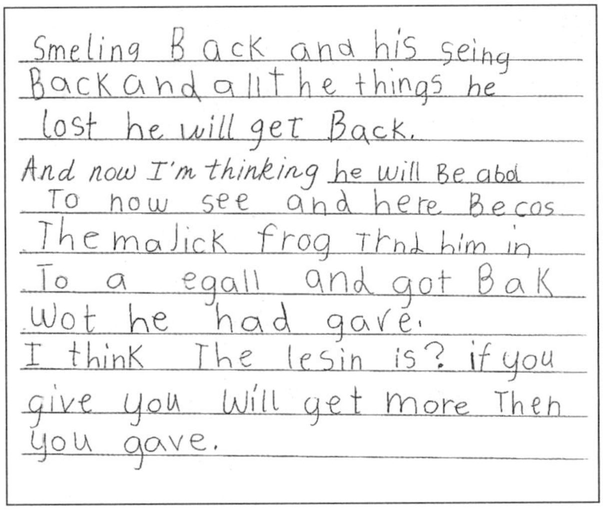

smeling Back and his seing Back and all the things he lost he will get Back.
And now I'm thinking he will Be abl To now see and here Becos The majick frog trnd him in To a egall and got Bak wot he had gave.
I think The lesin is? if you give you Will get more Then you gave.

FIGURE 8.6
Lilli's synthesis of The Story of Jumping Mouse *by John Steptoe*

FIGURE 8.7
Max's synthesis of The Story of Jumping Mouse *by John Steptoe*

Children love listening to fables, sitting with a partner to retell and infer their lessons, and of course just sharing them. Fables can take over work activity time, too, what with children acting them out, writing their own, and creating scenes, characters, and events from their favorites with wooden blocks, Legos, and Beanie Babies.

Once children have worked with fables for a while, I increase the sophistication of the read-alouds with stories like Lauren Mills's *The Rag Coat*, Byrd Baylor's *The Table Where Rich People Sit,* Estelle Condra's *See the Ocean*, John Steptoe's *The Story of Jumping Mouse*, and Arnold Lobel's *Fables*. It was right after the *Jumping Mouse* lesson that Whit and Frank created their *Oliver Button* chart. And as you may imagine, it wasn't long before other charts were vying for space on walls, cupboards, and doors.

As I finish this last chapter on synthesis, I'm thinking, as I always do when we finish a study, *What worked well? What didn't?* and *What might I do differently next year?* I'm also thinking about what I learned this year about synthesizing and learning from Whit, Ben, Lilli, and their twenty-four classmates. I'm struck again by their intelligence and the amazing potential they bring to the classroom.

Ben's artistic definition of synthesis helped me understand that as readers encounter new information, it doesn't necessarily change everything that has come before. Readers actively revise their synthesis as they read, but "some of the best thinking leaks right on through." Lilli and Max, through their synthesis of *The Story of Jumping Mouse*, taught me that the search for meaning is different for each child, because meaning is constructed from individual cognitive processes. And Whit's depiction of *Oliver Button* and the words *Be who you want to be. Trust your heart* showed me that keeping a cognitive synthesis during reading can help the reader identify and depict themes that connect to the overall meaning of the text.

Evidence of Understanding and Independence

What you see in this section are examples of some of the ways in which children have demonstrated evidence of understanding and independence. See page 91 for a more detailed explanation of what you will find in this section.

Synthesis is like inferring, only super-sized!
—Madi

If you don't ever change your mind, you're not really synthesizing.
—Mitchell

Synthesizing is like putting a puzzle together. You have to sort out your thinking and put it in the right place.
—Cory

Your whole life is a synthesis. First you are a baby and you learn a little bit of stuff. Then you get older and learn more and more and more.
—Frank

When you synthesize, it means you are ready to challenge your mind.
—Molly

When you synthesize, you say in your head, "I used to think this, but now I'm thinking this."
—Meghan

When I synthesize, my mind is changing, my ideas are changing, my thinking is changing.
—Brendan

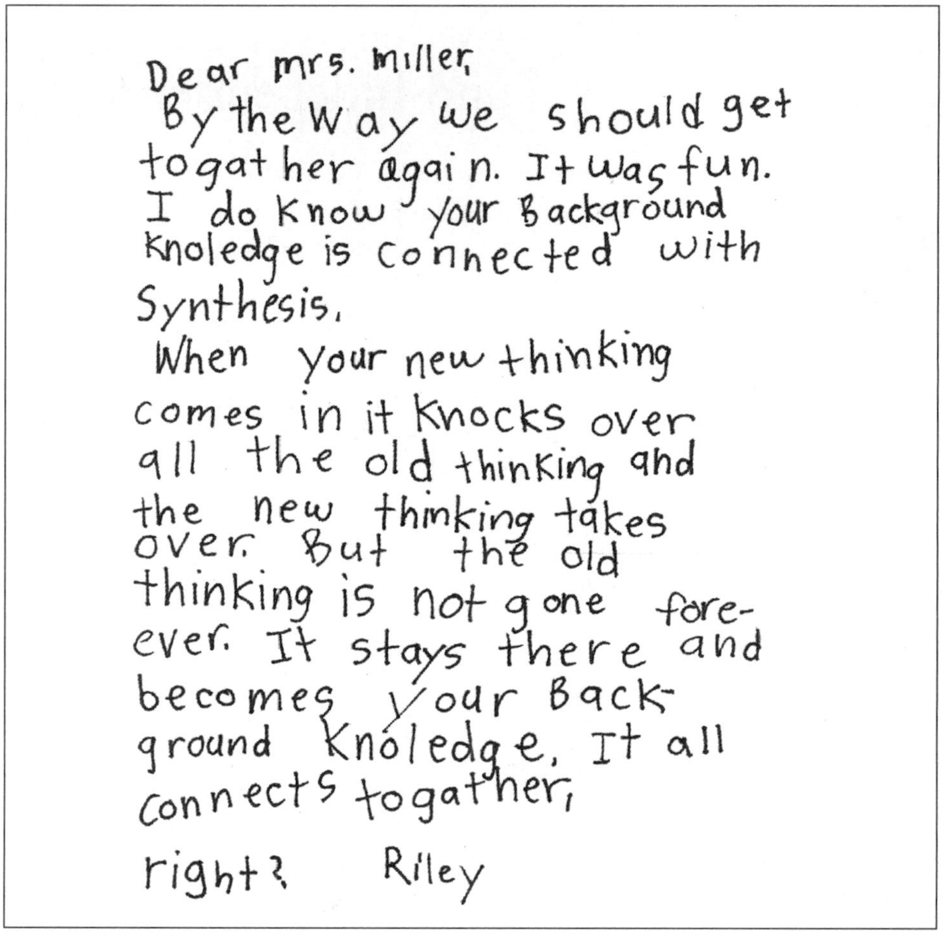

Dear mrs. miller,
  By the way we should get
togather again. It was fun.
I do know your Background
Knoledge is connected with
Synthesis.
  When your new thinking
comes in it knocks over
all the old thinking and
the new thinking takes
over. But the old
thinking is not gone fore-
ever. It stays there and
becomes your Back-
ground Knoledge, It all
connects togather,

right?   Riley

FIGURE 8.8
Riley was still contemplating synthesis in his summer letter.

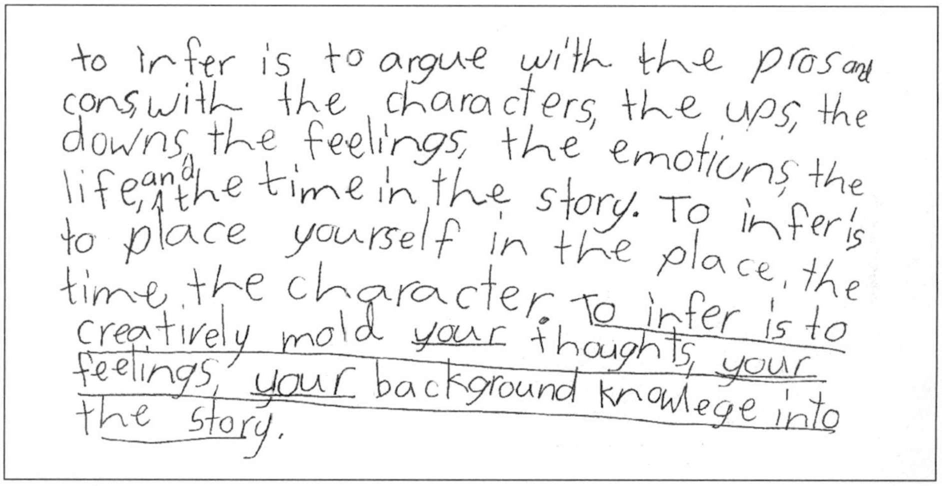

to infer is to argue with the pros and
cons with the characters, the ups, the
downs, the feelings, the emotions, the
life, and the time in the story. To infer is
to place yourself in the place, the
time, the character. To infer is to
creatively mold your thoughts, your
feelings, your background knowlege into
the story.

FIGURE 8.9
Isabella's synthesis of inferring, as a third grader

FIGURE 8.10
Rian's depiction of synthesis

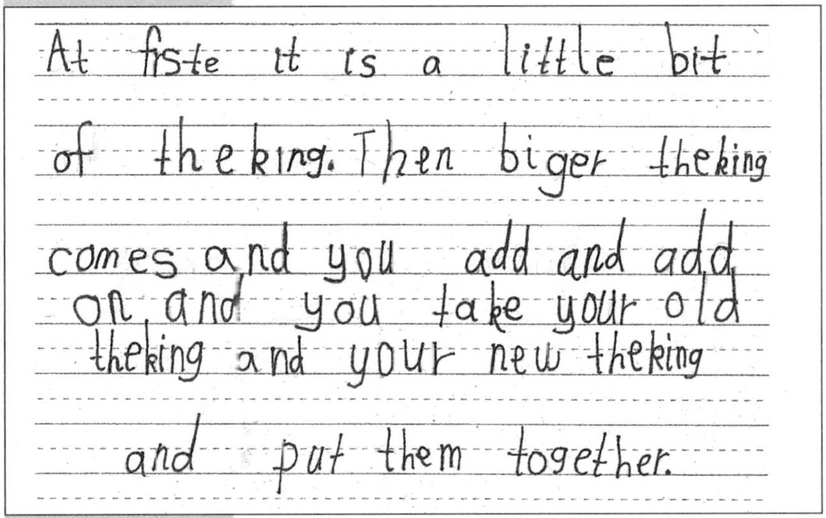

FIGURE 8.11
Frank's definition of synthesis

> At fiste it is a little bit
> of the king. Then biger the king
> comes and you add and add
> on, and you take your old
> the king and your new the king
> and put them together.

FIGURE 8.12
Madison's definition of synthesis

Epilogue
In June

By the end of the year, Christopher wouldn't dream of reading without a pencil in his hand.

"Wow! Take a look at this!"

186   *Reading with Meaning*

It's a late afternoon in June. The children have gone, and save for a lone cricket (could it possibly be the same one?) chirping from the bug box in a faraway corner, the room is quiet. It's the last day of school, and my desk is a heap of bath beads and oils, plates of candy and cookies, a pair of purple dangling earrings, roses, daisies, plants, and gift certificates for movies, a facial, and—glory be!—a ninety-minute massage.

But I know what lies underneath all the goodies. There are the cumulative records into which I need to glue children's pictures and record test scores, a ratty-looking register I must reconcile and ink in, and report cards I have to mail to those children who are already on summer vacation. And then there's the room that needs to be packed up, the plants that need to be wedged into my trunk for their yearly pilgrimage to their summer home, and piles of thank-you notes that need to be written and mailed.

What's a teacher to do? This one makes her way over to the once-white chair in the corner and settles in to watch the sunlight as it streams through the windows. I think about my animal lovers, Irish step dancers, and Kenny Loggins enthusiasts. I wonder what life will hold for them, and I wish for a peaceful world that appreciates all they have to offer.

Gone are the interviews and self-portraits with their too-high-on-the-forehead eyes, crinkled-paper hair, glued-on earrings, and bright red lips that once smiled back at me. Crayons and pencils, once pointed and lying just so, are but little nubs of lead and wax. Picture frames that held the smiles of this year's girls and boys are empty. And I'm feeling, as I always do at this time of year, just a little empty myself.

My eye catches the dry erase board across the way. "Dear First Graders," it reads. "Welcome to first grade! You are going to LOVE it!!! Love, the Second Graders."

Taped right below the message is a poem titled "Like Magic."

Just when I'm about to get misty, Ellie, whom I've known since she was three, races into the room and jumps into my arms. "I'm in first grade now!" she proclaims. "And guess what? You get to be my teacher!"

Like Majic
When
I
came
to
First Grade
I
did int
KNOW
how
to
read.
I
Just
hesutatid
and
Then
My
swch
turnd on
the
light
and
then in
a Flash
I learnd how to read, it was Butuful, like Majic.

Frequently Asked Questions

Charting children's thinking makes it visible and permanent and traces our work together.

Cory uses the same format for *Tut's Mummy Lost and Found* by Judy Donnelly.

Asking Questions   Day One

We are reading <u>Amelia's Road</u> This is the question we want to focus on tomorrow.

> Why is the box the answer to her problem?

What is a labor camp?

Why does she hate roads so much?

Why does she cry when her father pulls out the map?

Why do they have to work so much?

Why didn't the teacher bother to learn her name?

Did she get her wish?

Why did she want to belong to this place, and know it belonged to her?

Why does she put the map in the box?

Why didn't she cry the last time? Why does she like roads now?

Day Two
After rereading and focusing on our question today, we're thinking...

> When Amelia went down that accidental road and saw that most wonderous tree, she finally found a place where she felt like she belonged. She filled the box with "Amelia things"—they were the things she wanted to come back to.

What helped us?

rereading, using our schema,

thinking together, inferring

Name <u>Cory</u>

Day One

I am reading <u>Tut's MUMMY</u>

This is the burning question I want to focus on tomorrow:

> Why are his people so happe if the king is ded?

Day Two
After rereading and focusing on my question today, I'm thinking...
Maby it's becos he's to have a good life. Maby it's going to be beter for him.

How do I help my students go deep?

First, we go deeper ourselves. We increase the sophistication of our read-alouds, and challenge ourselves to work at least as hard as we're asking our students to work. When we struggle to make meaning—in front of children and in an intellectually honest way—we let them know that this is just what readers do.

We're also mindful of what children are reading. We want to ensure that what they're reading is worthy of what we're asking them to practice and do—they can't think deeply about nothing. What if children are just learning to read? What if they haven't yet cracked the code?

Wordless books are a great way for our youngest readers to practice thinking and deepen their interactions with text. (For a list of wordless books, see the appendix.) With wordless books, children can focus their attention entirely on making meaning, giving them opportunities to practice the deeper structure systems in an authentic way.

Handing off books we've read aloud ("Who would like to do some more thinking about *How to Heal a Broken Wing*?") is another early-reader strategy that moves children into thinking about big ideas. In this instance, they don't have to know how to read the words—they've heard the story already. Now they can focus their attention on enhancing understanding.

Book clubs also allow children to take their thinking deeper, whether the type of text they're discussing is fiction, nonfiction, or poetry, particularly when the text is one they've had some experiences with. (More on book clubs in Chapter 6.)

How come my kids talk so eloquently in response to read-alouds, but it doesn't transfer to independent reading?

It's often simply the difference between listening comprehension and reading comprehension. When children are listening, they're responsible only for the thinking. When they're working and reading independently, they're responsible for both the reading *and* the thinking. That's a big leap! This is where the gradual release model comes into play: in what ways might we support children as they move from whole-group experiences to independent practice?

Could they work with a partner? Practice strategies for accessing and understanding content using a short text that has big ideas? Come together in small child-led or teacher-led groups to practice applying strategies in texts that are easy to decode yet challenging to understand? Could the teacher read the beginning of the book, and then hand it off?

Listen to this from David Perkins:

> How can we engage youngsters in reading in any holistic sense when they can't even decode? Yes, research demonstrates clearly that the decoding side of reading benefits from a phonetics approach. However, the endeavor of understanding narratives, explanations,

and other such language forms involves much more than decoding and begins with oral exchanges. . . . Rich oral exchanges like careful listening to and discussion about a story should be considered work on the larger enterprise of reading, even when all the actual reading students are doing at that moment focuses on decoding. (2008, 41)

How does your model correspond to the Daily 5?

My friends Gail and Joan, "The Sisters," have many of the same goals for children as I do. We go about things a bit differently, but in the end, thoughtful teaching and learning is always in our hearts and minds. I know they join me in saying, "There really isn't one right way to teach children how to read. Our hope is that you'll find your way. What systems and structures for teaching and learning do you believe will work best for you and the children you teach?"

How do you know what to say when you confer?

I mostly think about three things: What do I know about this child? What do I know about myself as a reader? What do I know about reading? And then I go from there, asking myself these questions: Where is this child now? Where does he or she need to go? How can I help him or her get there?

What are your "go-to" questions for a conference?

How's your reading going? What's your book about so far?

Where are you with our learning target?

What's one thing you've learned about yourself as a reader since we last talked together?

What problems have you come across? (Johnston 2004; this question implies that this is normal, that everyone has problems—this is what learning is all about)

And then . . .

What did or what will you do?

Has this happened to you before? What did you do then?

Do you need help from me, or someone else in class?

Let's think about what's next for you. Let's set some goals.

When do you teach phonics and word work?

I had a twenty-minute block of time in the afternoon for working explicitly on letters, sound, and word work. This time was outside the reading workshop, and lessons were focused, fast, and fun. In most of the schools I work in now, teachers use a variety of systematic programs for teaching phonics, phonemic awareness, how to make words, and so on for those who need it. In addition, take a look at pages 46–49 for ways throughout the day for teaching phonics, word work, and more.

But here's the key: children practice applying these skills (in real books) during the independent practice portion of the reading workshop. That way these skills don't live in isolation, *and* children have daily opportunities to consolidate both the surface and deep structures during independent reading.

Do you put centers or stations in reading workshop?
I don't. I really want their hands, hearts, and minds on books, practicing what they're learning about how to read and about themselves as readers. Here are some questions I often ask colleagues to consider:

- Is the activity at the center more effective than giving children significant time every day to dig into a stack of yummy books?
- Will the activity at the center give me more information about my learners than a reading conference would?
- Does the activity at the center move children forward as readers, or does it serve as a classroom management tool to keep children busy while the teacher works with small groups?
- Does the activity at the center really move children toward independence? Does it lead to self-sustaining independence (that comes from within the child) or managed independence (that comes from the teacher)?

If you believe your children would benefit from centers or stations, or they are mandated, you might consider putting them outside reading workshop. They'd easily fit into your word-work block of time, or a stand-alone twenty-minute block, anytime during the day. Then, during reading workshop, children will have the time they need for the close, in-depth reading and thinking they are capable of and deserve.

How do you decide which books to use for your mini-lesson?
First, I think about the focus of our lesson—our learning target(s):

- *What* do I want children to learn about?
- What skills and strategies will they need me to show them to help them access, understand, and remember the content?

I look for the most interesting and engaging books I can find, asking, "Does this text meet my needs and those of the children sitting before me?" If it's part of a content-area study, I ask, "Is the information presented clearly? Is it accurate? Does it focus on big ideas and give students something to think about?" If it's a literary study, I ask, "Does the text focus on big ideas? Offer a variety of perspectives? Give students something to think about?"

Do you think aloud in every book? Do you ever "just read"?

It's really all about purpose. When the focus of the lesson is comprehension, it doesn't make sense to think aloud about my thinking when all is said and done. I need to think aloud "in real time" (as I read) because that's what active, thoughtful readers do.

Sometimes I'll read aloud a book one day, and the next day go back in and focus on something in particular—maybe phrasing, beautiful language, questions, inferring big ideas, content, or something else. This helps me keep the lesson short. They've heard it; now we go back in for some explicit teaching.

And yes, there are times I just read aloud. Sometimes children just need to *hear* and *feel* the words wash over them. Think *The Tin Man, I Want My Hat Back,* or *Songs of Myself.* And of course there are chapter book read-alouds, such as *The Trumpet of the Swan,* or the series My Father the Dragon.

What is your "go-to" when you feel stuck with a kid?

I let them know I'm stuck, and that I need their help to help me be a better teacher. I say something like, "Jamie, I've been thinking and thinking about what we can do to move forward. How can I help? Is there something specific that you need from me or someone else in the room? I believe in you, and I want you to believe in me, too. Can we work together on this?"

What about the kid who won't . . . no matter what I do? What questions do you ask yourself?

- What's my role in this? How can I think about this child in a different way?
- Who might give me some new insights? His parents? Other teachers? Students?
- What can I do to elevate this child, in her eyes and in the eyes of others? What can I do to change the way this child sees herself? What can I do to change the way others (students) view this child?
- What else might be going on in this child's life, either in or out of school?
- Are there read-alouds that might prompt discussion and make a difference?

Have you ever had a kid you couldn't reach? Couldn't help read better?

Yes. There have been times when I've wished I knew more about how to help a child become a better reader, writer, or thinker. When this happens, I collaborate with colleagues and support people, read up, and, of course, talk with the child's parents.

What if, for now, nothing seems to work? Do you know the book *The Four Agreements*? It says that when we are impeccable with our word, don't take things personally, don't make assumptions, and do our very best each day, there's not much more we can do. I try to live by that. When I do, particularly when the day has been rough, I go home with a clear head and heart. I'm not giving up on the child—I'm going to continue to work hard to find helpful answers. But knowing I've done the best I can do at the end of the day is really all I can ask of myself.

What about gifted students who don't need the strategies?

All kids need strategies. Whether a child is gifted or not, there is going to come a time when learning doesn't come easily. "Gifted" kids need to know what it's like to struggle. They, too, need to understand the power of hard work, effort, and determination. If we let them cruise on by, they might develop a fixed mind-set (Dweck 2007), where they believe they do well because they were born smart. But what about when things get difficult? (And they will.) If they can't do it right away, will they think that maybe they're not so smart after all? Will they be reluctant to take risks because they might not get it right on the first try? Might they even resort to cheating?

We need to put all children in learning situations where there is just the right amount of struggle. That way they can get to know themselves as learners: What do I know about myself? What will I try? How much work will I do, and how much effort will I put forth to make myself smarter? It's essential that children understand: smart isn't something you *have*, smart is something that you *get*.

If children think they don't use or don't need the thinking strategies, it is usually because the text is too easy. They need guidance on how to choose a more sophisticated text—an unfamiliar genre, new content, or both.

What if a student has no background knowledge?

All children have background knowledge! It might be different from ours, but every child has a wealth of background knowledge—they've lived at least five years before we've met them, right? So let's value, honor, and build on what they already know, *and* provide a range of experiences that build children's background knowledge in areas where they need it.

How do you know when to move on?

When we're intentional in our planning—when children and I are crystal clear about where we're going, and what we or they need to do to get there, things aren't as nebulous as they once were. When we have daily learning targets and matching assessments, we know right away who is where and who needs what. And then we—the child and I—take immediate action. Maybe it's an individual conference, creating a partnership with another student, creating an individual plan, or a small, needs-based group.

And for children who continue to struggle? I remain optimistic. I continue to see them as promising and capable; I have a "yet-to-get" frame of mind. To move children forward, chances are good I need to model more;

guide, release, and respond to their efforts;

give them time; and

understand that tomorrow is another day.

How long should my mini-lessons be?

Mini-lessons should be between twelve and fifteen minutes. I do my best to remember that the longer I keep students with me, the less time they have to practice, and the less time I have to confer with individual students, differentiate my instruction, and move children toward independence. Remember the one-third/two-thirds balance of teaching and learning? The one who is doing the reading, writing, and talking is also the one who is doing the thinking and the one who is getting smarter! Plus, over-scaffolding diminishes student energy, engagement, and motivation, and increases student conformity and compliance. So let's take an oath:

I, _____, pledge to allow my children to read, write, and talk a lot more than I do.

How do you teach children to hold thinking and make meaning as they read?

We teach during mini-lessons (of course!) but sometimes the most powerful teaching—both for individual children and the class as a whole—occurs during the individual conference. Maybe we suggest to one child that if she draws what she's learning on a sticky note, it might help her not only better understand her new learning, but also remember it. "This is kind of like research," I say. "Do you want to try it and see if it works for you?" Of course she does! (It's a pretty, pink sticky note!)

"I'll come back in five or so minutes to see how it's working—I can't wait to see what happens."

I come back, and sure enough, she's drawn what she's learned about firefighters. "Oh my goodness," I say. "You've got to share this with everyone when we come back together. I don't think everyone knows about this!" And so now Shawna becomes the teacher, and little by little, because of one little girl, more and more children try it out.

This happens a lot—thinking about authentic ways for children to demonstrate understanding often occurs within the conference. A child tries something out, shares it, and presto! It goes viral.

Do you do guided reading?

I don't do guided reading in a capital *G*, capital R kind of way. I like to think about small-group instruction as guiding readers rather than marching them through levels. When I bring a small group of children together, it's because they need support in a certain area. Their reading level might come into the equation, but I don't believe a letter or a number should define who a child is as a reader, or should be the only marker we consider when forming groups.

Think about the child who can decode almost anything, yet when we ask her to talk with us about the big ideas in her book, she's stumped. Or what about the child who struggles with decoding, yet during read-alouds, synthesizes information like no one else? Would their level-based guided reading group meet their needs as growing readers?

Maybe I notice that there are four children who, when it comes to decoding, can tell me lots of things they know to do when they encounter an unknown word. They talk about looking at the pictures, going back, going on, thinking about what makes sense, and so forth.

But even though they can *tell* me what to do, I've noticed that they don't really *do* it. They're really just stuck on sounding out the word. So now I have a group of children whom I can guide—support—as readers. It makes sense— it's efficient—to bring them together for more explicit teaching. But are they at the same level? No. They have the same needs, though. Will their books be the same? No. They'll bring books that are just right for them—in this instance those where they can read most of the words, but not all of them.

Guided reading was always intended to be part of a larger whole—all children still need time daily for independent practice, consistent, descriptive feedback from their teacher, and opportunities to reflect and share with each other what they're learning about themselves as readers. In some schools I work in, children and teachers have a thirty-minute block of time for guided reading and stations, and a sixty- to ninety-minute reading workshop. Now everyone's happy. Especially kids.

Appendix

A Collection of Books to Start the Year and Use All Year Long

Fiction Picture Books
How to Heal a Broken Wing by Bob Graham
My Lucky Day by Keiko Kasza
The Falling Raindrop by Neil Johnson
Duck! Rabbit! by Amy Rosenthal and Tom Lichtenheld
The Little Yellow Leaf by Carin Berger
How Rocket Learned to Read by Tad Hills
The Recess Queen by Alexis O'Neill
Stand Tall, Molly Lou Melon by Patty Lovell
Odd Velvet by Mary Whitcomb
Walk On! by Marla Frazee
Amber on the Mountain by Tony Johnston
Koala Lou by Mem Fox
Enemy Pie by Derek Munson
Oliver Button Is a Sissy by Tomie DePaola
The Little Hummingbird by Michael Nicoll
Ish by Peter Reynolds
Wolf's Coming! by Joe Kulka
Chrysanthemum by Kevin Henkes
Ruby in Her Own Time by Johnathan Emmett

Nonfiction Picture Books
Actual Size by Steve Jenkins
Prehistoric Actual Size by Steve Jenkins
Almost Gone by Steven Jenkins
Bones (and anything else) by Steve Jenkins
Under One Rock by Anthony D. Fredericks
Animals Nobody Loves by Seymour Simon
Owen and Mzee by Isabella Hatkoff
Bat Loves the Night by Nicola Davies
Ice Bear by Nicola Davies
Biblioburro by Jeannette Winter
Wangari's Trees of Peace by Jeannette Winter
One Tiny Turtle (and anything else) by Nicola Davies
Spiders by Nic Bishop
Growing Patterns by Sarah Campbell
Bugs Up Close by Diane Swanson
National Geographic Readers
Life Size Farm by Teruyuki Komiya
Life Size Zoo by Teruyuki Komiya
Life Size Aquarium by Teruyuki Komiya
Zoobooks (Wildlife Education)

Wordless Books
A Circle of Friends by Giora Carmi
Chalk by Bill Thomson
The Flower Man by Steve Ludy
A Ball for Daisy by Chris Raschka
The Umbrella by Ingrid and Dieter Schubert
Wave by Suzy Lee
The Boy, Frog, and Dog series by Mercer Mayer
Why? by Nicolai Popov
My Dog Carl series by Alexander Day
The Red Book (and others) by Barbara Lehman
The Lion and the Mouse by Jerry Pinkney
Looking Down by Steve Jenkins
Pancakes for Breakfast by Tomie dePaola

Songbooks
Consider multiple copies of these. Kids love them, the rhythms and rhymes are infectious, and they're fun to read with a partner!

Hush, Little Baby by Marla Frazee
Little Rabbit Foo Foo by Michael Rosen
The Lady with the Alligator Purse by Nadine Bernard Westcott
Five Little Ducks, This Little Light of Mine (and others) by Raffi
The Itsy Bitsy Spider by Iza Trapani
Miss Mary Mack by Nadine Bernard Westcott
Oh, A-Hunting We Will Go by John Langstaff
Hush, Little Dragon by Boni Ashburn

Predictable Books
Consider multiple copies—they're early reader favorites!

Tough Boris by Mem Fox
Brown Bear, Brown Bear, What Do You See? by Bill Martin, Jr.
Who Took the Cookies from the Cookie Jar? by Bonnie Lass and Philemon
    Sturge
I Went Walking by Sue Williams
Let's Go Visiting by Sue Williams
Who Hops? by Katie Davis
Witch, Witch Come to My Party by Arden Druce
Mary Wore Her Red Dress by Merle Peak
*Pete the Cat: I Love My White Shoes, Pete the Cat: Rocking in My School
    Shoes,* and *Pete the Cat and His Four Groovy Buttons* by Eric Litwin

One Red Rooster by Kathleen Sullivan Carroll
The Magic Fish by Freya Littledale
Does a Kangaroo Have a Mother, Too? by Eric Carle
We're Going on a Bear Hunt by Michael Ross

Alphabet Books
Chicka Chicka Boom Boom by Bill Martin, Jr.
Dr. Seuss's ABC by Dr. Seuss
Old Black Fly by Jim Aylesworth
If Rocks Could Sing by Leslie McGuirk
A, My Name Is Alice by Jane Bayer
Alphabet Adventure by Audrey Wood
Super Hero ABC by Bob McLeod
LMNO Peas by Keith Baker

Rhyming Books
Jazz Baby by Lisa Wheeler
Farmers Garden: Rhymes for Two Voices by David Harrison
Trucktown Truckery Rhymes by Jon Scieszka
Pigs Rock! by Melanie Davis Jones
Read Aloud Rhymes for the Very Young by Jack Pelutsky
Llama Llama Red Pajama by Anna Dewdney
In the Tall, Tall Grass (and others) by Denise Fleming
Jack and Jill and Other Nursery Rhymes by Mandy Stanley
One, Two, Buckle My Shoe by Anna Hines
Here Comes Mother Goose edited by Iona Opie
There's a Wocket in My Pocket! by Dr. Seuss
Silly Sally Went to Town by Audrey Wood
Oh Say Can You Say? by Dr. Seuss

References

Children's Literature

Abercrombie, Barbara. 1990. *Charlie Anderson.* New York: M. K. McElderry Books.

Adoff, Arnold. 2000. *Touch the Poem.* New York: Blue Sky Press.

Allen, Judy. 2000. *Are You a Snail?* London: Kingfisher.

Aliki. 1975. *The Two of Them.* New York: Mulberry Books.

Altman, Linda Jacobs. 1993. *Amelia's Road.* New York: Lee and Low Books.

Anderson, Hans Christian. 2007. *The Ugly Duckling.* Somerville, MA: Candlewick.

Arnold, Tedd. 1987. *No Jumping on the Bed.* New York: Penguin.

Atwater, Richard, and Florence Atwater. 1938. *Mr. Popper's Penguins.* Boston: Little, Brown.

Avi. 1995. *Poppy.* New York: Orchard Books.

———. 1998. *Poppy and Rye.* New York: Avon Books.

Barchas, Sarah. 1975. *I Was Walking Down the Road.* New York: Scholastic.

Bauer, Marion Dane. 2007. *A Mama for Owen.* New York: Simon and Schuster.

Baylor, Byrd. 1994. *The Table Where Rich People Sit.* New York: Macmillan.

Bentley, Dawn. 1998. *The Three Little Pigs.* Kansas City, MO: Piggy Toes.

Berger, Barbara. 1984. *Grandfather Twilight.* New York: Philomel Books.

———. 1997. *A Lot of Otters.* New York: Penguin Putnam.

Berger, Carin. 2008. *The Little Yellow Leaf.* New York: Greenwillow Books.

Boelts, Maribeth. 2007. *Those Shoes.* Somerville, MA: Candlewick.

Brewster, Hugh. 1997. *Inside the Titanic.* Toronto, ON, Canada: Morgan Press Books.

Brinkloe, Julie. 1986. *Fireflies.* Chicago: Scott Foresman.

Brothers Grimm. Retold by Barbara Cooney. 1965. *Snow White and Rose Red.* New York: Delacorte.

Brown, Margaret Wise. 2006. *Another Important Book.* New York: HarperCollins.

Brown, Marc Tolon. 1985. *Hand Rhymes.* New York: E. P. Dutton.

Brutschy, Jennifer. 1993. *Winter Fox.* New York: Knopf.

Bunting, Eve. 1988. *How Many Days to America? A Thanksgiving Story.* New York: Clarion Books.

———. 1991. *Fly Away Home.* New York: Clarion Books.

———. 1994. *Smoky Night.* San Diego: Harcourt Brace.

———. 2001. *The Wall.* New York: Clarion Books.

Carlstrom, Nancy White. 1987. *Wild, Wild Sunflower Child.* New York: Macmillan.

———. 1993. *What Does the Rain Play?* New York: Macmillan.

Carmi, Giora. 2003. *A Circle of Friends.* New York: Star Bright Books.

Coffelt, Nancy. 1993. *Dogs in Space.* San Diego: Harcourt Brace Jovanovich.

Coles, Robert. 2010. *The Story of Ruby Bridges.* New York: Scholastic.

Condra, Estelle. 1994. *See the Ocean.* Nashville, TN: Ideals Children's Books.

Cosmo, Mark. *Mountain Streams: Nature's Relaxing Sounds.* 1999. Sounds of Nature. Masters Series. Compact disc.

Davies, Nicola. 2001. *One Tiny Turtle.* Somerville, MA: Candlewick.

dePaola, Tomie. 1975. *Strega Nona.* New York: Prentice Hall.

———. 1979. *Oliver Button Is a Sissy.* San Diego: Harcourt Brace Jovanovich.

———. 1988. *Now One Foot, Now the Other.* New York: Trumpet Club.

Dodd, Anne Westcott. 1992. *Footprints and Shadows.* New York: Simon and Schuster Books for Young Readers.

Donnelly, Judy. 1987. *The Titanic Lost and Found.* New York: Random House.

————. 1988. *Tut's Mummy Lost and Found.* New York: Random House.

Downs, Robert Bingham. 1964. *The Bear Went Over the Mountain.* New York: Macmillan.

Dussling, Jennifer. 1998. *Bugs! Bugs! Bugs!* New York: DK Publishing.

Emmett, Jonathan. 2007. *Ruby in Her Own Time.* New York: Macmillan.

Eyewitness Books series. 1992. New York: DK Publishing.

Finch, Mary. 2001. *The Three Billy Goats Gruff.* New York: Barefoot Books.

First Discovery Books series. 1991. New York: Scholastic.

Fletcher, Ralph. 1997. *Twilight Comes Twice.* New York: Clarion.

Fox, Mem. 1988. *Koala Lou.* San Diego: Harcourt Brace Jovanovich.

————. 1994. *Tough Boris.* San Diego: Harcourt Brace Jovanovich.

Francen, Mike. 1999. *I Have a Dream.* Tulsa, OK: Francen World Outreach.

Frazee, Marla. 2006. *Walk On!* Orlando, FL: Harcourt.

French, Vivian. 2003. *Growing Frogs.* Somerville, MA: Candlewick.

Fujikawa, Gyo, ill. 2007. *Mother Goose.* New York: Sterling.

Gagliardi, Maria Francesca. 1969. *The Magic Fish.* New York: Putnam.

Galdone, Paul. 1977. *The Taileypo.* Boston: Houghton Mifflin.

Gannet, Ruth Stiles. 1987. My Father's Dragon Series. New York: Random House.

Garland, Sherry. 1993. *The Lotus Seed.* San Diego: Harcourt Brace Jovanovich.

Gibbons, Gail. 1989. *Monarch Butterfly.* New York: Holiday House.

Graham, Bob. 2008. *How to Heal a Broken Wing.* Somerville, MA: Candlewick.

Greenfield, Eloise. 1978. *Honey, I Love and Other Love Poems.* New York: Crowell.

Grindley, Sally. 1997. *Why Is the Sky Blue?* New York: Simon and Schuster Books for Young Readers.

Hallinan, P. K. 2009. *The Looking Book.* Nashville, TN: Ideals.

Harris, Beth Coombe. 1993. *Little Green Frog.* Lewisville, TX: School of Tomorrow.

Harrison, David L. 2005. *Farmer's Dog Goes to the Forest: Rhymes for Two Voices.* Honesdale, PA: Boyds Mills.

Hatkoff, Isabel. 2006. *Owen and Mzee: The True Story of a Remarkable Friendship.* New York: Scholastic.

Hazen, Barbara Shook. 1983. *Tight Times.* New York: Puffin.

Heard, Georgia. 1997. *Creatures of Earth, Sea, and Sky.* Honesdale, PA: Wordsong.

————, compiler. 2000. *Songs of Myself.* New York: Mondo.

Henkes, Kevin. 1991. *Chrysanthemum.* New York: Greenwillow Books.

————. 1996. *Lilly's Purple Plastic Purse.* New York: HarperCollins.

Hill, Barbara Tinker. 1976. *The Little Yellow Duck.* N.p.: Author.

Hills, Tad. 2010. *How Rocket Learned to Read.* New York: Schwartz and Wade.

Hoffman, Mary. 1991. *Amazing Grace.* New York: Dial Books for Young Readers.

Houston, Gloria. 1992. *My Great-Aunt Arizona.* New York: HarperCollins.

Howard, Jane R. 1985. *When I'm Sleepy.* New York: Dutton.

I Can Read About . . . Series. New York: Troll Associates.

Jenkins, Steve. 2004. *Actual Size.* Boston: Houghton Mifflin Books for Children.

————. 2003. *Looking Down.* Boston: Houghton Mifflin.

Johnson, Neil. 2010. *The Falling Raindrop.* New York: Crown.

Johnston, Tony. 1994. *Amber on the Mountain.* New York: Penguin.

Kasza, Keiko. 2003. *My Lucky Day.* New York: G. P. Putnam's Sons.

Keats, Ezra Jack. 1996. *The Snowy Day.* New York: Viking.

Kilborne, Sarah S. 1994. *Peach and Blue.* New York: Knopf.

Klassen, Jon. 2011. *I Want My Hat Back.* Somerville, MA: Candlewick.

Komiya, Teruyuki. 2010. *Life-Size Aquarium.* New York: Seven Footer Press.

Kramer, S. A. 1997. *Ice Stars.* New York: Grosset and Dunlap.

Kraus, Robert. 1970. *Whose Mouse Are You?* New York: Aladdin Books.

———. 1986. *Where Are You Going, Little Mouse?* New York: Greenwillow Books.

Kulka, Joe. 2007. *Wolf's Coming!* Minneapolis, MN: Carolrhoda.

Langstaff, John M. 1974. *Oh, a Hunting We Will Go.* New York: Atheneum.

Lee, Suzy. 2008. *Wave.* San Francisco: Chronicle Books.

LeGuin, Ursula. 1988. *Catwings.* New York: Orchard Books.

Let's Read and Find Out Science series. 2006. New York: HarperCollins.

Lewis, C. S. 2000. *The Lion, the Witch, and the Wardrobe.* New York: HarperCollins.

Levy, David H., ed. 1996. *Stars and Planets.* New York: Time-Life Books.

Lindgren, Astrid. 1950. *Pippi Longstocking.* Translated by Florence Lamborn. New York: Viking.

Lionni, Leo. 1968. *The Alphabet Tree.* New York: Dragonfly Books.

———. 1975. *A Color of His Own.* New York: Pantheon.

———. 1985. *Frederick's Fables: A Leo Lionni Treasury of Favorite Stories.* New York: Knopf.

Littledale, Freya. 1966. *The Magic Fish.* New York: Scholastic.

Litwin, Eric. 2010. *Pete the Cat: I Love My White Shoes.* New York: HarperCollins.

Lobel, Arnold. 1970–1979. Frog and Toad Series. New York: HarperCollins.

———. 1972. *Mouse Tales.* New York: Harper and Row.

———. 1977. *Mouse Soup.* New York: Harper and Row.

———. 1980. *Fables.* New York: HarperTrophy.

Long, Sylvia. 2000. *Hush Little Baby.* San Francisco: Chronicle Books.

Lovell, Patty. 2001. *Stand Tall, Molly Lou Melon.* New York: G. P. Putnam's Sons.

MacLachlan, Patricia. 1995. *What You Know First.* New York: HarperCollins.

Maestro, Betsy. 1994. *Why Do Leaves Change Color?* New York: HarperCollins.

Marshak, Suzanna. 1991. *I Am the Ocean.* New York: Arcade.

Martin, Bill, Jr. 1967. *Brown Bear, Brown Bear, What Do You See?* New York: Holt, Rinehart, and Winston.

———. 2006. *The Big Book of Poetry.* New York: Simon and Schuster Books for Young Readers.

Martin, Bill, Jr., and John Archambault. 1989. *Chicka Chicka Boom Boom.* New York: Simon and Schuster Books for Young Readers.

Marzollo, Jean. 1978. *Close Your Eyes.* New York: Dial.

Mayer, Mercer. 1977. *Just Me and My Dad.* Racine, WI: Western.

Mazer, Anne. 1991. *The Salamander Room.* New York: Knopf.

McKissack, Patricia. 1986. *Flossie and the Fox.* New York: Dial Books for Young Readers.

McLerran, Alice. 1992. *Roxaboxen.* New York: Puffin Books.

Mellonie, Bryan, and Robert Ingpen. 1983. *Lifetimes: A Beautiful Way to Explain Death to Children.* New York: Bantam Books.

Merriam, Eve. 1992. *Goodnight to Annie: An Alphabet Lullaby.* New York: Hyperion Books for Children.

———. 1993. *Quiet, Please.* New York: Simon and Schuster Books for Young Readers.

———. 1999. *The Wise Woman and Her Secret.* New York: Aladdin Picture Books.

Mills, Lauren. 1991. *The Rag Coat.* Boston: Little, Brown.

Milton, Joyce. 1992. *Wild, Wild Wolves.* New York: Random House.

Minarik, Else Holmelund. 1957. *Little Bear.* New York: Harper and Row.

———. 1978. *Father Bear Comes Home.* New York: HarperCollins.

———. 1979. *Little Bear's Visit.* New York: HarperCollins.

———. 1984a. *A Kiss for Little Bear.* New York: HarperCollins.

———. 1984b. *Little Bear's Friend.* New York: HarperCollins.

Munsch, Robert N. 1980. *The Paper Bag Princess.* Toronto, ON, Canada: Annick.

Munson, Derek. 2000. *Enemy Pie.* San Francisco: Chronicle Books.

Muse, Clarence. 1932. *Way Down South.* Hollywood, CA: D. G. Fischer.

Muth, Jon J. 2002. *The Three Questions.* New York: Scholastic.

Nicoll, Michael. 2010. *The Little Hummingbird.* Vancouver, BC, Canada: Greystone.

O'Neill, Alexis. 2002. *The Recess Queen.* New York: Scholastic.

Opie, Iona, ed. 1999. *Here Comes Mother Goose.* Cambridge, MA: Candlewick.

Oppenheim, Shulamith Levey. 1999. *Yanni Rubbish.* Honesdale, PA: Boyds Mills.

Park, Frances, and Ginger Park. 2000. *The Royal Bee.* Honesdale, PA: Boyds Mills.

Parish, Peggy. 1985. *Amelia Bedelia Goes Camping.* New York: Morrow.

Penn, Audrey. 1993. *The Kissing Hand.* Washington, DC: Child Welfare League of America.

Pinkney, Jerry. 2009. *The Lion and the Mouse.* New York: Little, Brown.

Popov, Nicolai. 1996. *Why?* New York: NorthSouth.

Prelutsky, Jack, compiler. 1983. *The Random House Book of Poetry for Children.* New York: Random House.

Raffi. 1989. *Five Little Ducks.* New York: Crown.

Read and Wonder series. 2001. Somerville, MA: Candlewick.

Reynolds, Peter. 2004. *Ish.* Somerville, MA: Candlewick.

Robinson, Martha. 1995. *The Zoo at Night.* New York: Margaret K. McElderry Books.

Rosen, Michael. 1990. *Little Rabbit Foo Foo.* New York: Simon and Schuster Books for Young Readers.

Rosenthal, Amy Krouse, and Tom Lichtenheld. 2009. *Duck! Rabbit!* San Francisco: Chronicle Books.

Ryder, Joanne. 1992. *The Chipmunk Song.* New York: Penguin.

Rylant, Cynthia. 1983. *Miss Maggie.* New York: Dutton.

———. 1985. *The Relatives Came.* New York: Bradbury.

———. 1988. *All I See.* New York: Orchard Books.

———. 1991. *Night in the Country.* New York: Macmillan.

———. 1992. *An Angel for Solomon Singer.* New York: Orchard Books.

Saunders, Dave, and Julie Saunders. 1990. *Dibble and Dabble.* New York: Bradbury.

Say, Allen. 1993. *Grandfather's Journey.* Boston: Houghton Mifflin.

———. 1999. *Tea with Milk.* Boston: Houghton Mifflin.

Schubert, Ingrid, and Dieter Schubert. 2011. *The Umbrella.* The Netherlands: Lemniscaat.

Sendak, Maurice. 1962. *Chicken Soup with Rice: A Book of Months.* Nutshell Library. New York: HarperCollins.

———. 1963. *Where the Wild Things Are.* New York: Harper and Row.

Seuss, Dr. 1963. *Dr. Seuss's ABC: An Amazing Alphabet Book.* New York: Beginner Books.

Shaw, Charles Green. 1947. *It Looked Like Spilt Milk.* New York: Harper.

Southgate, Vera. 2012. *Ladybird Tales: Hansel and Gretel.* London: Ladybird.

Squire, Ann. 2002. *Gemstones.* New York: Children's Press.

Steptoe, John. 1972. *The Story of Jumping Mouse: A Native American Legend.* New York: Lothrop, Lee and Shepard.

Stevenson, Robert Louis. 1981. *A Child's Garden of Verses.* New York: Simon and Schuster Books for Young Readers.

Stewart, Sarah. 1995. *The Library.* New York: HarperCollins.

Stock, Catherine. 1993. *Where Are You Going, Manyoni?* New York: Morrow Junior Books.

Stoltz, Mary. 1993. *Say Something.* New York: HarperCollins.

Swanson, Diane. 2007. *Bugs Up Close.* Tonawanda, NY: Kids Can Press.

Taylor, Barbara. 1999. *Nature Watch Spiders.* New York: Lorenz Books.

Thomas, Shelley Moore. 1995. *Putting the World to Sleep.* Boston: Houghton Mifflin.

Thomson, Bill. 2010. *Chalk.* Seattle: Amazon Children's Publishing.

Underwood, Deborah. 2010. *The Quiet Book.* New York: Houghton Mifflin.

Van Allsburg, Chris. 1986. *The Stranger.* Boston: Houghton Mifflin.

Waber, Bernard. 1972. *Ira Sleeps Over.* Boston: Houghton Mifflin.

Wang, Mary Lewis. 1989. *The Ant and the Dove: An Aesop Tale Retold.* Chicago: Children's Press.

Ward, Cindy. 1988. *Cookie's Week.* New York: Putnam.

Ward, Helen. 2003. *The Tin Forest.* New York: Puffin.

Weeks, Sarah. 2007. *Without You.* New York: HarperCollins.

Wells, Rosemary. 1981. *Timothy Goes to School.* New York: Dial Books for Young Readers.

———. 1985. *Hazel's Amazing Mother.* New York: Dial Books for Young Readers.

———. 1994. *Night Sounds, Morning Colors.* New York: Dial Books for Young Readers.

Westcott, Nadine Bernard. 1998. *The Lady with the Alligator Purse.* Boston: Little, Brown.

Whitcomb, Mary. 1998. *Odd Velvet.* San Francisco: Chronicle Books.

White, E. B. 1970. *The Trumpet of the Swan.* New York: Harper and Row.

———. 1999. *Stuart Little.* New York: HarperTrophy.

Wildsmith, Brian. 1973. *The Lazy Bear.* Oxford: Oxford University Press.

Willems, Mo. 2010. *City Dog and Country Frog.* New York: Hyperion.

Winter, Jeannette. 2005. *The Librarian of Basra.* Boston: Harcourt Children's.

———. 2008. *Wangari's Trees of Peace.* Boston: Harcourt Children's.

———. 2009. *Nasreen's Secret School.* New York: Beach Lane.

Wood, Audrey. 1984. *The Napping House.* San Diego: Harcourt Brace Jovanovich.

———. 1992. *Twenty-Four Robbers.* Swindon, UK: Child's Play International.

———. 2001. *Heckedy Peg.* Saint Paul: Minnesota Humanities Commission.

Worth, Valerie. 1994. *all the small poems and fourteen more.* New York: Farrar, Straus and Giroux.

Wright, Blanche Fisher. 2000. *My First Real Mother Goose Board Book.* New York: Scholastic.

Wyeth, Sharon Dennis. 1998. *Something Beautiful.* New York: Doubleday Books for Young Readers.

Yolen, Jane. 1981. *Sleeping Ugly.* New York: Coward, McCann and Geoghegan.

————. 1991. *Greyling.* New York: Philomel Books.

————. 1996. *Mother Earth, Father Sky.* Honesdale, PA: Wordsong/Boyds Mills.

————. 2000. *Color Me a Rhyme.* Honesdale, PA: Wordsong/Boyds Mills.

Yolen, Jane, and Andrew Fusek Peters, compilers. 2007. *Here's a Little Poem.* Somerville, MA: Candlewick.

Zolotow, Charlotte. 1972. *William's Doll.* New York: Harper and Row.

————. 1980. *If You Listen.* New York: Harper and Row.

————. 1984. *I Know a Lady.* New York: Puffin Books.

Professional Literature

Anderson, R. C., C. Chinn, M. Commeyras, A. Stallman, M. Waggoner, and I. Wilkinson. 1992. The Reflective Thinking Project. In *Understanding and Enhancing Literature Discussion in Elementary Classrooms.* Symposium, 42nd Annual Meeting of the National Reading Conference, San Antonio, Texas.

Anderson, R. C., and P. D. Pearson. 1984. "A Schema-Theoretic View of Basic Processes in Reading." In *Handbook of Reading Research*, ed. P. D. Pearson. White Plains, NY: Longman.

Atwell, Nancie. 2007. *The Reading Zone: How to Help Kids Become Skilled, Passionate, Habitual, Critical Readers.* New York: Scholastic.

Bennett, Samantha. 2007. *That Workshop Book: New Systems and Structures for Classrooms That Read, Write, and Think.* Portsmouth, NH: Heinemann.

Block, Cathy, and Michael Pressley, eds. 2002. *Comprehension Instruction: Research-Based Best Practices.* New York: Guilford.

Brown, A. L., J. D. Day, and E. S. Jones. 1983. "The Development of Plans for Summarizing Texts." *Child Development* 54: 968–979.

Calkins, Lucy. 1983. *Lessons from a Child.* Portsmouth, NH: Heinemann.

Calkins, Lucy, Mary Ehrenworth, and Christopher Lehman. 2011. *Pathways to the Common Core.* Portsmouth, NH: Heinemann.

Chappuis, Jan. 2009. *Seven Strategies of Assessment for Learning.* Boston: Pearson.

Common Core State Standards. 2010. www.corestandards.org.

Daniels, Harvey, ed. 2011. *Comprehension Going Forward: Where We Are and What's Next.* Portsmouth, NH: Heinemann.

Dweck, Carol. 2007a. "The Perils and Promises of Praise." *Educational Leadership* 65 (2): 34 and 39.

————. 2007b. *Mindset: The New Psychology of Success.* New York: Ballantine.

Guthrie, J. T., and N. M. Humenick. 2004. "Motivating Students to Read: Evidence for Classroom Practices That Increase Motivation and Achievement." In *The Voice of Evidence in Reading Research*, ed. P. McDardle and V. Chhabra. Baltimore: Paul Brookes.

Hansen, J. 1981. "The Effects of Inference Training and Practice on Young Children's Reading Comprehension." *Reading Research Quarterly* 16: 391–417.

Harvey, Stephanie, and Anne Goudvis. 2007. *Strategies That Work: Teaching Comprehension to Enhance Understanding.* 2nd ed. Portland, ME: Stenhouse.

Johnston, Peter. 2004. *Choice Words: How Our Language Affects Children's Learning.* Portland, ME: Stenhouse.

————. 2012. *Opening Minds: Using Language to Change Lives.* Portland, ME: Stenhouse.

Keene, Ellin Oliver. 2012. *Talk About Understanding: Rethinking Classroom Talk to Enhance Comprehension.* Portsmouth, NH: Heinemann.

Keene, Ellin, and Susan Zimmermann. 2007. *Mosaic of Thought: Teaching Comprehension in a Reader's Workshop.* 2nd ed. Portsmouth, NH: Heinemann.

Miller, Debbie. 2008. *Teaching with Intention: Defining Beliefs, Aligning Practice, Taking Action.* Portland, ME: Stenhouse.

Moline, Steve. 2011. *I See What You Mean, Second Edition: Visual Literacy K–8.* Portland, ME: Stenhouse.

National Reading Panel. 2000. Summary report. http://www.nationalreadingpanel .org/publications/publications.htm.

Palincsar, A., and A. L. Brown. 1984. "Reciprocal Teaching of Comprehension—Fostering and Monitoring Activities." *Cognition and Instruction* 1: 117–175.

Pearson, P. D., J. A. Dole, G. G. Duffy, and L. R. Roehler. 1992. "Developing Expertise in Reading Comprehension: What Should Be Taught and How Should It Be Taught?" In *What Research Has to Say to the Teacher of Reading.* 2nd ed., ed. J. Farstup and S. J. Samuels. Newark, DE: International Reading Association.

Pearson, P. D., and M. C. Gallagher. 1983. "The Instruction of Reading Comprehension." *Contemporary Educational Psychology* 8: 317–344.

Perkins, David. 1992. *Smart Schools: Better Thinking and Learning for Every Child.* New York: The Free Press.

————. 1993. "Creating a Culture of Thinking." *Educational Leadership* 51 (3): 98–99.

————. 2008. *Making Learning Whole: How Seven Principles of Teaching Can Transform Education.* San Francisco: Jossey-Bass.

Piaget, Jean. 1970. "Piaget's Theory." In *Carmichael's Manual of Child Psychology*, ed. P. Mussen. New York: John Wiley and Sons.

Pressley, G. M. 1976. "Mental Imagery Helps Eight-Year-Olds Remember What They Read." *Journal of Educational Psychology* 68: 355–359.

Raphael, T. E. 1984. "Teaching Learners About Sources of Information for Answering Questions." *Journal of Reading* 27: 303–311.

Resnick, Lauren B., and Sally Hampton, with the New Standards Primary Literacy Committee. 2008. *Reading and Writing Grade by Grade.* Newark, DE: International Reading Association.

Rothstein, Dan, and Luz Santana. 2011. *Make Just One Change: Teach Students to Ask Their Own Questions.* Cambridge, MA: Harvard Education Press.

Samuels, S. Jay, and Alan E. Farstrup. 2011. *What Research Has to Say About Reading Instruction.* 4th ed. Newark, DE: International Reading Association.

Stiggins, R. J., J. A. Arter, J. Chappuis, and S. Chappuis. 2004. *Classroom Assessment for Student Learning: Doing It Right—Using It Well.* Portland, OR: ETS Assessment Training Institute.

Wiggins, Grant, and Jay McTighe. 2005. *Understanding by Design.* 2nd ed. Alexandria, VA: Association for Supervision and Curriculum Development.

Index